The District Controll<
THE NORTH LON____
RAILWAY

Known as 'Coffeepots' on the North London, an LNW Super-D 0-8-0 49078 shunts at Maiden Lane in August 1956 whilst working Willesden Target 119. Willesden was responsible for a significant proportion of trip and goods working west of Broad Street and many turns were covered by 0-8-0's. (A E Bennet/transporttreasury.co.uk)

If, as chroniclers of Railway Operating History, we performed no other task except that of drawing attention to the post-war North London Railway and the prodigious amount of work it did, we should not have existed in vain. Several works have appeared on the North London system but none, so far as we know, have devoted much attention to minutiae of traffic or motive power operations. We hope, therefore, that this book will add a further dimension to what has already been published about the North London Railway.

As new entrants to the railway, we quickly discovered that the first thing to do was to throw away the railway map that we had acquired in our role as enthusiasts! This was true of almost all the BR network but especially so of the North London where the trunk route was not Broad Street to Richmond but Temple Mills to Acton and - accepting the North & South Western Junction Joint as being an extension of the North London - Cricklewood to Feltham.

There is a tendency to think that because distances were short that North London goods trains were no more than a series of long shunts with engines running here and there as traffic built up. In fact, nothing could be further from the truth and each service - and there were a great many of them - were as fixed as anything that ran from Kings Cross or Paddington. Each train had its place in the timetable backed with a diagrammed engine and crew. Rather surprisingly, in view of the type of traffic carried, there were no trip engines of the type familiar elsewhere: workings where an engine, crew and guard had no timings but ran as directed by the District Controller.

Another North London myth is the idea that its trains were worked solely by 3F 0-6-0 tank engines from Devons Road. It is certainly true that Devons Road and its thirty-odd Standard 3F tanks did an extraordinary amount of work on the main line, it is also true that the North London was almost certainly the most cosmopolitan of any railway in Britain where '700' and Q1 0-6-0's were regular visitors to the Great Eastern and, conversely, where J17 0-6-0's from Stratford penetrated as far west as Acton and Feltham. Adding to the variety were a considerable number of Great Northern engines: J6 0-6-0's working to Feltham, J52 0-6-0T's on local work over the Western section of the system to Poplar and J50 pannier tanks making regular appearances at Acton.

The Great Northern also played a major part in the running of Broad Street's remaining steam passenger workings; the result of a policy reversal during the war. The North London and Great Northern were linked by a connection that ran from Finsbury Park to Canonbury and for many years the North London had operated a service of trains from Broad Street to a number of inner-suburban stations on the Great Northern. The services remained - albeit cut back to the rush hour - after the war but were worked in their entirety by the Great Northern: the majority of trains being handled by 0-6-2T's with one B1 4-6-0 making an appearance morning and evening.

The LNWR sheds at Camden and Willesden also played a part in the North London's fortunes, not merely with 3F 0-6-0T's and Super-D 0-8-0's on local trip workings, but with a large number of 4-6-0's which each evening made their way in two's and three's from Willesden to Broad Street to work the large number of express goods trains that nightly left Broad Street for destinations down the West Coast Main Line.

The nature of operations on the North London has not made this an easy book to compile and we reinforce the usual caveat that accompanies our publications: it is not a work of art but a medium of information, pure and simple. For artistry, we recommend a visit to the Louvre but for a reasonably definitive description of the train and traffic working on the North London Railway in the 1950's we hope this offering will not only serve as a substitute but give value for money.

Credits for assistance with text & photographs: B. Hornsey, W.S.Becket, Steve Standbridge, Colin Dymock, Tim Bourne, M. Bentley, John Turner, Barry Hoper, Pat Webb, T.Bradshaw, The Signalling Record Society, J. Challis, and the Gentlemen of http://groups.yahoo.com/group/BritishRailways/

WORKING TIMETABLE : 1953

m.Ch	Train From	ECS · EMU · 66/31	K · 3F 0-6-0T · DR 4	00.15 Broad St · Light · 3F 0-6-0T · DR 20	Light · 3F 0-6-0T · DR 49	Light · 3F 0-6-0T · DR 3	00.50 Plaistow · Lght · 3F C-6-0T · DR 26	00.40 Broad St · Light · 3F 0-6-0T · DR 14	EBV · 3F 0-6-0T · DR 4	H · 3F 0-6-0T · DR 6	ECS · 4 2-6-0 · DR 7	00.30 W'den · H · 3F 0-6-0T · 1B 84	23.58 H.Green · J17 0-6-0 · SX 103	00.20 Feltham · H · Q1 0-6-0 · FEL 121	02.05 Plaistow · Light · 3F 0-6-0T · DR 6	H · 3F 0-6-0T · DR 25	01.00 Feltham · F · S15 4-6-0 · FEL 114	00.40 H.Green · H · J17 0-6-0 · SX 100	01.45 Ken O · Milk · 4 2-6-0 · DR 7	J · J52 0-6-0T · HSY 11	01.27 B'sea · 4F 0-6-0 · 14A/121	01.35 Feltham · J6 0-6-0 · HSY 5	19.00 Wyre Dk · C · SMT 4-6-0 · 1B/23	Plistow · Light · 3F 0-6-0T · DR 25	02.57 Stratfod · Milk · 4 2-6-0 · DR 7	Light · 4 2-6-0 · DR 7	K · 4F 0-6-0 · 1A/125
0.00	**KEW EAST JCN**																										
0.49	Bollo Lane																										
	RICHMOND	00.04																									
	Kew Gardens	00/10																									
	Gunnersbury	00/11																									
0.61	South Acton																										
1.37	**ACTON CENTRAL**	00.13																									
	ACTON YARD									00.25						01.25				01.58							
2.47	Acton Wells Jcn	00/15								00.30						01/31	01/38	01/34		02/03	02/07	02/12					
2.73	Old Oak Sidings										00.40																
3.22	**WILLESDEN (HL)**	00.18								00.33			01/18			01/34	01/57	01/53		02/06		02/16					
	WILLESDEN (HL Sdgs)																						02/21				
3.53	Kensal Green Jcn									00.35	ECS to Mitre Bge CS		01/20			01/36	02/00	01/55		02/08		02/18	02/26		02/36		
4.32	Kensal Rise																										
4.79	Brondesbury Park																										
5.38	Brondesbury																										
5.77	West End Lane																										
6.28	Finchley Road									00/43			01/30			01/46	02/08	02/01		02/16		02/25	02/33		02/45		
7.18	Hampstead Heath																										
7.66	**GOSPEL OAK**									00.48			01/35			01/51	02/12	02/06 (via)		02/21		02/35 (via)	02/37		02/50		
8.26	Kentish Town West												(via)					(via)		(T&H)							
	CAMDEN											00/55						(T&H)									
	Primrose Hill											00/58															
8.72	**CAMDEN ROAD**									00.53		01/00	(T&H)			01/56	02/16			02/26		(T&H)	02/41		02.55		03.00
9.16	Maiden Lane																										
9.34	St Pancras Sidings		00.11	00.25																							
10.09	Caledonian Road																										
10.45	Highbury		00.19						00.40																		
10.67	**Canonbury Jcn**			00/29	00/29			00/48	00/48	00/59		01/14	01/53			02/02	02/21	02/36		02/36		02/46					
11.65	Dalston W. Jcn			00/31				00/50	00/50	01/01		01/16	01/55			02/04	02/22	02/38				02/48					
12.02	Dalston Jcn											01.45	02.13	02.16						02.45		02.50					
13.56	Broad St Goods							01.04														02.57					
14.41	**BROAD STREET**						00/48	00/54				01/24															
11.76	Kingsland			00/34				00/52				01/18					01/10			02w08							
11.76	Kingsland						00/52					01/19					01w10	01/18	02/24		02w13						
12.16	**Dalston E. Jcn**			00/36			00/54									01/12		01/57	02/26		02/16						
12.41	Graham Road																			02.41							
12.46	Hackney																			R/R							
13.29	Homerton																										
13.73	Hackney Wick																					R/R					
14.03	**VICTORIA PARK**			00/40			00/58					01/24				01/20			02/30				03.02				
16.48	TEMPLE MILLS						01.04																				
21.02	GOODMAYES																										
17.33	THAMES WHARF																										
17.40	VICTORIA DOCKS																										
14.48	Old Ford																										
14.76	Tredegar Road						R/R															R.R			03.06	03.16	
14.76	Fairfield Road			00/43	00/45		00.58									01/26								02.58			03.18
14.76	**TILBURY JCN**				00/47			01/01								02.16							02.27				
16.74	PLAISTOW									01.35													02.31				
21.71	RIPPLE LANE																										
15.10	Bow Junction			00/44	00/48		01.02									01/02							02/59			03.19	
15.40	**Devons Road**																										
15.40	Devon's Rd Loco			00/47	00/50		01/02	01/04															03.02			03.21	
16.36	POPLAR DOCKS																										
	Destination	Kensington															Toton	Ilford	C.Yard	Brent (M)	F. Park						

2

WORKING TIMETABLE : 1953

m.xh / Station	1	2	3	4	5	6	7	8	9	10	11	12	13	14	15	16	17	18	19	20	21	22	23	24	25	26	27
Train	00.05	00.28	Light	Light	Light	F	00.58	00.15			01.10		Light	Light			23.06	02.25			01.58		Light	03.00	03.00	03.25	03.25
From	Brent	Brent					W. End	F. Park			W'den						Cambs	Brent (M)			Acton	Acton		Kens Milk	Kens Milk	Kens Milk	Brent (M)
Class	J						K			H		H			K	K	H	H	H	H	K						J
Engine	4F 0-6-0	8F 2-8-0	3F 0-6-0T	3F 0-6-0T	SMT 4-6-0	8F 2-8-0	3F 0-6-0T	J6 0-6-0	H16 4-6-2T	4 2-6-0	3F 0-6-0T	3F 0-6-0T	3F 0-6-0T	3F 0-6-0T	3F 0-6-0T	3F 0-6-0T	J17 0-6-0	700 0-6-0	3F 0-6-0	3F 0-6-0T	J52 0-6-0T	4F 0-6-0	7F 0-8-0	3P 2-6-2T	3P 2-6-2T	3P 2-6-2T	4F 0-6-0
Shed	14A/120	14A/150	DR 20	DR 14	1A/56	1A/127	14A/84	HSY 4	FEL 144	DR 23	1A/75	DR 12	DR 22	DR 8	DR 2	1A/75	SX 100	FEL 136	DR 8	DR 22	HSY 11	1A/125	1A/119	1A/150	1A/150	1A/150	14A/121
0.00 **POPLAR DOCKS**																											
0.76 Devon's Rd Loco																											
0.76 **Devons Road**						00.35							01.00	01.05	01.13												
1.26 Bow Junction						00/40							01/03	01/08	01/17												
RIPPLE LANE																											
PLAISTOW																			02.00								
1.40 **TILBURY JCN**						00/41	00/53						01/04	01.09 R/R To Plaistow					02/09								
1.40 Fairfield Road																											
1.40 Tredegar Road																											
1.68 Old Ford																											
VICTORIA DOCKS																											
THAMES WHARF																											
GOODMAYES																											
TEMPLE MILLS																	01.05			01.55							
2.33 **VICTORIA PARK**						00/45	00/50			00/57			01.08 R/R To T. Mills		01/21		01/39		02/13	02/20							
2.43 Hackney Wick																											
3.07 Homerton																											
3.70 Hackney																											
3.75 Graham Road																											
4.20 **Dalston E. Jcn**																				02/28							
4.40 Kingsland						00/53				00/57					01/28		01/47		02w22	02/32	02/50						
4.40 Kingsland																											
2.35 **BROAD STREET**																											
2.60 Broad St. Goods			00/15	00/40																							
4.34 **Dalston Jcn**			00/24	00/46																							
4.51 Dalston W Jcn					00/51	00/55				00/59					01/30		01/49		02/30	02/34	02/54						
5.49 **Canonbury Jcn**					00/57	00/57				01/01					01/32		01/51		02/32	02/36	02/57 To GN						
5.71 Highbury																											
6.27 Caledonian Road																											
7.02 St Pancras Sidings																						03.15	03.30				
7.20 Maiden Lane																							03.40				
7.44 **CAMDEN RD**					00/58	01/07				01/10					01/38		02/02		02/40	02/50		03/20					
8.11 Primrose Hill						01/10																03/22					
8.23 **CAMDEN**						01/12																03.25					
8.10 Kentish Town West																											
8.50 **GOSPEL OAK**								01/06		01/15					01/43		02/07		02/45	02/54							
9.18 Hampstead Heath																											
10.08 **Finchley Road**								01/04		01/19					01/47		02/11		02/49	02/58							
10.39 West End Lane																											
10.78 Brondesbury																											
11.37 Brondesbury Park																											
12.04 Kensal Rise																											
12.63 **Kensal Green Jcn**					01/13			01/19		01/28					01/56		02/20		02/59	03/13							
14.50 **WILLESDEN (BRENT)**								01/22		01/31	01/36				02/10		02/23	03/10	03/10	03/15							
13.43 Old Oak Sidings							01.25																				
13.69 Acton Wells Jcn	00/34	00/45					01/28	01/25		01/34	01/39						02/27	02/47	03/18					03/35		03/56	
14.45 **ACTON YARD**										01.40						01.28	02.33		03.25	03.25							
14.79 **ACTON CENTRAL**																02.15											
15.55 South Acton	00/40	00/51						01/30		01/34						02/19		02/53						03/41			04/02
16.20 Gunnersbury								01/34																			
17.34 Kew Gardens																											
18.64 **RICHMOND**																											
15.67 Bollo Lane																											
16.36 **KEW EAST JCN**	00/43	00/54					01/37	01/33		01/37						02/23		03/00						03/44	03/55	03/59	04/05
Destination	Battersea	Feltham	To D. Rd	T. Mills	1A Loco	Overseal	Feltham	Feltham	Kew Nth	Feltham						Feltham		Feltham			C. Yard	C. Yard	GN	B'sea	B'sea	R/R	B'sea

3

Train	01.50	02.37	03.00	03.08	14.40	02.15	02.45	23.08	04.00	03.16	04.18	02.35		04.55		04.15	04.25		03.50	04.03	05.05		05.15	
From	Feltham				Pe'th	Norwood	B'sea	Stockp't	D.Road	Feltham	E.Gds	H.Green	Milk	B.St		Mitre B	Mitre B		H.Green	Feltham	Mitre B		W'den	Pcls
Class	K	J	H	K	Fish	J	K	C	Pass	J	K	J		Pass	K	ECS	ECS	H	H	K	ECS	K	Pcls	Pass
Engine	Q1 0-6-0	3F 0-6-0	7F 0-8-0	7F 0-8-0	SMT 4-6-0	Q 0-6-0	4F 0-6-0	SMT 4-6-0	4 2-6-0	8F 2-8-0	J50 0-6-0T	8F 2-8-0	3P 2-6-2T	4 2-6-0	4F 0-6-0	EMU	EMU	4 2-6-0	J17 0-6-0	J6 0-6-0	EMU	3F 0-6-0	4F 0-6-0	EMU
Shed	FEL 125	14A/84	1A/108	1A/119	1B/24	NWD 583	14A/120	9A/57	DR 7	14A/150	HSY 20	14A/125	1A/140	DR 7	1A/125	16	19	DR 23	SX 104	HSY 4	15	DR 21	1A/109	13/50
KEW EAST JCN	02/28						03/23			03/39		03/53	04/09		04/26			04/05	04/21	04/36				
RICHMOND																								
Kew Gardens																								
Gunnersbury																								
South Acton	02/31						03/28			03/43		03/57	04/12					04/30		04/39				
ACTON CENTRAL																								
ACTON YARD		02.45								03.55			04.17						04.20					
Acton Wells Jcn		02.50					03.36			04.00		04.08			04.40	04.27	04.38	04.35	04.35	04.45	05.20		05.27	
Old Oak Sidings		02.42																						
WILLESDEN (HL)		Brent(M)			03/25		to Brent(M)			to Brent(M)		to Brent(M)	Cwood	04.10	04.42				04.42	04.49	K.Grn CS		05.18	
WILLESDEN (HL Sdgs)								03/30					04.05	04.26	04.44	04.29	04.40		04.51		05.07		05.33	
Kensal Green Jcn						03/27		03/38					04.21								05.20			
Kensal Rise																To W'den	To K.Grn CS				To K.Grn CS			
Brondesbury Park																								
Brondesbury																								
West End Lane																								
Finchley Road						03/38		03/45		04/14			04/30	04/40										
Hampstead Heath																								
GOSPEL OAK						03/43		03/50		04/19			04/35	04/45						04/56			05/22	
Kentish Town West						via				via										via			via	
CAMDEN			03.00/03.04			T&H				T&H		04.32/04.34							T&H				05.23/05.25	
Primrose Hill			03.04									04.34											05.25	
CAMDEN ROAD			03.06	03.11	03.30			03.55		04.24		04.35		04.50					05.01				05.27	05.33
Maiden Lane																								
St Pancras Sidings				03.16																				
Caledonian Road				03.16																				
Highbury																			05.07				05.37	
Canonbury Jcn			03.12/03.14		03.34/03.36			03.59/04.01		04.31/04.33	04.25/04.27	04.41/04.43		04.56/04.58				04.50/04.52	05.08/05.10				05.31/05.33	05.38/05.39
Dalston W. Jcn			03.14		03.36			04.01		04.33	04.27	04.43		04.58				04.52	05.10				05.33	05.39
Dalston Jcn			03.16/03.24		03.37			04.03/04.10	04.14		04.45/04.54			05.00/05.08	05.01				05.00		05.31	05.35	05.35	05.42
Broad St Goods					03.45																			
BROAD STREET									04.20													05.41		05.48
Kingsland													04.30			04.54	04.40		05.12					
Kingsland																								
Dalston E. Jcn															04.42	04.56	05.03		05.14					
Graham Road																05.08								
Hackney																								
Homerton																								
Hackney Wick																05.35	05.05							
VICTORIA PARK																04.53	05.08		05.19					
TEMPLE MILLS																					06.00			
GOODMAYES																								
THAMES WHARF																								
VICTORIA DOCKS																	05.52							
Old Ford																								
Tredegar Road																								
Fairfield Road																			05.25					
TILBURY JCN																			05/31					
PLAISTOW																								
RIPPLE LANE																								
Bow Junction													05/13								05/32			
Devons Road													05.16											
Devon's Rd Loco																								
POPLAR DOCKS																								
Destination		Ferme Pk						Ferme Pk															Haydon Sq	

4

Train				04.05 Brent (M)										05.00 Brent (M)		04.52 F. Park		05.10 Brent (M)								
Class	K	H	Light	H	H	Light	Pass	Pass	Light	Pass	H	EBV	Light	K	J	J	Light	Light		Pass	H	Light	Pass	Pass	H	Light	Pass
Engine	Q1 0-6-0	3F 0-6-0T	7F 0-8-0	S15 4-6-0	3F 0-6-0T	4F 0-6-0	EMU	4MT 2-6-0	7F 0-8-0	EMU	Q1 0-6-0	3F 0-6-0T	5MT 4-6-0	J15 0-6-0	3F 0-6-0T	3F 0-6-0T	Q 0-6-0	J50 0-6-0	3F 0-6-0T	4MT 2-6-0	4F 0-6-0T	3F 0-6-0T	EMU	EMU	J15 0-6-0	3F 0-6-0T	EMU
Shed	FEL 125	1B/84	1A/108	FEL 114	DR 14	DR 15	16/53	DR 7	1A/119	19/55	FEL 121	DR 30	1B/24	SX 113	14A/70	DR 30	NWD 583	HSY 20	14A/67	DR 7	DR 15	DR 21	15/52	13/50	SX 114	DR 9	CW 17/54
POPLAR DOCKS																											
Devon's Rd Lcco						03.55																05.00				05.05	
Devons Road						03.59		04.00				04.14									05.00						
Bow Junction								04.03				04.17										05.03				05.08	
RIPPLE LANE																											
PLAISTOW																											
TILBURY JCN					04.00							04.19										05.08		05.09			
Fairfield Road																											
Tredegar Road																											
Old Ford																											
VICTORIA DOCKS																											
THAMES WHARF																											
GOODMAYES											04.00			03.50							04.30				04.45		
TEMPLE MILLS	03.00	03.15																									
VICTORIA PARK	03.27	03.40				04.04		04.06			04.16	04.23		04.37							05.00				05.05	05.12	
Hackney Wick								04.08																			
Homerton																											
Hackney																											
Graham Road																									05.12	05.19	
Dalston E. Jcn		03w52						04.12				04.30															
Kingsland	03.35	03w57									04.23			04.44												05.21	
BROAD STREET																04.55								05.09			05.24
Broad St Goods			03.40																								
Dalston Jcn			03.47												05.00									05.15			05.30
Dalston W. Jcn	03.37	04.00	03.49								04.25			04.46		04.52							05.22	05.16			05.31
Canonbury Jcn	03.39	04.02	03.51								04.27			04.48		04.54	04.56	04.59					05.24	05.17			05.32
Highbury																		05.01						05.19			05.33
Caledonian Road														04.52													
St Pancras Sidings									04.17																		
Maiden Lane									04.21																		
CAMDEN RD	03.46	04.10	03.57								04.33					05.01	05.07	05.07						05.24			05.38
Primrose Hill			03.59						04.24				04.39														
CAMDEN			04.00						04.27				04.45														
Kentish Town West																											
GOSPEL OAK											04.38					05.06	05.17			05.22							05.40
Hampstead Heath																											05.42
Finchley Road											04.42					05.10	05.19			05.26							05.44
West End Lane																											05.46
Brondesbury							Ex Mitre Bge CS																				05.48
Brondesbury Park										Ex Siding																	05.50
Kensal Rise							04.33			04.48																	05.53
Kensal Green Jcn	04.04	04.28									04.55					05.20	05.24			05.37			05.30				05.56
WILLESDEN (BRENT)	04.15	04.30																									
Old Oak Sidings	03.58																										
Acton Wells Jcn	04.03	04.34		04.20							05.02				05.15	05.25			05.28						05.35		
ACTON YARD		04.40														05.30											
ACTON CENTRAL										04.57													05.38				06.02
South Acton	04.09			04.26						05.00									05.21				05.40		05.34		06.04
Gunnersbury										05.02													05.43				06.07
Kew Gardens																							05.46				06.10
RICHMOND										05.07													05.50				06.13
Bollo Lane																											
KEW EAST JCN	04.12			04.29										04.15										05.20			
Destination	Feltham	W'den	W'den	Feltham	T. Mills	W'den	B. St	W'den	W'den		Norwood	E. Gds	Ken (H)	Devons Rd	W'den										Feltham		

5

WORKING TIMETABLE : 1953

Train	05.20			05.05			05.20	05.02	05.18		06.05							05.45	05.40		05.35	06.29				06.14	
From	T. Mills			C'ham Jn			Mitre B	Feltham	Watford		E. Gds							Watford	Feltham		B'sea	W'den				Watford	
Class	Light	H	ECS	Pcls	Pass	K	ECS	H	Pass	K	K	ECS	ECS	K	Light	H	Pass	Pass	K	ECS	J	Pass	K	Light	Pass	Pass	K
Engine	3F 0-6-0T	J15 0-6-0	EMU	3P 2-6-2T	EMU	3F 0-6-0T	EMU	Q1 0-6-0	EMU	2F 0-6-0T	J50 0-6-0T	EMU	EMU	3F 0-6-0T	3F 0-6-0T	3F 0-6-0T	EMU	EMU	H16 4-6-2T	EMU	4F 0-6-0	EMU	3F 0-6-0T	3F 0-6-0T	EMU	EMU	3F 0-6-0T
Shed	DR 12	SX 113	31/66	1A/151	19	DR 2	30	FEL 123	4	DR 38/40	HSY 20	25/60	8	DR 8	1B/103	DR 22	23/59	21/57	FEL146	15/52	14A/121	27/62	1B/132	DR 8	17/54	16/53	DR 14
KEW EAST JCN								**05/29**											**06/03**		**06/14**						
Bollo Lane																											
RICHMOND					**05.20**															**06.03**					**06.23**		
Kew Gardens					05.23															06.06					06.26		
Gunnersbury					05.26															06.09					06.29		
South Acton					**05.28**			05/35											06/06	**06.11**	06/17				**06.31**		
ACTON CENTRAL					**05.31**												*ECS ex*			**06.14**					**06.34**		
ACTON YARD																**05.46**											**06.30**
Acton Wells Jcn					**05/33**			**05/41**								**05/53**	*Mitre*		**06/12**	**06/16**	**06/23**				**06/36**		**06/40**
Old Oak Sidings								*to*									*Bge*		06.17		*to*						
WILLESDEN (HL)				**05/29**	**05.37**		**05/39**	*Brent(M)*								**05/56**	**06.10**			**06.20**	*Brent(M)*				**06.40**		**06/43**
WILLESDEN (HL Sdgs)						**05.25**								**05.30**													
Kensal Green Jcn				**05/30**	**05/38**	**05/39**	**05.41**							**05/47**		**05/58**	**06/11**			**06/21**					**06/41**		**06/45**
Kensal Rise					**05.39**												**06.12**			**06.22**					**06.42**		
Brondesbury Park																											
Brondesbury					**05.42**												**06.15**			**06.25**					**06.45**		
West End Lane					**05.44**												**06.17**			**06.27**					**06.47**		
Finchley Road					**05.46**	05/50								05/58		06/07	**06.19**			**06.29**					**06.49**		06/53
Hampstead Heath					**05.48**												**06.21**			**06.31**					**06.51**		
GOSPEL OAK					**05.50**	**05/55**								06/03		06/11	**06.23**			**06.33**					**06.53**		06/58
Kentish Town West					**05.52**												**06.25**			**06.35**					**06.55**		
CAMDEN									**06/00**						**06.05**			**06/26**				**06/39**	**06.42**			**06/56**	
Primrose Hill									06.01						06/10			06.27				06.40	06/44			06.57	
CAMDEN ROAD				**05/47**	**05.55**	**06/00**			**06/03**					**06/09**	**06/12**	**06/18**	**06.27**	**06.30**		**06.38**		**06.43**	**06/46**		**06.57**	**07.00**	**07/03**
Maiden Lane															06.15												
St Pancras Sidings		05.44																					06.52				
Caledonian Road									**06.06**								**06.30**	**06.33**		**06.41**		**06.46**			**07.00**	**07.04**	
Highbury					**05.58**				**06.08**								**06.32**	**06.35**		**06.43**		**06.48**			**07.02**	**07.06**	
Canonbury Jcn		**05/50**		**05/57**	**06/00**	**06/06**			**06.10**		**06/12**			**06/18**		**06/27**	**06/33**	**06.37**		**06.45**		**06.50**			**07.04**	**07.08**	**07/11**
Dalston W. Jcn		05/52		05/58	06/01	06/08			06/12		06/15			06/20		06/29	06/34	06/38		06/46		06/51			07/05	07/09	07/13
Dalston Jcn			**05.57**	**05/59**	**06.02**				**06.13**			**06.16**	**06.21**				**06.36**	**06.40**		**06.48**		**06.53**			**07.07**	**07.11**	
Broad St Goods																											
BROAD STREET			**06.03**	**06.08**	**06.07**				**06.18**			**06.23**	**06.31**				**06.41**	**06.45**		**06.53**		**07.00**			**07.12**	**07.16**	
Kingsland																											
Kingsland		05/54				06/10					06/17			06/22		06/31											07/15
Dalston E. Jcn		**05/56**				**06/12**					**06/19**			**06/24**		**06/33**											**07/17**
Graham Road																											
Hackney																											
Homerton																											
Hackney Wick	R/R																										
VICTORIA PARK	**05.42**	**06/03**				**06/17**					**06/25**			**06/37**		**06.43**											**07/22**
TEMPLE MILLS		06.15														07.00											
GOODMAYES																											
THAMES WHARF																											
VICTORIA DOCKS																											
Old Ford														06.42										07.10			
Tredegar Road																											
Fairfield Road																											
TILBURY JCN	**05/45**																										**07/25**
PLAISTOW																											
RIPPLE LANE																											
Bow Junction	05/46					06.22					06/30													07/13			07/26
Devons Road											**06/35**																**07/29**
Devon's Rd Loco	05.49									06.27														07.15			
POPLAR DOCKS										**06.34**	**06.42**																**07.34**
Destination							H. Square																				

WORKING TIMETABLE : 1953

Note: This is a very wide multi-column working timetable. Columns are numbered 1–27; each column's Class, Engine, Shed and (where shown) originating "Train From" are given in the header block. Times shown with a dot (e.g. 06.20) are booked stops; times shown with a slash (e.g. 06/20) are pass/junction times.

Train From			05.50 Brent (M)									06.35 Brent (M)									06.42 H.Sq						
Class	Light	Light	Pass	Pass	J	Pass	EBV	Light	K	Pass	K	J	J	Pass	Pass	Pass	Pass	Pass	Pass	K	Light	Pass	K	Pass	Light	Light	Pass
Engine	5MT 4-6-0	4F 0-6-0	EMU	EMU	3F 0-6-0	EMU	3F 0-6-0T	3F 0-6-0T	3F 0-6-0T	EMU	7F 0-8-0	8F 2-8-0	3F 0-6-0T	EMU	EMU	EMU	EMU	EMU	EMU	3F 0-6-0T	3F 0-6-0T	EMU	3F 0-6-0T	EMU	3F 0-6-0	SMT 4-6-0	EMU
Shed	1B/23	1A/125	30/65	18	14A/35	9	DR 39	DR 39	DR 9	13/50	1A/108	14A/151	DR 49	51/66	4	19/55	8	60/25	23/59	1B/132	DR 21	21/57	DR 9	15/52	DR 48	9A/57	27/62
POPLAR DOCKS																											
Devon's Rd Loco																									07.06		
Devons Road							05.38	05/51																	07.09		
Bow Junction							05/41	05/52													06/55						
RIPPLE LANE																											
PLAISTOW																											
TILBURY JCN							05/42														06/56				07/10		
Fairfield Road																											
Tredegar Road																											
Old Ford																									07/12		
VICTORIA DOCKS																											
THAMES WHARF																											
GOODMAYES																											
TEMPLE MILLS																											
VICTORIA PARK							05/45	05.57													06/59						
Hackney Wick																											
Homerton																											
Hackney																											
Graham Road																											
Dalston E Jcn							05/50														07/02						
Kingsland							05/52														07/04						
BROAD STREET	05.33			05.38		05.50				06.05				06.20	06.25	06.35	06.47	06.50	06.54			07.03		07.07		07.10	07.18
Broad St Goods		05.35									06/07																
Dalston Jcn	05.40	05.42		05.44		05.56				06.11	06/15			06.26	06.31	06.41	06.53	06.56	07.00			07.09		07.13		07/18	07.24
Dalston W. Jcn	05.41	05.44		05.45		05.57				06.12	06/17			06.27	06.32	06.42	06.54	06.57	07.01		07/06	07.10		07.14		07/19	07.25
Canonbury Jcn	05.43	05.46		05.46		05.58				06.13	06/19			06.28	06.33	06.43	06.55	06.58	07.02		07/08	07.11		07.15		07/21	07.26
Highbury				05.48		06.00				06.15				06.30	06.35	06.45	06.57	07.00	07.04			07.13		07.17			07.28
Caledonian Road				05.50		06.02				06.17				06.32	06.37	06.47	06.59	07.02	07.06			07.15		07.19			07.30
St Pancras Sidings																				07.09							
Maiden Lane																											
CAMDEN RD	05.48	05.50		05.54		06.05			06/09	06.20	06/25			06.35	06.40	06.50	07.02	07.05	07.09	07/13	07/15	07.18		07.22		07/28	07.33
Primrose Hill	05.49	05.51				06.07					06/27				06.43		07.05		07.12	07/15	07/18	07.21				07/32	07.36
CAMDEN	05.50	05.52	06.00			06.08			06/25		06/28				06.45		07.06		07.13	07/16	07/20	07.22				07/35	07.37
Kentish Town West				05.56						06.22				06.37		06.52		07.07						07.24			
GOSPEL OAK				05.58						06.24				06.39		06.54		07.09						07.26			
Hampstead Heath				06.00						06.26				06.41		06.56		07.11						07.28			
Finchley Road				06.02						06.28				06.43		06.58		07.13						07.30			
West End Lane				06.04						06.30				06.45		07.00		07.15						07.32			
Brondesbury				06.06						06.32				06.47		07.02		07.17						07.34			
Brondesbury Park																07.04		07.19						07.36			
Kensal Rise				06.09						06.35				06.50		07.06		07.21						07.38			
Kensal Green Jcn				06.12						06.38				06.54		07.09		07.25						07.42			
WILLESDEN (BRENT)																											
WILLESDEN (HL)			06.05	06.13						06.39				06.55		07.10		07.26						07.43			
Old Oak Sidings												06/40											07/35				
Acton Wells Jcn			06.07	06.15						06.41		06/50	06/18	06.57		07.12		07.28					07/40	07.45			
ACTON YARD																							07/46				
ACTON CENTRAL			06.09	06.18						06.44		06/56		07.01		07.15		07.31						07.48			
South Acton			06.11	06.20						06.46				07.03		07.17		07.33						07.50			
Gunnersbury			06.13	06.25						06.50				07.06		07.20		07.36						07.53			
Kew Gardens			06.16	06.28						06.53				07.09		07.23		07.39						07.56			
RICHMOND			06.19	06.31						06.56				07.12		07.26		07.42						07.59			
Bollo Lane																											
KEW EAST JCN			06/27									07/01															
Destination	W'den		Kew	Kew		Watford				Feltham		Feltham	Bow (M)		Watford		Watford		Watford		Watford	Watford			Camden	Camden	Watford

Notes: col. 8 (DR 39, Light) shows "R/R" at Victoria Park. col. 3 (30/65) is shown "Ex Siding" at Camden (06.00).

7

	07.10	06.25			06.09		07.03		07.35	06.44	07.05	07.38			07.32	07.45		06.54	07.19			07.30		07.35	07.46	07.50
From	E. Gds	Watford			Feltham		Kew N		Fins Pk	Watford	Watford	E. Gds			G. Hill	F. Park		Feltham	Watford			Hertford		Bushey	Watford	Welwyn
Class	K	Pass	Pass	K		Pass	K	H	Light	Pass		K	H	Pass	Pass	J	Pass	F	Pass	K	Light	Pass	Pass	Pass	XP	Pass
Engine	J50 0-6-0T	EMU	EMU	7F 0-8-0	700 0-6-0	EMU	3P 2-6-2T	J15 0-6-0	N2 0-6-2T	EMU	EMU	J50 0-6-0T	3F 0-6-0T	EMU	N2 0-6-2T	J50 0-6-0T	EMU	Q1 0-6-0	EMU	3F 0-6-0T	3F 0-6-0T	N2 0-6-2T	EMU	EMU	EMU	N2 0-6-2T
Shed	HSY 21	28/63	30/65	1A/108	FEL138	18	1A/150	SX 114	KX 195	1/38	9/46	HSY 22	DR 21	13/50	KX 196	HSY 24	31/66	FEL 124	12/49	DR 30	DR 18	KX 197	19/55	32/67	4/41	KX 198
KEW EAST JCN					06/49													07/34								
Bollo Lane																										
RICHMOND		06.40				06.54								07.10			07.25						07.40			
Kew Gardens		06.43				06.57								07.13			07.28						07.43			
Gunnersbury		05.46				07.00								07.16			07.31						07.46			
South Acton		06.48			06/53	07.02	07/06							07.18			07.33	07/37					07.48			
ACTON CENTRAL		06.51				07.05								07.21			07.36						07.51			
ACTON YARD																				07.50						
Acton Wells Jcn		06/53			06/59		07/12							07/23			07/38	07/43		07/57			07/53			
Old Oak Sidings					to Neasden		to C'wood											to Toton		08.03						
WILLESDEN (HL)		06.57				07.10								07.26			07.42						07.57			
WILLESDEN (HL Sdgs)																										
Kensal Green Jcn		06.58				07/11								07/27			07/43						07/58			
Kensal Rise		06.59				07.12								07.28			07.44						07.59			
Brondesbury Park						07.14								07.30			07.46						08.01			
Brondesbury		07.02				07.16								07.32			07.48						08.03			
West End Lane		07.04				07.18								07.34			07.50						08.05			
Finchley Road		07.06				07.20								07.36			07.52						08.07			
Hampstead Heath		07.08				07.22								07.38			07.54						08.09			
GOSPEL OAK		07.10				07.24								07.40			07.56						08.11			
Kentish Town West		07.12				07.26								07.42			07.58						08.13			
CAMDEN	07/05	07.14		07.14						07/27	07/48		07.36							08/00					08/13	08/23
Primrose Hill	07.06			07/17#						07.28	07.49		07.38							08.01					08.14	08.24
CAMDEN ROAD	07.09	07.14		07/19		07.28				07.31	07.52		07.40	07.44			08.00			08.04			08.15		08.17	08.27
Maiden Lane																										
St Pancras Sidings																					08.10					
Caledonian Road	07.12	07.17				07.31				07.35	07.55			07.47			08.03			08.07			08.18		08.21	
Highbury	07.14	07.19				07.33				07.37	07.57			07.49			08.05			08.09			08.20		08.23	
Canonbury Jcn	07.16	07.21		07/26		07.35			07/38	07.39	07.59			07.51	08.02	08.07	08.07			08.11	08/14	08/19	08.22	08.25		08.34
Dalston W. Jcn	07/17	07/22		07/28		07/35			07/40	07/40	08.00			07/52	08.03	08.10	08.08			08/12	08/16	08/20	08/23	08/26	08/32	08/35
Dalston Jcn	07.19	07.24		07/30		07.38			07/42	07.42	08.02			07.54	08.06		08.10			08.14	08/18	08.23	08.25	0828	08.33	08.38
Broad St Goods				07/38																						
BROAD STREET		07.29				07.43			07.48	07.47	08.08			08.00	08.12		08.15			08.20	08.24	08.29	08.30	08.33	08.38	08.44
Kingsland	07/23											07/50				08/12										
Kingsland																										
Dalston E. Jcn	07/25											07/52				08/14										
Graham Road								07.40																		
Hackney																										
Homerton																										
Hackney Wick																										
VICTORIA PARK	07/31							07/45				07/57				08/19										
TEMPLE MILLS								08.00																		
GOODMAYES																										
THAMES WHARF																										
VICTORIA DOCKS	08.05																									
Old Ford																										
Tredegar Road																										
Fairfield Road																										
TILBURY JCN												08/00														
PLAISTOW																										
RIPPLE LANE																										
Bow Junction												08.01														
Devons Road								08.10				08.05														
Devon's Rd Loco																										
POPLAR DOCKS								08.18				08.10														
Destination																										

Train / From									08.05 Mitre B				07.35 V.Docks		08.05 Mitre B						08.54 Neasden			09.00 Brent(M)		
Class	K	K	Pass	Pass	K	Pass	Pass	Pass	Milk	Pass	H	Pass	H	EBV	Milk	Light	ECS	Pass	Pass	Light	H	ECS	Pass	J	ECS	Pass
Engine	3F 0-6-0T	H16 4-6-2T	EMU	EMU	3F 0-6-0T	EMU	EMU	EMU	3P 2-6-2T	EMU	4MT 2-6-0	EMU	4MT 2-6-0	3F 0-6-0T	3P 2-6-2T	3F 0-6-0T	N2 0-6-2T	EMU	EMU	3F 0-6-0T	700 0-6-0T	N2 0-6-2T	EMU	4F 0-6-0	EMU	EMU
Shed	DR 49	FEL 146	54/17	53/16	1B/103	62/28	30/65	18	1B/150	1/38	DR 23	50/13	DR 23	DR 17	1B/150	DR 14	KX 195	46/9	31/66	DR 49	FEL 138	KX 196	49/12	14A/120	32/67	19/55
POPLAR DOCKS																08.05										
Devon's Rd Loco																										
Devons Road											07.30					08.08										
Bow Junction											07.34															
RIPPLE LANE																										
PLAISTOW																										
TILBURY JCN					07.35																					
Fairfield Road																										
Tredegar Road																										
Old Ford																										
VICTORIA DOCKS													07.35													
THAMES WHARF																										
GOODMAYES																										
TEMPLE MILLS																										
VICTORIA PARK													07.38	08.04												
Hackney Wick																										
Homerton																										
Hackney																										
Graham Road																										
Dalston E. Jcn													07.43	08.09												
Kingsland													07.45	08.11												
BROAD STREET			07.22	07.28		07.35	07.38	07.53		08.06		08.10					08.20	08.23	08.26			08.35	08.40		08.43	08.47
Broad St Goods																										
Dalston Jcn			07.28	07.34		07.41	07.44	07.59		08.12		08.16					08.25	08.29	08.32			08.41	08.46		08.50	08.53
Dalston W. Jcn			07.29	07.35		07.42	07.45	08.00		08.13		08.17					08.27	08.30	08.33			08.43	08.47		08.54	
Canonbury Jcn			07.30	07.36		07.43	07.46	08.01		08.14		08.18					To Fins Park	08.31	08.34			08.46	08.48		08.55	
Highbury	07.25		07.32																							
Caledonian Road	07.35		07.34																							
St Pancras Sidings																										
Maiden Lane															08.38											
CAMDEN RD		07.43	07.37		07.47			08.08		08.21		08.25	08.33*			08.42	08.38		08.41				08.55			09.02
Primrose Hill		07.46			07.49					08.24			08.36			08.44			08.43							09.04
CAMDEN		07.49			07.51					08.25			08.38			08.46			08.44							09.05
Kentish Town West			07.39	07.52								08.27						08.40					08.57			
GOSPEL OAK			07.41	07.54		08.00						08.29						08.42					08.59			
Hampstead Heath			07.43	07.56								08.31						08.44					09.01			
Finchley Road			07.45	07.58		08.04						08.33						08.46					09.03			
West End Lane			07.47	08.00								08.35						08.48					09.05			
Brondesbury			07.49	08.02								08.37						08.50					09.07			
Brondesbury Park			07.51	08.04								08.39						08.52					09.09			
Kensal Rise			07.53	08.06								08.41						08.54					09.11			
Kensal Green Jcn		07.56		08.09								08.43						08.57					09.13			
WILLESDEN (BRENT)																										
WILLESDEN (HL)		07.57		08.10			08.15	08.28	08.33			08.44		08.45				08.58						09.14		
Old Oak Sidings	07.47			08.12			08.20	08.30	08.35			08.46		08.53				09.00							09.16	09.23
Acton Wells Jcn	07.50	07.59					08.25							08.58							09.06					
ACTON YARD																										
ACTON CENTRAL				08.15				08.33				08.49						09.03			09.15			09.18		
South Acton	07.56			08.17				08.35	08.38			08.51						09.05						09.20		09.30
Gunnersbury				08.20				08.38				08.54						09.09						09.23		
Kew Gardens				08.23				08.41				08.57						09.12						09.26		
RICHMOND			08.14	08.26				08.44				09.00						09.15						09.29		
Bollo Lane															09.00											
KEW EAST JCN	07.59													09.05							09.18			09.34		
Destination	Feltham	Watford			Watford				Watford				Acton	Acton	Watford		Fins Pk			Watford	Feltham	Fins Pk		B'sea	B'sea	Watford

9

WORKING TIMETABLE : 1953

Location	1	2	3	4	5	6	7	8	9	10	11	12	13	14	15	16	17	18	19	20	21	22	23	24	25	26	27
Train From			07.30 Feltham	08.07 Harrow	07.57 Watford	07.58 Hertford	07.50 Tring		08.09 Watford	08.23 Watford	08.15 Hertford				08.36 Bushey	08.30 Welwyn		08.37 Watford	08.49 Brentford	08.48 Watford	09.04 G. Hill		09.00 W'den	08.40 Tring	09.00 Bollo L	08.46 Hitchin	09.00 W'den
Class	Pass	Pass	H	Pass	Pass	Pass	Pass	Pass	Pass	Pass	Pass	Pass	Light	Light	Pass	Pass	Pass	Pass	F	XP	Pass	Pass	K	Pass	Milk	Pass	K
Engine	3F 0-6-0T	EMU	Q1 0-6-0	EMU	EMU	N2 0-6-2T	4 2-6-4T	EMU	EMU	EMU	N2 0-6-2T	EMU	2F 0-6-0T	4MT 2-6-0	EMU	N2 0-6-2T	EMU	EMU	S15 4-6-0	EMU	N2 0-6-2T	EMU	4F 0-6-0	4 2-6-4T	3P 2-6-2T	B1 4-6-0	4F 0-6-0
Shed	DR 21	25/60	FEL 125	21/57	10/47	KX 199	WAT 131	15/52	3/40	2/39	KX 190	17/54	DR 41	DR 23	33/68	KX 191	28/63	27/62	FEL 115	48/11	KX 192	18	DR 15	WAT 135	1A/150	HN 201	DR 15
KEW EAST JCN			08/11																08/55						09.12		
Bollo Lane																											
RICHMOND		07.56						08.15				08.29					08.44					08.56					
Kew Gardens		07.59						08.18				08.32					08.47					08.59					
Gunnersbury		08.02						08.21				08.35					08.50					09.02			09.15		
South Acton		08.04	08/14					08.23				08.37					08.52		08/58			09.04					
ACTON CENTRAL		08.07						08.26				08.40					08.55					09.07					
ACTON YARD																											
Acton Wells Jcn		08/09	08/20					08/28				08/42					08/57		09/04			09/09					
Old Oak Sidings			to Neasden																To Toton								
WILLESDEN (HL)		08/12						08/31				08/46					09.00					09.12					
WILLESDEN (HL Sdgs)																											
Kensal Green Jcn		08/13						08/32				08/47					09/01					09/13					
Kensal Rise		08.14						08.33				08.48					09.02					09.14					
Brondesbury Park		08.16						08.35				08.50					09.04					09.16					
Brondesbury		08.18						08.37				08.52					09.06					09.18					
West End Lane		08.20						08.39				08.54					09.08					09.20					
Finchley Road		08.22						08.41				08.56					09.10					09.22					
Hampstead Heath		08.24						08.43				08.58					09.12					09.24					
GOSPEL OAK		08.26						08.45				09.00					09.14					09.26					
Kentish Town West		08.28						08.47				09.02					09.16					09.28					
CAMDEN				08/32	08/39		08/44		08/50	08/59				09.02	09/12			09/18		09/24			09/30	09/34			
Primrose Hill				08/33	08/40		08/45		08.51	09/00				09.05	09/13			09/19		09/27			09/31	09/35			
CAMDEN ROAD		08.30		08/36	08/43		08/47	08/49	08.54	09/02		09/04		09.06	09/15		09/18	09.21		09/27		09/30	09/33	09/37			
Maiden Lane																											
St Pancras Sidings																											
Caledonian Road		08.33						08.52				09.07					09.21	09.24				09.33					
Highbury		08.35*		08/41	08/49			08.54	09.00			09.09					09.23	09.26				09.35	09.39*				09.42*
Canonbury Jcn				08/43		08/47	08/52	08.56	09.01	09/06	09/07	09.11			09/19	09/20	09.25	09.28		09/32	09/35	09.37		09/41		09/41	09.43
Dalston W. Jcn		08/38		08/44	08/50	08/48	08/53	08/57	09/01	09/07	09/08	09/12			09/20	09/22	09/26	09/29		09/33	09/37	09/38		09/42		09/42	09.45
Dalston Jcn		08.40		08/46	08/51	08.51	08.55	08.59	09.03	09.08	09.11	09.14			09.21	09.24	09.28	09.31		09.34	09.39	09.40		09/43		09.45	
Broad St Goods																											
BROAD STREET		08.45		08/51	08/56	08.57	09.01	09.04	09.08	09.13	09.17	09.19			09.26	09.30	09.33	09.36		09.39	09.45	09.45		09.48		09.51	
Kingsland														09/18													09/47
Dalston E. Jcn														09/20													09/49
Graham Road																											
Hackney																											
Homerton																											
Hackney Wick																											
VICTORIA PARK														09/25													09/57
TEMPLE MILLS																											10.10
GOODMAYES																											
THAMES WHARF																											
VICTORIA DOCKS																											
Old Ford	08.50																										
Tredegar Road																											
Fairfield Road																											
TILBURY JCN	08/53													09/28													
PLAISTOW																											
RIPPLE LANE																											
Bow Junction	08.54													09.29													
Devons Road	08.57												09.25														
Devon's Rd Loco														09.32													
POPLAR DOCKS													09.30														
Destination																									Ken		

10

WORKING TIMETABLE : 1953

Train				09.20 Brent(M)									09.17 C'wood					09.45 Brent(M)			09.45 Brent(M)					
From																										
Class	EBV	ECS	Pass	J	ECS	K	ECS	Pass	K	ECS	J	ECS	J	Pass	Light	H	Pass	ECS	Light	K	J	ECS	Light	Light	ECS	ECS
Engine	3F 0-6-0T	EMU	EMU	Q1 0-6-0	N2 0-6-2T	3F 0-6-0T	EMU	EMU	J50 0-6-0T	EMU	3F 0-6-0T	N2 0-6-2T	3F 0-6-0T	EMU	4P 2-6-4T	J17 0-6-0	EMU	N2 0-6-2T	3F 0-6-0T	3F 0-6-0T	3F 0-6-0T	EMU	3F 0-6-0T	3F 0-6-0T	EMU	N2 0-6-2T
Shed	DR 31	4/41	6/25	FEL 123	KX 197	DR 43	57/21	47/10	HSY 20	40/3	DR 26	KX 198	14A/70	15	WAT 131	SX 103	2/39	KX 199	DR 45	DR 13	14A/86	54/17	DR 10	DR 27	33/68	KX 190
POPLAR DOCKS						08.45			08.55																	
Devon's Rd Loco	08.35														09.10								09.23			
Devons Road						08.54					09.03									09.14				09.28		
Bow Junction	08.38								09.02		09.07									09.18			09.26	09.32		
RIPPLE LANE																										
PLAISTOW																										
TILBURY JCN	08/39								09/03		09/08												09/27	09/33		
Fairfield Road																										
Tredegar Road																										
Old Ford	R/R																		R/R							
VICTORIA DOCKS																										
THAMES WHARF																										
GOODMAYES																										
TEMPLE MILLS																09.00										
VICTORIA PARK	08/42								09/06		09/11					*Via T&H*							09/31	09/37		
Hackney Wick	R/R																		R/R							
Homerton																										
Hackney																										
Graham Road									09/12														09/40			
Dalston E. Jcn											09/16															
Kingsland									09/14		09/18												09/42			
Kingsland																09/33										
BROAD STREET		08.53	08.58		09.00		09.06	09.09		09.14		09.16		09.23	09.25		09.30	09.20				09.34			09.40	09.40
Broad St Goods																										
Dalston Jcn		09/01	09.04		09/06		09/11	09/15		09/19		09/25		09.29	09.32		09.36	09/26				09/40	09/43		09.45	09/46
Dalston W. Jcn			09/05		09/08		09/12	09/16	09/16	09/20		09/26		09/30			09/38	09/28							09/47	
Canonbury Jcn			09.06		09/14		09/14	09/17	09/20	09/22		09/28		09/31			09/41	09/31				09/42	09/45			09/53
Highbury			09.08					09/19																		
Caledonian Road			09.10					09/21																		
St Pancras Sidings																							09.52			
Maiden Lane																										
CAMDEN RD			09.13				09/18	09/24		09/28	09/31			09.38	09/40	09/45	09/45	09/48				09/48				
Primrose Hill								09.26						09/42	09/42		09/48									
CAMDEN								09/27						09/44	09/44		09/49									
Kentish Town West			09.15																							
GOSPEL OAK			09.17							09/33	09/36					09/45										
Hampstead Heath			09.19								09/38					09/48										
Finchley Road			09.21							09/37	09/40					09/50										
West End Lane			09.23																							
Brondesbury			09.25																			10/11				
Brondesbury Park			09.27																							
Kensal Rise			09.29																							
Kensal Green Jcn			09.31							09/44	09/50					10/00						10/15				
WILLESDEN (BRENT)											10/05															
WILLESDEN (HL)			09.33				09/37			09/45						10/02						10/16				
Old Oak Sidings																					10/07					
Acton Wells Jcn			09.35	09/42									09/52													
ACTON YARD													09.57													
ACTON CENTRAL			09.38																			10.02				
South Acton			09.40																			10.04				
Gunnersbury			09.43																			10.07				
Kew Gardens			09.46																			10.10				
RICHMOND			09.49																			10.13				
Bollo Lane																										
KEW EAST JCN				09/53																						
Destination	Vic Dks	Fins Pk		Feltham	Fins Pk	Mitre B	Watford	E. Goods	Mitre B	Fins Pk	Watford	1A Loco	H. Green	Watford	E. Goods	Mitre B	Fins Pk	Plaistow	Bow Gas	W. Ken	Mitre B	Vic Dks	Fins Pk			

11

WORKING TIMETABLE : 1953

Train	Light	08.58	09.50	09.09	09.28			09.40	09.32	08.57			10.25				10.48		10.12	10.55	09.46		09.53
From		Watford	Bow Gas	Watford	Richmond			W'den	Watford	Feltham			Hornsey				F.Park		Watford	T.Mills	Feltham		Feltham
Class		Pass	J	Pass	Pass	H	K	H	Pass	H	Pass	K	Light	H	Pass	H		K	Pass	Coupled	K	J	H
Engine	3F 0-6-0T	EMU	3F 0-6-0T	EMU	EMU	3F 0-6-0T	3F 0-6-0T	7F 0-8-0	EMU	700 0-6-0	EMU	3F 0-6-0T	J50 0-6-0T	3F 0-6-0T	EMU	4F 0-6-0	J52 0-6-0T	5F 2-6-0	EMU	3F & 4F	S15 4-6-0	7F 0-8-0	8F 2-8-0
Shed	DR 21	23/59	DR 13	24	9/46	DR 18	1B/03	1A/119	14/51	FEL 137	12/49	1B/104	HSY 25	DR 30	25/60	1A/128	HSY 11	1A/117	8	DR 15/17	FEL 114	1A/100	14A/151
KEW EAST JCN										09/35									10.12		10.12	10.18	10/25
Bollo Lane																							
RICHMOND		09.15		09.28						09.45	10.02												
Kew Gardens		09.18		09.31						09.48	10.05												
Gunnersbury		09.21		09.34						09.51	10.08												
South Acton		09.23		09.36						09.53	10.10								10/18		10/18		10/28
ACTON CENTRAL		09.25		09.38						09.55	10.12												
ACTON YARD						09.27								10.00									
Acton Wells Jcn		09/27		09/32	09/40			09/43		09/57	10/14		10/05	10/05							10/27		10/34
Old Oak Sidings																					10/32		To Brent/M
WILLESDEN (HL)		09.30		09.35	09/43			09/51		10.00	10.17		10/08	10/08					10.18				
WILLESDEN (HL Sdgs)																09.55	10.10						
Kensal Green Jcn		09/31		09/37	09/44			09/53		10.01	10/18		10/10	10/10		10/21	10/26		10/33				
Kensal Rise		09.32			09.45					10.02	10.19												
Brondesbury Park		09.34			09.47					10.04	10.21												
Brondesbury		09.36			09.49					10.06	10.23												
West End Lane		09.38			09.51					10.08	10.25												
Finchley Road		09.40		09/46	09.53			10/02		10.10	10.27		10/20	10/20		10/30		10/41				10.45	
Hampstead Heath		09.42			09.55					10.12	10.29												
GOSPEL OAK		09.44		09/51	09.57			10/07		10.14	10.31		10/25	10/25		10/35		10/47					
Kentish Town West		09.46			09.59					10.16	10.33												
CAMDEN	09/39			09/50			09.55	10/13			10.18	10.05			10.18				10/52				
Primrose Hill	09.40			09.51			10/01	10.14			10.21	10/08			10.21				10.53				
CAMDEN ROAD	09.42	09.48		09.53	09/56		10/03	10.16		10/12	10.23	10/10		10/23		10/40		10/52	10.55				
Maiden Lane																							
St Pancras Sidings			09.55									10.15											
Caledonian Road		09.51		09.56							10.38								10.58				
Highbury		09.53		09.58							10.40								11.00				
Canonbury Jcn		09.55	09/46	10.00	10/01	10/04	10/11	10/19	10/20		10.42	10/25	10/35	10/29		10/46	10/48	10/57	11.02				
Dalston W Jcn		09.58	09/47	10.01	10/03	10/06	10/13	10.21	10/21		10.43	10/26	10/37	10/31		10/48	10/50	10/59	11.03				
Dalston Jcn	09.48	09.58		10.03	10/11		10/15	10.22	10.22		10.45		10/51	10/37				11/01	11.05				
Broad St Goods							10/23											11.17					
BROAD STREET	09.53	10.03		10.08	10.16			10.27	10.27		10.50								11.10				
Kingsland						10w09							10w42				10.55						
Kingsland			10/05			10w14				10/23			10w47			10/50	R/R						
Dalston E. Jcn			10/07		10/17					10/25			10/46	10/50		10/52							
Graham Road																							
Hackney																							
Homerton																							
Hackney Wick																				R/R			
VICTORIA PARK				11/07	10/24				10/30				10/51	10.58		11/07				11.12			
TEMPLE MILLS					10.36				10.42														
GOODMAYES																							
THAMES WHARF													11.15										
VICTORIA DOCKS													11.09	11.25									
Old Ford																							
Tredegar Road			R/R																				
Fairfield Road			10.11																				
TILBURY JCN	10.16		10/13		10.15											11.11				11/16			
PLAISTOW					10.26																		
RIPPLE LANE														11.37									
Bow Junction	10/14		10/14																	11/17			
Devons Road	10.18	10.16								10.42													
Devon's Rd Loco																				11/20			
POPLAR DOCKS	10.21	10.21								10.50													
Destination																Acton							

WORKING TIMETABLE : 1953

						09.52		10.15			09.10		09.50				10.20							10.40	10.45					
Train						C'wood		Neasden			F. Park		Bow Gas				Hendon							Brent (M)	Brent (M)					
From																														
Class	Pass	Light	ECS	J	Pass	H	ECS	Pcls	J	H	J	D	ECS	ECS	J	H	H	Pass	2 LE	Pass	K	J	Light	ECS	H	Light	K
Engine	EMU	3F 0-6-0T	EMU	4F 0-6-0	EMU	Q1 0-6-0	EMU	3P 2-6-2T	J6 0-6-0	3F 0-6-0T	3F 0-6-0T	7F 0-8-0	N2 0-6-2T	EMU	8F 2-8-0	3F 0-6-0T	J50 0-6-0T	EMU	B1/N2	EMU	Q1 0-6-0	3F 0-6-0T	4P 2-6-4T	EMU	3F 0-6-0T	3F 0-6-0T	3F 0-6-0T
Shed	27/62	DR 3	28/63	14A/121	18	FEL 125	4E/11	1A/101	HSY 4	DR 22	DR 13	1A/108	KX 191	50/13	14A/125	DR 45	HSY 21	23	201/192	24	FEL 124	14A/70	WAT 135	46/9	DR 31	DR 36	DR 10
POPLAR DOCKS																											
Devon's Rd Loco		09.35																						10.25			
Devons Road		09.38									09/55														10.28		
Bow Junction																											
RIPPLE LANE																											
PLAISTOW											09.50																
TILBURY JCN		09/39									09/57	09/57					10/01									10/29	
Fairfield Road												09/58															
Tredegar Road												R/R															
Old Ford																											
VICTORIA DOCKS				10.00						10.00																	
THAMES WHARF																	09.05										
GOODMAYES																											
TEMPLE MILLS																09.35											
VICTORIA PARK		09/42									10/04					09/53	10/09							10/25	10/32		
Hackney Wick																									R/R		
Homerton																											
Hackney																											
Graham Road																											
Dalston E. Jcn		09/49									10/11					10/02	10/18									10/32	
Kingsland		09/51									10w17					10/04	10/20									10/34	
BROAD STREET	09.45		09.47		09.53		09.55	10.00					10.05	10.12				10.18	10.20	10.23			10.28	10.30			
Broad St Goods												10.04															
Dalston Jcn	09.51	09/55			09.59			10/07				10/11	10/13	10/18				10.24	10.26	10.29			10.35	10.38			
Dalston W. Jcn	09.52	09/56			10.00			10.08				10/13	10/14	10/19				10.25	10/27	10.30			10.37				
Canonbury Jcn	09.53	09/57			10.01			10.09		10/08		10/15	10/17	10/20		10/22		10.26	10/32	10.31			10.39				
Highbury	09.55				10.03													10.28		10.33							
Caledonian Road	09.57		10/07		10.05								10.30				10/32	10.30		10.35							
St Pancras Sidings																											10.52
Maiden Lane										10/40				10/40													11.02
CAMDEN RD	10.00	10/02	10/05					10/15				10/22		10/26		10/20	10/30	10.33		10.38			10/43				10/47
Primrose Hill	10.03	10/04						10/20				10/24						10.35					10/45				
CAMDEN	10.04	10/05						10/22				10/25						10/36					10/46				
Kentish Town West																											
GOSPEL OAK					10.12				10/20							10/25				10.40				10.52			
Hampstead Heath					10.14															10.42							
Finchley Road					10.16				10/25							10/30				10.44				10.57			
West End Lane					10.18															10.46							
Brondesbury			10/07		10.20		10/25													10.48							
Brondesbury Park					10.22															10.50							
Kensal Rise					10.24															10.52							
Kensal Green Jcn			10/11		10.26		10/29		10/34					10/44		10/39				10.54				10/59			
WILLESDEN (BRENT)				10.12																							
WILLESDEN (HL)			10/12		10.27		10/30		10/36					10/45		10/41				10.57							
Old Oak Sidings																											
Acton Wells Jcn				10/24		10/32			10/39						10/45	10/44					11/04	11/16					
ACTON YARD																10.50											
ACTON CENTRAL					10.32															11.02			11.18				
South Acton				10.30	10.34	10.40			10.45						10.54					11.04	11.13	11.24					
Gunnersbury					10.37															11.07							
Kew Gardens					10.40															11.10							
RICHMOND					10.43															11.13							
Bollo Lane																					11.16						
KEW EAST JCN				10/33		10/43			10/48						10/57												
Destination	Watford	Mitre B	B'sea	Feltham		Mitre B	W'den	Feltham	W'den	W'den	D. Road	Wood G	Mitre B	Feltham		H. Green	Fins Pk	W'den	Brentford	Brentford	W. Ken	C'sea	W. Ken	C'sea			

13

WORKING TIMETABLE : 1953

Train				Light	10.58 W'den	11.05 E.Gds				10.29 W.Ken	11.00		11.30 Hornsey					11.28 W'den		11.09 Ken(High)	10.10 W'den		12.01 Bow Gas	Light	11.57 E.Goods	11.58 W'den	12.15 T.Mills
Class	Pass	K			Pass	H	J	H	J		Pass	TPO	K	K	K	K	Pass	J			Pass			K	Pass	
Engine	EMU	3F 0-6-0T	7F 0-8-0		EMU	J50 0-6-0T	J50 0-6-0T	3F 0-6-0T	3F 0-6-0T	3F 0-6-0T	EMU	N2	3F 0-6-0T	3F 0-6-0T	3F 0-6-0T	4F 0-6-0	EMU	7F 0-8-0	3F 0-6-0T	7F 0-8-0	EMU	3F 0-6-0T	2F 0-6-0T	J50 0-6-0T	EMU	3F 0-6-0T
Shed	15	DR 3	1A/119		23	HSY 20	HSY 24	DR 9	14A/70	14A/70	18	KX	DR 43	DR 10	DR 12	1A/121	59	1A/119	14A/67	1A/100	24	DR 13	DR 40	HSY 21	8	DR 9
KEW EAST JCN																										
Bollo Lane																										
RICHMOND	10.26										10.56										11.26					
Kew Gardens	10.29										10.59										11.29					
Gunnersbury	10.32										11.02										11.32					
South Acton	10.34								10/55		11.04								11/25		11.34					
ACTON CENTRAL	10.36							10.50			11.06										11.36					
ACTON YARD																										
Acton Wells Jcn	10/38							10/57	11/00	11/05	11/08								11/32		11/38					
Old Oak Sidings									To Brent(M)	To Brent(M)									To Brent(M)							
WILLESDEN (HL)	10.41							11/00	11/00 Brent(M)	11.00 Brent(M)	11.11						11/41				11.41					
WILLESDEN (HL Sdgs)																11.00										
Kensal Green Jcn	10.42					10/47		11/02			11/12					11/17					11/42					
Kensal Rise	10.43										11.13										11.43					
Brondesbury Park	10.45										11.15										11.45					
Brondesbury	10.47										11.17										11.47					
West End Lane	10.49										11.19										11.49					
Finchley Road	10.51					11/00		11/11			11.21					11/29					11.51					
Hampstead Heath	10.53										11.23										11.53					
GOSPEL OAK	10.55					11/08		11/16			11.25					11/34					11.55					
Kentish Town West	10.57										11.27										11.57					
CAMDEN	10.58				11/08						11.29						11/38				11.59				12/08	
Primrose Hill		11.01			11.09												11.39								12.09	
CAMDEN ROAD	10.59	11.03			11.11	11/10		11/21			11.32	11/40				11/39	11.41				12.02				12.11	
Maiden Lane			11.05			11w30																				
St Pancras Sidings			11/19											11.28	11.47											
Caledonian Road	11.02				11.14	11w34					11.34		11.36	11/38			11.44				12.04				12.14	
Highbury	11.04				11.16						11.36						11.46				12.06				12.16	
Canonbury Jcn	11.06				11.18	11/16		11/32			11/37	11/43			12.04	11/48	11.48				12/07				12.18	
Dalston W. Jcn	11.07				11.19	11/18		11/34			11/37	11.45				11/50	11.49		12/10						12.19	
Dalston Jcn	11.09				11.21						11.39	11.45					11.51				12.09				12.21	
Broad St Goods																										
BROAD STREET	11.14				11.26						11.44						11.56				12.14				12.26	
Kingsland		11/15					11/40						11/47		11/52											
Dalston E. Jcn		11/17				11/23	11/43					11/45	11/49		11/54				12/14							
Graham Road							11/45																			
Hackney															12.14											
Homerton																								12.19		
Hackney Wick																								R/R		12.36
VICTORIA PARK		11/23				11/28		11L54					11/56			12/02								12/23		
TEMPLE MILLS						12.04		12.11																		
GOODMAYES																										
THAMES WHARF																										
VICTORIA DOCKS						11.50																				
Old Ford																										
Tredegar Road																						12.23				
Fairfield Road																						12/25				
TILBURY JCN		11/29											12/00											12/32		
PLAISTOW													12/14													
RIPPLE LANE																										
Bow Junction		11.30														12/06						12/26		12/33		12/41
Devons Road															12.00	12/07						12/30		12/36		12/44
Devon's Rd Loco																							12.30			
POPLAR DOCKS															12.07	12.12							12/35	12.40		
Destination		H.Squ																								

WORKING TIMETABLE : 1953

Train / From / Class / Engine / Shed	DR 43	51/14	59	14A/124	12/49	HSY 11	DR 2	1B/103	DR 21	DR 13	FEL 115	8	15	FEL 114	DR 36	HSY 24	1B/132	23	18	1A/92	DR 27	DR 18	HSY	1B/76	DR 37	59	DR 40
Train				11.05		10.00	10.30				11.27				11.10					11.50							
From				Brent(M)		F.Park	Haydon S				Brent(M)				C'sea					W'den							
Class	Light	ECS	Pass	J	Pass	K	K	K	K	J	J	Pass	Pass	K	H	EBV	J	Pass	Pass	Light	H	H	TPO	K	K	Pass	
Engine	3F 0-6-0T	EMU	EMU	4F 0-6-0	EMU	JS2 0-6-0T	3F 0-6-0T	3F 0-6-0T	3F 0-6-0T	3F 0-6-0T	S15 4-6-0	EMU	EMU	S15 4-6-0	3F 0-6-0T	JS2 0-6-0T	3F 0-6-0T	EMU	EMU	7F 0-8-0	3F 0-6-0T	3F 0-6-0T	N2 0-6-0T	7F 0-8-0	3F 0-6-0T	EMU	3F 0-5-0T
POPLAR DOCKS									10.46															11.54			12.00
Devon's Rd Loco																											
Devons Road	10.30									11.15																	
Bow Junct on	10/33								10/54	11/19														12/00			
RIPPLE LANE																											
PLAISTOW																							11.22				
TILBURY JCN	10.37						10/53																		12/01		
Fairfield Road																											
Tredegar Road																											
Old Ford																											
VICTORIA DOCKS																					10.25						
THAMES WHARF																											
GOODMAYES																											
TEMPLE MILLS																											
VICTORIA PARK						10.40	10/55								11/15						11/38	11/44			12/04		
Hackney Wick																11.25 (Pro-pel)											
Homerton																											
Hackney																											
Graham Road																											
Dalston E. Jcn							11/02								11/21	11/28					11/45	11/53	12.05	12/10			
Kingsland						11/00	11/04								11w24	11/30					11w47	11w56	12/07	12W13			
BROAD STREET		10.45	10.48		10.53							11.18	11.23					11.48	11.53							12.18	
Broad St Goods																											
Dalston Jcn		10/51	10/54		10/59		11/15					11/24	11/29		11/32		11/40	11/54	11/59							12.24	
Dalston W Jcn		10/52	10/55		11/00		11/17					11/25	11/30				11/49	11/55	12/00							12/25	
Canonbury Jcn		10/53	10/56		11/01		11/19					11/26	11/31		11/34		11/51	11/56	12/01		11/57				12/06	12/26	
Highbury			10/58		11/03							11/28	11/33					11/58	12/03							12/28	
Caledonian Road			11.00		11/05							11/30	11/35					12.00	12/05							12/30	
St Pancras Sidings						11.15											11/59					12.12					
Maiden Lane																											
CAMDEN RD			11/03		11/08		11/26					11/33	11/38		11/43			12/03	12/08		12/12					12/33	
Primrose Hill			11/05				11/28					11/35						12/05								12/35	
CAMDEN			11/06				11/29					11/36						12/06								12/36	
Kentish Town West																											
GOSPEL OAK				11/08	11/10								11/40		11/48				12/10		12/17			12/34			
Hampstead Heath					11/12								11/42						12/12								
FINCHLEY ROAD					11/16								11/46		11/53				12/16		12/22			12/39			
West End Lane					11/18								11/48						12/18								
Brondesbury					11/20								11/50						12/20								
Brondesbury Park					11/22								11/52						12/22								
Kensal Rise					11/24								11/54						12/24	R/R							
Kensal Green Jcn		11/21			11/26								11/56		12/03				12/26	12.30	12/35				12/47		
WILLESDEN (BRENT)		11/22		11/24	11/27						11/47		11/57		12/05				12/27	12/32	12/50				13.05		
Old Oak Sidings											11/58									12/43					12/50		
Acton Wells Jcn											12/04				12/10					12/35							
ACTON YARD															12/15												
ACTON CENTRAL					11/32								12/02														
South Acton				11/30	11/34								12/04	11/53						12.42				12.57			
Gunnersbury					11/37								12/07														
Kew Gardens					11/40								12/10														
RICHMOND					11/43								12/13						12/43								
Bollo Lane																											
KEW EAST JCN				11/34							12/24			11/56													
Destination	Mitre B	W'den		B'sea		W'den			Feltham		Feltham			Feltham	W'den	Bow Gas	W'den			W'den		Hornsey	Hornsey	H'smith	W'den		

Train From																		
Train From	12.28 W'den			12.40 1B/loco	10.10 W'den		12.17 Feltham	12.58 W'den	13.15 E. Gds		12.27 Feltham	12.13 Ken	13.00 W'den	13.37 Plaistow	12.25 B'sea	13.28 W'den	13.00 Feltham	14.05 T. Mills	13.55 Camden
Class	Pass	Pass	H	2 LE	J	Light	K	Pass	J	H	K	J	H	Light	K	Pass	K	Light	K
Engine	EMU	EMU	3F 0-6-0T	3F5MT	7F 0-8-0	3F 0-6-0T	Q1 0-6-0	EMU	J50 0-6-0T	3F 0-6-0T	Q1 0-6-0	3F 0-6-0T	3F 0-6-0T	3F 0-6-0T	4F 0-6-0	EMU	S15 4-6-0	3F 0-6-0T	4F 0-6-0
Shed	23	15	DR 45	DR2/122	1A/100	DR 48	FEL 123	59	HSY 26	DR 31	FEL 125	14A/86	DR 26	1B/76	14A/120	8	FEL 110	DR 22	1A/111

KEW EAST JCN (Bollo Lane)	12/49						12/41		12/49							13/09	13/23		
RICHMOND	11.56	12.26						12.56											13.26
Kew Gardens	11.59	12.29						12.59											13.29
Gunnersbury	12.02	12.32						13.02											13.32
South Acton	12.04	12.34		12/53	12.55		12/44	13.04			12/58			13.09		13/14	13/26		13.34
ACTON CENTRAL	12.06	12.36		12.55?	13.03			13.06											13.36
ACTON YARD	11.52		12.20					12.50								13.20			
Acton Wells Jcn	11/57	12.08	12/27	12.38			12/50	12.57	13/08		12/59	13/04	13/08	13/15	13/20	13/27	13/32	13/38	13.55
Old Oak Sidings		To					To		To		13.04	To		R/R	To		To		13.59
WILLESDEN (HL)	12/00	12.11	12/30	12.41			Brent(M)	13.11	Brent(M)	13/00		Brent(M)	13/11	13/18	Brent(M)	13/30	Neasden	13.41	14/01
WILLESDEN (HL Sdgs)										13.00									14.05
Kensal Green Jcn	12/12	12.42	12/32					13.12		13/02		13/17	13/17	13/20		13/32	13/42		
Kensal Rise	12.13	12.43						13.13						R/R		13.43			
Brondesbury Park	12.15	12.45						13.15								13.45			
Brondesbury	12.17	12.47						13.17								13.47			
West End Lane	12.19	12.49						13.19								13.49			
Finchley Road	12/10	12.51	12/41					13.21	13/10			13/28	13/28			13.51	13/40		
Hampstead Heath	12.23	12.53						13.23								13.53			
GOSPEL OAK	12/15	12.55	12/46					13.25	13/15			13/33	13/33			13.55	13/45		
Kentish Town West	12.27	12.57						13.27								13.57			
CAMDEN	12/38			12.40				13/08		13/28			13/38		13.38	13/38	13.55		13.55
Primrose Hill	12.39			12.46				13.09		13.30					13.39		13.59		13.59
CAMDEN ROAD	12/20	12.59	12/51	12.48				13.11		13/31		13/38	13/38	13/38	13.41	13/50			14/01
Maiden Lane																			14.05
St Pancras Sidings																			
Caledonian Road	12.32	13.02						13.14							13.44		14.02		
Highbury	12.34	13.04						13.16							13.46		14.04		
Canonbury Jcn	12.36	13.06	12/58	12/53				13.18	13/23	13/30		13/39	13/48	13/48	13.48	13/57	14.06		
Dalston W. Jcn	12.37	13.07	13.00	12/55				13/19	13/25	13/32		13/41	13/50	13/50	13.49	13/59	14.07		
Dalston Jcn	12.39	13.09		12/57				13.21					13.39		13.51		14.09		
BROAD STREET	12.44	13.14						13.26					13.44		13.56		14.14		
Kingsland	12/39		13v03						13v28			13v44				14.02			
Kingsland			13v08	13.05					13v49			13w49				R/R			
Dalston E. Jcn	12/41		13/10						13/30	13/36		13/52	13/52	13/55			14/03	14.14	
Graham Road																	14.07	14/09	
Hackney																			
Homerton																			
Hackney Wick																	R/R		
VICTORIA PARK	12/54		13/18						13/40	13.43		13/59	14/04			14/26			
TEMPLE MILLS	13.07																		
GOODMAYES																			
THAMES WHARF										14.05									
VICTORIA DOCKS										14.10									
Old Ford					13.00														
Tredegar Road																			
Fairfield Road																			
TILBURY JCN			13/22		13/02							14/03	14/07	14.09				14/29	
PLAISTOW			13.34									14.14							
RIPPLE LANE					13.03														
Bow Junction														14.08		14.15		14/30	
Devons Road					13.06									14.11				14.33	
Devon's Rd Loco														14.15					
POPLAR DOCKS																14.22			
Destination											1A Loco					C. Yard			

WORKING TIMETABLE : 1953

Train	12.01		12.35																							13.20	
From	Bow Gas		Brent(M)																							Acton	
Class	K	Light	H	H	Pass	H	K	J	Pass	Pass	Light	K	Light	K	Pass	Pass	K	D	K	H	K	H	Pass	Pass	H	K	J
Engine	3F 0-6-0T	2F 0-6-0T	8F 2-8-0	J50 0-6-0	EMU	700 0-6-0	3F 0-6-0T	J50 0-6-0T	EMU	EMU	3F 0-6-0T	3F 0-6-0T	7F 0-8-0	SF 2-6-0	EMU	EMU	3F 0-6-0T	SMT 4-6-0	Q1 0-6-0	3F 0-6-0T	J50 0-6-0T	J50 0-6-0T	EMU	EMU	3F 0-6-0T	J52 0-6-0T	7F 0-8-0
Shed	DR 13	DR 40	14A/152	HSY 25	24	FEL 37	DR 18	HSY 24	8	49	1B/132	DR 12	1A/119	1A/117	25	15	DR 12	1B/22	FEL 125	DR 43	HSY 22	HSY 20	59	18	DR 49	HSY 11	1A/119
POPLAR DOCKS																											
Devon's Rd Loco																											
Devons Road												12.40								13.27	13/30						
Bow Junction	12/06											12/49									13/33						
RIPPLE LANE																											
PLAISTOW																				13.05							
TILBURY JCN	12/07											12/50								13.23	13/35						
Fairfield Road																											
Tredegar Road	12.10																										
Old Ford	R/R																										
VICTORIA DOCKS								12.40																			
THAMES WHARF																											
GOODMAYES			11.40																								
TEMPLE MILLS						12.05																13.15					
VICTORIA PARK				12/17		12/26						12/54								13/28	13/38	13/43			13/50		
Hackney Wick																											
Homerton																											
Hackney																											
Graham Road																											
Dalston E. Jcn				12/22		12/31		12/45				13/00								13/35	13/44	13/48			13/58		
Kingsland				12/24		12/33		12/47				13/02								13w38/13w43	13/46	13/50			14/00	14.10 R/R	
BROAD STREET					12.23				12.48	12.53					13.18	13.23							13.48	13.53			
Broad St Goods													13.00	13.10													
Dalston Jcn					12.29				12.54	12.59			13/09	13/18	13.24	13.29		13.32					13.54	13.59			
Dalston W. Jcn				12/25	12.30	12/35			12.55	13.00		13/04	13/11	13/20	13.25	13.30		13/39				13/52	13.55	14.00			
Canonbury Jcn				12/29	12.31	12/37			12.56	13.01		13/06	13/12	13/22	13.26	13.31		13/41				13/56	13.58	14.01			
Highbury					12.33				12.58	13.03					13.28	13.33		13/43						14.03			
Caledonian Road					12.35				13.00	13.05					13.30	13.35							14.00	14.05			
St Pancras Sidings							12.53				13.05	13/12	13/19				13.40										
Maiden Lane																									14.10	14.13	
CAMDEN RD					12.38	12/45	12/57		13.03	13.08	13/11			13/27	13.33	13.38	13/44	13/48		13/57	14/08		14.03	14.08		14/17	
Primrose Hill							12/59		13.05		13/14			13/29	13.35			13/49					14.05				
CAMDEN							13.00		13.06		13/20			13/31	13.36			13.51					14.06				
Kentish Town West					12.40					13.10						13.40								14.10			
GOSPEL OAK					12.42	12/50				13.12						13.42	13/49			14/02			To W'den	14.12	14/13	14/22	
Hampstead Heath					12.44					13.14						13.44								14.14			
Finchley Road					12.46	12/55				13.16						13.46	13/54			14/07				14.16	14/15	14/27	
West End Lane					12.48					13.18						13.48								14.18			
Brondesbury					12.50					13.20						13.50								14.20			
Brondesbury Park					12.52					13.22						13.52								14.22			
Kensal Rise					12.54					13.24						13.54								14.24			
Kensal Green Jcn					12.56	13/03				13.26						13.56								14.26		14/37	
WILLESDEN (BRENT)			13/03		12.57	13/05				13.27						13.57	14/03			14/16	14/18			14.27		14.50	
Old Oak Sidings																			14.10								
Acton Wells Jcn					12.59	13/08				13.29						13.59	14/10		14/16	14/25	14/29			14.29			
ACTON YARD																	14.15			14.30							
ACTON CENTRAL			13/08		13.02					13.32						14.02								14.32			
South Acton					13.04					13.34						14.04			14/24					14.34			
Gunnersbury					13.07					13.37						14.07								14.37			
Kew Gardens					13.10					13.40						14.10								14.40			
RICHMOND					13.13					13.43						14.13								14.43			
Bollo Lane																											
KEW EAST JCN			13/11																								
Destination	Devons Rd		Feltham	Ferme Pk		Ferme Pk	Ferme Pk	W'den	W'den						W'den		W'den	Glasgow	Feltham	Feltham	W'den	Ferme Pk	W'den		W'den	C' Yard	

17

WORKING TIMETABLE : 1953

Location	13.35 Kew B N	13.30 W'den	13.58 W'den			10.10 W'den	13.26 Feltham	14.28 W'den		14.35 Broad St		13.50 B'sea	14.47 Bow Gas			14.58 W'den	14.50 Mitre B			13.45 H. Green		15.03 Camden		15.40 T. Mills		14.25 B'sea
Class	K	K	Pass	H	Pass	J	J	Pass	K	K	Pass	J	J	Light	ECS	Pass	ECS	K	K	H	Pass	K	K	Light	ECS	
Engine	3F 0-6-0T	3F 0-6-0T	EMU	3F 0-6-0T	EMU	7F 0-8-0	J6 0-6-0	EMU	4F 0-6-0	3F 0-6-0T	EMU	4F 0-6-0	3F 0-6-0T	3F 0-6-0T	EMU	EMU	EMU	3F 0-6-0T	3F 0-6-0T	J17 0-6-0	EMU	3F 0-6-0T	3F 0-6-0T	3F 0-6-0T	EMU	4F 0-6-0
Shed	1A/75	1A/95	25	DR 36	12/49	1A/100	HSY 4	59	1A/111	DR 2	15	14A/121	DR 13	DR 3	46/9	23	28	DR 18	DR 49	SX 103	18	DR 18	DR 10	DR 36	33/68	14A/124
KEW EAST JCN	13/37						14/04					14/34														15/04
Bollo Lane																										
RICHMOND			13.56								14.26										14.56					
Kew Gardens			13.59								14.29										14.59					
Gunnersbury			14.02								14.31										15.02					
South Acton	13/40		14.04				14/08					14/37									15.04					15/07
ACTON CENTRAL			14.06	13.50																	15.06					
ACTON YARD																										
Acton Wells Jcn	13/48	13/57					14/14					14/44 *To Brent(M)*														15/14 *To Brent(M)*
Old Oak Sidings	13.52																									
WILLESDEN (HL)	14/00		14.11				14/19					15/02				15.11				15/05				15.00		
WILLESDEN (HL Sdgs)																15/16										
Kensal Green Jcn		14/02	14/12				14/21				14/42					15.04 *R/R*				15/07				15/16		
Kensal Rise			14.13								14.43										15.13					
Brondesbury Park			14.15								14.45										15.15					
Brondesbury			14.17								14.47										15.17					
West End Lane			14.19				14/28				14.49									15/16	15.19			15/25		
Finchley Road	14/10		14.21								14.51										15.21			15/30		
Hampstead Heath			14.23								14.53										15.23					
GOSPEL OAK	14/15		14.25				14/33				14.55									15/21	15.25					
Kentish Town West			14.27				*via*				14.57									*via*	15.27					
CAMDEN		14/00						14/38								15.08										
Primrose Hill		14/03						14.39								15.09										
CAMDEN ROAD		14/05	14.29					14.41			14.59					15.11		15.35		*T&H*	15.29					
Maiden Lane		14.10																					15.30			
St Pancras Sidings									14.47										15.17				15.40			
Caledonian Road			14.32					14.44			15.02					15.14			15.27		15.32					
Highbury			14.34					14.45			15.04					15.16					15.24					
Canonbury Jcn			14.36					14.48	14/53		15.06					15.18					15.36					
Dalston W. Jcn			14.37					14.49	14/55		15.07					15.19					15.37					
Dalston Jcn			14.39					14.51	14/57		15.09				15.19	15.21					15.39					
Broad St Goods									15/05						15.25											
BROAD STREET			14.44					14.56			15.14				15.25	15.26	15.53				15.44					
Kingsland																				15.20		15.45		15w47		
Kingsland																				15.23				15w54		
Dalston E. Jcn				14.38						14/44										15.22		15.47		15.57		
Graham Road																										
Hackney																										
Homerton																										
Hackney Wick																						R/R				
VICTORIA PARK				15.00						14/50			15/27			15/31				16.00		16.02				
TEMPLE MILLS																										
GOODMAYES																										
THAMES WHARF																										
VICTORIA DOCKS																										
Old Ford																										
Tredegar Road									R/R														15.45			
Fairfield Road									15.07													16.06				
TILBURY JCN									15.08	14/53			15.30									16/12	16/06			
PLAISTOW																										
RIPPLE LANE																										
Bow Junction									15.09	14.54			15.31									16/13	16/07			
Devon's Road									15.13	14.58			15/31									16/15	16/13	16/10		
Devon's Rd Loco																						16.20				
POPLAR DOCKS									15.36				15.55													
Destination																										

F. Park

WORKING TIMETABLE : 1953

Train		13.30							13.45		13.30							15.10				15.25	14.47	15.28			
From		Haydon							F, Park		Haydon							Brent(M)				Neasden	Bow	W'den			
Class	H	K	K	K	Pass	Pass	K	J	J	Pass	K	Light	K	H	Pass	Pass	Light	K	H	K	Milk	H	J	Milk	H	Pass	K
Engine	3F 0-6-0T	3F 0-6-0T	3F 0-6-0T	4F 0-6-0	EMU	EMU	3F 0-6-0T	3F 0-6-0T	J6 0-6-0	EMU	3F 0-6-0T	4MT 2-6-0	3F 0-6-0T	3F 0-6-0T	EMU	EMU	3F 0-6-0T	Q1 0-6-0	4F 0-6-0	7F 0-8-0	4MT 2-6-0	S15 4-6-0	3F 0-6-0T	3P 2-6-2T	J17 0-6-0	EMU	3F 0-6-0T
Shed	1B/104	DR 3	DR 48	1A/121	23	24	DR 10	DR 13	HSY 5	28/63	DR 3	DR 23	DR 2	DR 30	8	12/49	1A/95	FEL 123	1A/128	1A/100	DR 23	FEL 110	DR 13	1A/150	SX 100	25/60	DR 44
POPLAR DOCKS				**13.57**																							**15.10**
Devon's Rd Loco												14.20															
Devons Road			**13.55**	**14/00**				**14.10**				**14/22**															
Bow Junction		13/50	13/58	14/03				14.15				14/23											14.56				15/17
RIPPLE LANE																			14.05								
PLAISTOW																											
TILBURY JCN		**13/53**	**14/00**	**14/04**								**14/24**							**14/35**				**14/57**				**15/18**
Fairfield Road																							14.59				
Tredegar Road												14.25									14.40						
Old Ford		13.55	14.02								14.24																
VICTORIA DOCKS	13.40													14.08													
THAMES WHARF																											
GOODMAYES																											
TEMPLE MILLS																									14.45		
VICTORIA PARK	**14/03**			**14/08**							**14/28**			**14.38**					**14/41**		**14.45**				**15/05**		**15/21**
Hackney Wick																					R/R						
Homerton																											
Hackney																											
Graham Road																											
Dalston E. Jcn	**14/11**			**14/15**							**14/36**			**14/45**					**14/52**						**15/14**		**15/26**
Kingsland																											
Kingsland	14/13			14/17							14/38			14/47					14/54						15/16		15/28
BROAD STREET					**14.18**	**14.23**									**14.48**	**14.53**										**15.18**	
Broad St Goods													14.35														
Dalston Jcn					**14.24**	**14.29**							**14/42**		**14.54**	**14.59**										**15.24**	
Dalston W. Jcn	14/15			14/19	14/25	14/30					14/40			14/49	14/55	15/00			14/56						15/18	15/25	15/30
Canonbury Jcn	**14/17**			**14/21**	**14.26**	**14.31**					**14/42**			**14/51**	**14.56**	**15.01**			**14.58**						**15/20**	**15.26**	**15/32**
Highbury					**14.28**	**14.33**									**14.58**	**15.03**										**15.28**	
Caledonian Road					**14.30**	**14.35**									**15.00**	**15.05**										**15.30**	
St Pancras Sidings							14.26																				15.38
Maiden Lane							14.36		*Via*								15.05			15.14							
CAMDEN RD	**14/28**			**14/29**	**14.33**	**14.38**			*T&H*		**14/51**			**15/00**	**15.03**	**15.08**	**15/10**		**15/13**	**15/18**					**15/35**	**15.33**	
Primrose Hill	14/29				14.35						14/53				15.05		15/12									15.35	
CAMDEN	**14.30**				**14/36**						**14.55**				**15/06**		**15/18**									**15/36**	
Kentish Town West					*To*	**14.40**										**15.10**											
GOSPEL OAK				**14/34**	***W'den***	**14.42**			**14/47**					**15/05**		**15.12**			**15/18**	**15/23**					**15/40**		
Hampstead Heath						**14.44**										**15.14**											
Finchley Road				**14/39**		**14.46**			**14/52**					**15/10**		**15.16**			**15/23**	**15/28**					**15/45**		
West End Lane						**14.48**										**15.18**											
Brondesbury						**14.50**				*Ex*						**15.20**											
Brondesbury Park						**14.52**				*Mitre*						**15.22**											
Kensal Rise						**14.54**			15/03	*Bge CS*						**15.24**											
Kensal Green Jcn				**14/48**		**14/56**			**15/05**	**15.10**				**15/19**		**15/26**			**15/31**	**15/36**				**15/49**	**15/55**		
WILLESDEN (BRENT)				**15.00**															**15.43**								
WILLESDEN (HL)						**14.57**				**15.12**				**15/21**		**15.27**				**15/38**				**15/51**	**15/57**		
Old Oak Sidings																				*To*							
Acton Wells Jcn						**14/59**			**15/08**	**15/14**				**15/25**		**15/29**		**15/34**		***W'den***		**15/43**		**15/55**	**16/00**		
ACTON YARD														**15.30**											**16.07**		
ACTON CENTRAL						**15.02**				**15.17**						**15.32**											
South Acton						15.04			15/14	15.19						15.34		15/39				15/51		16/03			
Gunnersbury						15.07				15.22						15.37											
Kew Gardens						15.10				15.25						15.40											
RICHMOND						**15.13**				**15.28**						**15.43**											
Bollo Lane																								16.06			
KEW EAST JCN									**15/17**									**15/42**				**15/54**					
Destination					W'den			Bow Gas	Feltham				Devons Rd		Watford		1A Loco	Feltham		W'den	C'sea	Feltham				Watford	

WORKING TIMETABLE : 1953

Train	15.40	15.04	14.08			15.58	15.50		16.10	16.10	15.50	15.50	15.45	15.33		15.45		16.15		16.22	15.46	16.35		15.30	16.10	16.35	16.02
From	Fbury Pk	Watford	H. Green			Fbury Pk	Fbury Pk		Fbury Pk	E. Goods	Mitre B	W'den	IA Loco	Watford		Feltham		Fbury Pk		Fbury Pk	Watford	Fbury Pk		W'den	IA Loco	Fbury Pk	Watford
Class	ECS	Pass	J	H	Pass	Light	ECS	ECS	Light	H	ECS	K	2 LE	Pass	EBV	H	ECS	ECS	Pass	ECS	Pass	ECS	Pass	K		ECS	Pass
Engine	B1 4-6-0	EMU	8F 2-8-0	3F 0-6-0T	EMU	N2 0-6-2T	N2 0-6-2T	EMU	N2 0-6-2T	J50 0-6-0T	EMU	3F 0-6-0T	2 x 2-6-4T	EMU	3F 0-6-0T	8F 2-8-0	EMU	N2 0-6-2T	EMU	N2 0-6-2T	EMU	N2 0-6-2T	EMU	3F 0-6-0T	SMT 4-6-0	N2 0-6-2T	EMU
Shed	KX 41	22/58	14A/125	DR 12	24	KX 190	KX 191	32/67	KX 192	HSY 20	21/57	DR 37	130/131	7/44	DR 44	14A/152	4/41	KX 193	28/63	KX 194	30/65	KX 195	3/40	DR 37	1A/57	KX 195	27/62
KEW EAST JCN			15/21													16/12											
Bollo Lane																											
RICHMOND					15.25														15.53								
Kew Gardens					15.28														15.56								
Gunnersbury					15.31														15.59								
South Acton			15/25		15.33														16.01								
ACTON CENTRAL					15.35											16/16	ECS		16.03								
ACTON YARD				15.23																							
Acton Wells Jcn			15/31	15/28	15/37											16/23	ex Mitre B		16/05								
Old Oak Sidings			To Brent(M)													To Brent(M)											
WILLESDEN (HL)					15.40						16.03								16.08				16.20				
WILLESDEN (HL Sdgs)																											
Kensal Green Jcn					15.41						16.05 R/R								16.09				16/21				
Kensal Rise					15.42														16.10				16.22				
Brondesbury Park					15.44														16.12				16.24				
Brondesbury					15.46														16.14				16.26				
West End Lane					15.48														16.16				16.28				
Finchley Road					15.50														16.18				16.30				
Hampstead Heath					15.52														16.20				16.32				
GOSPEL OAK					15.54														16.22				16.34				
Kentish Town West					15.56														16.24				16.36				
CAMDEN		15/45											16/03	16/14	16/08										16/39		16/41
Primrose Hill		15.46											16/06	16/15	16/10										16/41		16/44
CAMDEN ROAD		15.48			15.58								16/08	16/18	16/13				16.26				16.38		16/42		16/46
Maiden Lane																											
St Pancras Sidings															16.22												
Caledonian Road		15.51			16.01									16.22					16.29		16.35						16.49
Highbury		15.53			16.04									16.24					16.31		16.37						16.51
Canonbury Jcn	15/57	15.55			16.06	16/04	16/09		16/15					16.26				16/26	16.33	16/34		16/40					16.53
Dalston W. Jcn		15/56			16/07	16/08	16/13		16/16					16/27				16/30	16/34	16/36	16/40	16/42					16.54
Dalston Jcn		15.58			16.08	16.09	16.14	16.18	16.20					16.29				16.31	16.36	16.39	16.42	16.45					16.56
Broad St Goods																						16.45				16.55	
BROAD STREET	16.03	16.04			16.13	16.15	16.20	16.25	16.27					16.34				16.40	16.42	16.50	16.47						17.01
Kingsland	16w04												16.27														
Kingsland	16w07														16.33									16.50			
Dalston E. Jcn	16/09									16/25			16/23											16/53			
Graham Road																											
Hackney																											
Homerton																											
Hackney Wick																								16.55			
VICTORIA PARK	16/20									16/34															17/00		
TEMPLE MILLS	16.40																										
GOODMAYES																											
THAMES WHARF																											
VICTORIA DOCKS																											
Old Ford																											
Tredegar Road																											
Fairfield Road																											
TILBURY JCN																									17/03		
PLAISTOW																											
RIPPLE LANE																											
Bow Junction																									17/04		
Devons Road																									17.07		
Devon's Rd Loco																											
POPLAR DOCKS																											
Destination																											

WORKING TIMETABLE : 1953

Station	DR 16	9	DR 23	DR 49	HSY 26	DR 1	15	14A/84	1A/150	DR 15	DR 13	21/57	23/59	1A/111	33/68	18/52	22/58	KX 190	32	KX 41	7/44	24	4/41	KX 191	28/63	65/30	DR 27
Train / From			15.20 C'sea					15.32 C'wood	15.28 W'den																		
Class	Light	Pass	Milk	Light	H	Light	Pass	K	Milk	Light	J	Pass	Pass	K	Pass	Pass	Pass	Pass	Pass	Pass	Pass	Pass	Pass	Pass	Pass	Pass	Light
Engine	3F 0-6-0T	EMU	4MT 2-6-0	3F 0-6-0T	J50 0-6-0	4MT 2-6-0	EMU	3F 0-6-0T	3P 2-6-2T	4F 0-6-0	3F 0-6-0T	EMU	EMU	4F 0-6-0	EMU	EMU	EMU	N2 0-6-2T	EMU	B1 4-6-0	EMU	EMU	EMU	N2 0-6-2T	EMU	EMU	3F 0-6-0T
POPLAR DOCKS	15.18																										16.30
Devon's Rd Loco																											
Devons Road						15.39				15.45	16.02																16.35
Bow Junction	15.21					15.40				15.48	16.07																
RIPPLE LANE											R/R																
PLAISTOW																											
TILBURY JCN				R/R		15/41				15/49																	
Fairfield Road																											
Tredegar Road																											
Old Ford																											
VICTORIA DOCKS					15.10																						
THAMES WHARF																											
GOODMAYES																											
TEMPLE MILLS																											
VICTORIA PARK			15/25		15/39	15/45				15/55																	
Hackney Wick						R/R																					
Homerton																											
Hackney																											
Graham Road																											
Dalston E. Jcn			15/30		15/44					16/00																	
Kingsland					15/46	16/02																					
Kingsland			15/32																								
BROAD STREET		15.37					15.48						16.00		16.15	16.22	16.33	16.35	16.37	16.43	16.44	16.49	16.53	16.56	16.58	17.02	
Broad St Goods														16.06													
Dalston Jcn		15.43					15.54						16.06	16/13	16.21	16.28	16.39	16.41	16.43	16.48	16.50	16.55	16.59	17.02	17.04	17.08	
Dalston W. Jcn		15/44					15/55			16.04			16/07	16/15	16/22	16/29	16/40	16/42	16/44	16/50	16/51	16/56	17/00	17/04	17/05	17/09	
Canonbury Jcn		15/45					15/56			16.06			16/08	16/17	16/23	16/30	16/41	16/45	16/46	16/51	16/52	17/00	17/01	17/06	17/06	17/10	
Highbury		15/47					15/58						16/10		16/25	16/31	16/43		16/48		16/54		17/03		17/08	17/12	
Caledonian Road		15/49					16.00						16/12		16/27		16/45		16/50		16/56		17/05		17/10	17/14	
St Pancras Sicings																											
Maiden Lane																											
CAMDEN RD		15.52		15.55			16.03			16.10			16.15	16/23	16.30	16.35	16.48		16.53		16.59	17.01	17.08		17.13	17.17	
Primrose Hill				15/58			16.06							16/25		16.38			16.55			17.03	17/10		17/15		
CAMDEN				16.05			16/07							16/26		16/39			16/56			17/04	17/11		17/16		
Kentish Town West		15.54													16.32		16.50				17.01					17.19	
GOSPEL OAK		15.56													16.34		16.52				17.03					17.21	
Hampstead Heath		15.58													16.36		16.54				17.05					17.23	
Finchley Road		16.00													16.38		16.56				17.07					17.25	
West End Lane		16.02										Ex			16.40		16.58				17.09					17.27	
Brondesbury		16.04										Mitre			16.42		17.00				17.11					17.29	
Brondesbury Park		16.06										Bge CS			16.44		17.02				17.13					17.31	
Kensal Rise		16.08													16.46		17.04				17.15					17.33	
Kensal Green Jcn		16/10										16.23			16/49		17/07				17/18					17/36	
WILLESDEN (BRENT)																											
WILLESDEN (HL)		16.11										16.27			16.50		17.08				17.19					17.37	
Old Oak Sidings																											
Acton Wells Jcn		16/13						16/21				16/29			16/52		17/10				17/21					17/39	
ACTON YARD								16.26																			
ACTON CENTRAL		16.16										16.32			16.55		17.13				17.24					17.42	
South Acton		16.18										16.34			16.57		17.15				17.26					17.44	
Gunnersbury		16.21										16.37			17.00		17.18				17.30					17.48	
Kew Gardens		16.24										16.40			17.03		17.21				17.33					17.51	
RICHMOND		16.27										16.43			17.06		17.24				17.36					17.54	
Bollo Lane									16.20																		
KEW EAST JCN									16.23																		
Destination	H. Squ	S. Bush		Camden	Watford	Barking	Watford	Bow Gas	W'den	W'den	R/R			Camden		Watford		Hertford	Watford	Royston		Watford	Watford	G. Hill	Watford	Watford	

WORKING TIMETABLE : 1953

Train	16.13	15.57	16.20	16.46	—	16.21	16.30	17.05	17.05	—	16.30	17.10	16.46	—	16.40	—	17.17	16.24	—	16.40	16.39	16.40	16.55	—	—	17.52
From	W. Ken	Feltham	Bollo L	F'bury Pk	—	Bushey	Mitre B	F'bury Pk	Bow (M)	—	—	F'bury Pk	1A/Loco	—	1A loco	—	F'bury Pk	Feltham	—	1A loco	Watford	1A loco	Watford	—	—	F'bury Pk
Class	Pass	K	Milk	ECS	Pass	Pass	ECS	ECS	Light	Light	J	ECS	Light	Pass	Light	Pass	ECS	K	Pass	Light	Pass	ECS	Pass	Pass	K	ECS
Engine	EMU	H16 4-6-2T	3P 2-6-2T	N2 0-6-2T	EMU	EMU	EMU	N2 0-6-2T	3F 0-6-0T	3F 0-6-0T	3F 0-6-0T	N2 0-6-2T	4F 0-6-0	EMU	4F 0-6-0	EMU	N2 0-6-2T	S15 4-6-0	EMU	4F 0-6-0	EMU	4F 0-6-0	EMU	EMU	3F 0-6-0T	N2 0-6-2T
Shed	12/49	FELI43	1A/150	KX 196	13/50	34/69	14/51	KX 197	DR 39	DR 9	DR 13	KX 198	1A/147	9/46	1A/144	11/48	KX 199	FEL 114	21/57	1A/144	25/60	1A/147	19/37	23/59	DR 49	KX 189
KEW EAST JCN		16/28	16.32																							
Bollo Lane																										
RICHMOND	16.16													16.36					16.52					17.08		
Kew Gardens	16.19													16.39					16.55					17.11		
Gunnersbury	16.21	16.32												16.42					16.58					17.14		
South Acton	16.24	16.36												16.44					17.00					17.16		
ACTON CENTRAL	16.26													16.46					17.02					17.19		
ACTON YARD																										
Acton Wells Jcn		16.38	16.42											16.50					17.04					17.21		
Old Oak Sidings		16.42																								
WILLESDEN (HL)					16.37									16.52		17.00								17.25		
WILLESDEN (HL Sdgs)																										
Kensal Green Jcn					16/38									16/53		17/01			17/09					17/26		
Kensal Rise					16.39									16.54		17.02			17.10					17.27		
Brondesbury Park					16.41									16.56		17.04			17.12					17.29		
Brondesbury					16.43									16.58		17.06			17.14					17.31		
West End Lane					16.45									17.00		17.08			17.16					17.33		
Finchley Road					16.47									17.02		17.10			17.18					17.35		
Hampstead Heath					16.49									17.04		17.12			17.20					17.37		
GOSPEL OAK					16.51									17.06		17.14			17.22					17.39		
Kentish Town West					16.53									17.08		17.16			17.24					17.41		
CAMDEN						16/57									17/15						17/20		17/36			
Primrose Hill						16.58									17/18						17.21		17.37			
CAMDEN ROAD					16.55	17.01	17.04							17.10	17/20	17.18			17.27		17.23		17.39	17.44		
Maiden Lane																										
St Pancras Sidings																										
Caledonian Road					16.58	17.04								17.13		17.21			17.30		17.26		17.42			
Highbury					17.00	17.06								17.15	17.24*	17.23			17.32		17.28		17.44	17.48		
Canonbury Jcn					17.02	17.08	17/12	17/10				17/18		17.17		17.25	17/31		17.34		17.30		17.46	17.50		
Dalston W Jcn					17.03	17.09	17/13	17/13				17/20		17.19		17.26	17/32		17.35		17.31		17.47	17.51		
Dalston Jcn				17.00	17.05	17.11	17/14	17.14				17/22		17.20		17.28	17/35		17.37		17.33		17.49	17.53		18.00
Broad St Goods																										
BROAD STREET				17.05	17.12	17.16	17.20	17.21				17.29		17.26		17.33	17.42		17.42		17.38		17.54	17.58		18.10
Kingsland																										
Dalston E. Jcn																										
Graham Road																										
Hackney																										
Homerton																										
Hackney Wick																										
VICTORIA PARK									17.21 R/R																17.24	
TEMPLE MILLS																										
GOODMAYES																										
THAMES WHARF																										
VICTORIA DOCKS																										
Old Ford											17.10															
Tredegar Road																										
Fairfield Road																										
TILBURY JCN											17/11														17.24	
PLAISTOW																										
RIPPLE LANE																										
Bow Junction											17/12														17.25	
Devons Road										17.40	17.15														17.29	
Devon's Rd Loco										17.45																
POPLAR DOCKS																										
Destination																										

Notes appearing in the body: "To S. Bush", "To Brent(M)", "To Neasden", "ex Mitre B", "R/R", and starred time 17.24*.

22

WORKING TIMETABLE : 1953

Station	K 3F 0-6-0T DR 18	16.40 Bow J 3F 0-6-0T DR 13	Pass N2 0-6-2T KX 192	Pass EMU 3/40	17.00 H'smith K 7F 0-8-0 1A/92	Pass EMU 62/27	Pass N2 0-6-2T KX 193	K H16 4-6-2T FEL 143	Pass EMU 49/12	XP 4P 2-6-4T WAT 130	Pass EMU 13/50	Pass N2 0-6-2T KX 194	Pass EMU 69/34	Pass EMU 51/14	Light 3F 0-6-0T DR 10	Pass N2 0-6-2T KX 195	XP EMU 46/9	Pass EMU 48/11	K J50 0-6-0T HSY 21	Pass N2 0-6-2T KX 196	Pass EMU 60/25	Pcls 3F 0-6-0T DR 10	Pass N2 0-6-2T KX 197	Pass EMU 57/21	18.30 Brent(M) J 8F 2-8-0 14A/153	Pass 4P 2-6-4T WAT 131	Pass EMU 57/21	Pass EMU 37/19
POPLAR DOCKS	16.37																											
Devon's Rd Loco	16.45																		17.25									
Devons Road																			17/29									
Bow Junction		16/44																	17/32									
RIPPLE LANE																												
PLAISTOW																												
TILBURY JCN		16/46																	17/33									
Fairfield Road		16.47																										
Tredegar Road																												
Old Ford																												
VICTORIA DOCKS																												
THAMES WHARF																												
GOODMAYES																			17/38									
TEMPLE MILLS																												
VICTORIA PARK																												
Hackney Wick																												
Homerton																												
Hackney																			17/46									
Graham Road																												
Dalston E. Jcn																												
Kingsland																			17/48									
BROAD STREET			17.06	17.09		17.12	17.15		17.17	17.22	17.25	17.26	17.28	17.31		17.36	17.40	17.43		17.45	17.47		17.53	17.56		18.02		18.05
Broad St Goods																												
Dalston Jcn			17.12	17.15		17.18	17.21		17.23	17.27	17.31	17.32	17.34	17.37		17.42	17.46	17.49		17.51	17.53		17.59	18.02		18.08		18.11
Dalston W. Jcn			17/14	17/16		17/19	17/23		17/24	17/28	17/32	17/34	17/35	17/38		17/44	17/47	17/50		17/52	17/54		18/01	18/03		18/09		18/12
Canonbury Jcn			17/16	17/17		17/20	17/25		17/25	17/29	17/33	17/36	17/36	17/39		17/46	17/48	17/51		17/55	17/55		18/03					18/13
Highbury				17.18		17.22							17.38	17.41				17.53			17.57			18.05				18.15
Caledonian Road						17.24							17.40	17.43				17.55			17.59							18.17
St Pancras Sidings															17.46													
Maiden Lane															17.56							18.00						
CAMDEN RD				17.21		17.27				17/33	17.37		17.43	17.46			17.52	17.58			18.02	18/04		18.08		18/18		18.20
Primrose Hill				17/24						17/35	17/39						17/54	18.01				18/06		18/11		18/21		
CAMDEN				17/25						17/36	17/40						17/55	18/02				18/07		18/12		18/22		
Kentish Town West						17.29								17.48							18.04							18.22
GOSPEL OAK						17.31								17.50							18.06							18.24
Hampstead Heath						17.33								17.52							18.08							18.26
Finchley Road						17.35								17.54							18.10							18.28
West End Lane						17.37								17.56							18.12							18.30
Brondesbury						17.39								17.58							18.14							18.32
Brondesbury Park						17.41								18.00							18.16							18.34
Kensal Rise						17.43								18.02							18.18							18.36
Kensal Green Jcn						17/47								18/04							18/21							18/39
WILLESDEN (BRENT)						17.47								18.05							18.22							18.40
Old Oak Sidings								17.52																				
Acton Wells Jcn						17/49		17/58						18/07							18/24							18/42
ACTON YARD																												
ACTON CENTRAL						17.52								18.10							18.27							18.45
South Acton					17.50	17.54		18/04						18.12							18.30				18.54			18.47
Gunnersbury						17.56								18.16							18.33							18.50
Kew Gardens						17.59								18.19							18.36							18.53
RICHMOND						18.02								18.22							18.39							18.56
Bollo Lane																												
KEW EAST JCN					17/53			18/07																	18/57			
Destination	W G City	Watford	Hertford	Watford	Kew B		Tring	Feltham	Watford	Watford	Watford	Cuffley	Watford		Watford	Hertford	Watford	Watford	C. Yard	Hatfield		Camden	Barnet	Watford	Feltham	Watford	Tring	

23

	17.06 / Watford / Pass / EMU / 20/56	K / 3F 0-6-0T / 14A/84	Pass / EMU / 33/68	17.48 / W'den Pcis / 4 2-6-0 / DR 23	Light / 3F 0-6-0T / DR 20	17.21 / Watford / Pass / EMU / 31/66	Pass / EMU / 22/58	17.34 / Watford / Pass / EMU / 29	H / J17 0-6-0 / SX 100	18.18 / D. Road / Light / 3F 0-6-0T / DR 4	Pass / EMU / 7	18.28 / Camden / Light / 3F 0-6-0T / DR 10	17.55 / Brentford / H15 4-6-0 / NE 79	17.50 / Watford / Pass / EMU / 32	18.05 / 1A loco / 3 LE / 2 X 5MT, 4F / 262/52/147	Pass / EMU / 30/65	18.10 / W'den / K / 4F 0-6-0 / DR 15	K / 3F 0-6-0T / DR 30	18.14 / Kew / K / 7F 0-8-0 / 1A/92	18.09 / Watford / Pass / EMU / 28/63	Pass / EMU / 27/62	17.55 / Feltham / J 6 0-6-0 / HSY 5	Lght / 3F 0-6-0T / DR 30	Pass / EMU / 14/51	Light / 3F 0-6-0T / DR 11	18.27 / Feltham / H / S15 4-6-0 / FEL 108	18.33 / Watford / EMU / 10/2
KEW EAST JCN													18/01						18/16			18/30				18/49	
Bollo Lane																											
RICHMOND	17.23						17.38				17.54					18.06					18.23			18.38			
Kew Gardens	17.26						17.41				17.57					18.09					18.26			18.41			
Gunnersbury	17.29						17.44				18.00					18.12					18.29			18.44			
South Acton	17.31						17.46				18.02		18/06			18.14			18/19		18.31	18/35		18.46		18/52	
ACTON CENTRAL	17.33						17.49				18.05					18.17					18.34			18.49			
ACTON YARD		17.26							17.50									18.15									
Acton Wells Jcn		17/32	17/35				17/51		17/55		18/07		18/11			18/19		18/23	18/27		18/36	18/41		18/51		18/59	
Old Oak Sidings																			18/32								
WILLESDEN (HL)			17.39				17.55		18.00		18.11		to Neasden			18.24		18/27			18.40	18/44		18.55		To Neasden	
WILLESDEN (HL Sdgs)																											
Kensal Green Jcn			17.40				17/56		18/02		18/12				18/16	18/25		18/29				18/46		18/56			
Kensal Rise			17.41				17.57				18.13					18.26								18.57			
Brondesbury Park			17.43				17.59				18.15					18.28								18.59			
Brondesbury			17.45				18.01				18.17					18.30								19.01			
West End Lane			17.47				18.03				18.19					18.32								19.03			
Finchley Road			17.49				18.05		18/13		18.21				18/28	18.34		18/37				18/55		19.05			
Hampstead Heath			17.51				18.07		18/18		18.23					18.36								19.07			
GOSPEL OAK			17.53				18.09				18.25				18/33	18.38		18/42				19/00		19.09			
Kentish Town West			17.55				18.11				18.27					18.40						via		19.11			
CAMDEN				17.56		18.03		18.15				18.28		18.32			18.40			18.51							
Primrose Hill				17.57		18.04		18.19				18.30		18.33			18.42			18.52							
CAMDEN ROAD			17.57	17.59		18.08	18.13	18.19	18.23		18.29	18.31		18.35		18.42	18.44	18.47		18.55	18.58	T&H		19.13			
Maiden Lane				18.03																							
St Pancras Sidings																	18.49	18.52					19.04				
Caledonian Road			18.00			18.11	18.16	18.22	18.29		18.32			18.38		18.45				18.58	19.01			19.16			
Highbury			18.02			18.13	18.18				18.34			18.40		18.47				19.00	19.03			19.18			
Canonbury Jcn			18.04			18.15	18.20		18/29		18.36	18/39		18.42	18/44	18.49				19.02	19.05		19/09	19.20			
Dalston W Jcn			18/05			18/16	8/21		18/27	18/31	18/37	18/41		18/43	18/46	18/50				19/03	19/06		19/11	19/21			
Dalston Jcn			18.07			18.18		18.23		18/33	18.39			18.45	18/48	18.52				19.05	19.08			19.23			
Broad St Goods										18/41					18.55												
BROAD STREET			18.12			18.23		18.28			18.44			18.51		18.58				19.10	19.14			19.29			
Kingsland									18/33			18/43													19/13		
Dalston E. Jcn									18/35			18/44													19/15		
Graham Road																											
Hackney																											
Homerton																											
Hackney Wick																											
VICTORIA PARK									18/41			18/54													19/19		
TEMPLE MILLS									18.55																		
GOODMAYES																											
THAMES WHARF																											
VICTORIA DOCKS																											
Old Ford																											
Tredegar Road																											
Fairfield Road																											
TILBURY JCN												18/58													19/22		
PLAISTOW																											
RIPPLE LANE																											
Bow Junction												18/59													19/23		
Devons Road					18.30							19.02													19.26		
Devon's Rd Loco																									19.32		
POPLAR DOCKS					18.35																				19.37		
Destination																									F. Park		

Column key (the five header lines — Train / From / Class / Engine / Shed — for each train column):

Col	Train	From	Class	Engine	Shed
C1			Pass	N2 0-6-2T	KX 198
C2			Pass	EMU	59/23
C3			D	SMT 4-6-0	1A/57
C4			Pass	EMU	20/56
C5			Pass	EMU	68/33
C6	17.50		Light	2F 0-6-0T	DR 41
C7	17.17	Ferme Pk	J	J6 0-6-C	HSY 4
C8	18.10		K	3F 0-6-0T	DR 9
C9			Pass	N2 0-6-2T	KX 199
C10			Light	N2 0-6-2T	KX 189
C11			Pass	EMU	66/31
C12	18.55	Brent(M)	J	4F 0-6-0	14A/120
C13			Pass	EMU	58/22
C14			Light	3F 0-6-0T	DR 4
C15			D	4F 0-6-0	1A/144
C16			Light	3F 0-6-0T	DR 3
C17			EBV	3F 0-6-0T	DC2
C18	18.28	H.Squ	E	3F 0-6-0T	DR 16
C19			Pass	EMU	29
C20	18.10	Poplar	K	3F 0-6-0T	DR 9
C21	19.20	Neasden	H	H15 4-6-0	NE 79
C22			H	3F 0-6-0T	DR 31
C23			H	J50 0-6-0T	HSY 20
C24			Pass	EMU	7
C25			K	3F 0-6-0T	DR 3
C26			Pass	EMU	32
C27	19.00		K	3F 0-6-0T	DR 20

Timings (station × train column):

Station	C1	C2	C3	C4	C5	C6	C7	C8	C9	C10	C11	C12	C13	C14	C15	C16	C17	C18	C19	C20	C21	C22	C23	C24	C25	C26	C27
POPLAR DOCKS						17.50		18.10																			19.00
Devon's Rd Loco						18.00								18.18		18.21											
Devons Road								18/14						18/21		18/24	18.27										19.03
Bow Junction								18/17									18/30	18/41									19.06
RIPPLE LANE																											
PLAISTOW																											
TILBURY JCN								18/18						18/22		18/25	18/31	18/42									19/08
Fairfield Road																											
Tredegar Road																											
Old Ford																18/27	R/R					18.15	18.25		19.00		
VICTORIA DOCKS																											
THAMES WHARF																											
GOODMAYES																											
TEMPLE MILLS																											
VICTORIA PARK								18/21						18/26			18.35 (To Vic Dks)	18/47				18.52	18.58		19/04		19/10
Hackney Wick																											
Homerton																											
Hackney																											
Graham Road																											
Dalston E. Jcn								18/28						18/33				18/52				19/00	19/06		19/10		19/17
Kingsland								18w30										18/54				19/02	19/08		19/12		19/19
Kingsland								18w35																			
BROAD STREET	18.06	18.09		18.18	18.23				18.32	18.35	18.35		18.40						18.52					19.05			
Broad St Goods			18.11												18.45												
Dalston Jcn	18.12	18.15	18/18	18.24	18.29				18.38	18/41	18.41		18.46		18/51				18.58					19.11		19.16	
Dalston W. Jcn	18/14	18/16	18/20	18/25	18/30				18/40	18/42	18/42		18/47		18/53				18/59					19/12		19/17	
Canonbury Jcn	18/16	18.17	18/22	18.26	18.31				18/42	18/44	18.43		18.48		18/55				19.00					19.13		19.18	
Highbury		18.19		18.28	18.33						18.45		18.50						19.02					19.15		19.20	
Caledonian Road		18.21		18.30	18.35						18.47		18.52						19.04					19.17		19.22	
St Pancras Sidings																											
Maiden Lane							Via																				
CAMDEN RD		18.24	18/28	18.33	18.38						18.50		18.55		19.00				19.07	19.10*				19.20	19/15	19.25	19.29
Primrose Hill		18.27	18/30	18.41	18.41						18.58		18.58		19.02									19.23	19/17		19.32
CAMDEN		18.28	18.32	18/42	18/42			18.50*			18/59		18/59		19.03									19/24	19/18	19.25	19.34
Kentish Town West																											
GOSPEL OAK							18.45												19.09	19.15						19.27	
Hampstead Heath																			19.11							19.29	
Finchley Road							18.50												19.13	19.20						19.31	
West End Lane																			19.15							19.35	
Brondesbury																			19.17							19.37	
Brondesbury Park																			19.19							19.39	
Kensal Rise																			19.21							19.41	
Kensal Green Jcn							19.00												19.23	19.33							
WILLESDEN (BRENT)																											
WILLESDEN (HL)							19.02												19.26	19.35						19.44	
Old Oak Sidings																											
Acton Wells Jcn							19.05					19/11							19.28	19.38	19.41					19.46	
ACTON YARD												19.15								19.45							
ACTON CENTRAL																			19.31		19.47					19.49	
South Acton							19.11												19.33							19.51	
Gunnersbury																			19.37							19.54	
Kew Gardens																			19.40							19.57	
RICHMOND																			19.43							20.00	
Bollo Lane																											
KEW EAST JCN							19.14					19/14									19/52						
Destination	Hertford	Watford		Bushey	Watford		Feltham		Cuffley	Fins Pk	Watford	B'sea	Watford		Broad St		Vic Dks		Richmond	C.Yard	Feltham			Watford		Watford	Broad St

WORKING TIMETABLE : 1953

Station	5A/39	25/60	DR 15	6	8B/1	19/37	FEL 133	DR 3	20	FEL 115	DR 13	23/59	1A59/58	1B/94	DR 48	29/56	31/66	1A/58	DR 44	HSY 21	FEL 108	29	29	32	FEL137	67/57
Train	18.50			18.55	19.10		19.00			19.15	19.57	19.23	19.50	20.05		19.53		18.50		20.25	19.57				19.55	20.20
From	1A loco			Watford	1A loco		Feltham			Feltham	Bow Gas	Watford	1A loco	W'den		Richmond		W'den		F. Park	Neasden				Feltham	1A loco
Class	Light	Pass	Light	Pass	Light	Pass	H	Light	Pass	K	H	Pass	2 LE		Light	ECS	Pass	K	J	J		Pcls	ECS	Pass	H	2 LE
Engine	5XP 4-6-0	EMU	4F 0-6-0	EMU	5MT 4-6-0	EMU	700 0-6-0	3F 0-6-0T	EMU	S15 4-6-0	3F 0-6-0T	EMU	2 SMT	3F 0-6-0T	3F 0-6-0T	EMU	EMU	4F 0-6-0	3F 0-6-0T	J50 0-6-0T	S15 4-6-0	EMU	EMU	EMU	700 0-6-0	2 SMT
KEW EAST JCN							19/24			19/39															20/21	
Bollo Lane																										
RICHMOND		18.55				19.15			19.30							19.53	19.50							20.10		
Kew Gardens		18.58				19.18			19.33								19.53							20.13		
Gunnersbury		19.01				19.21			19.36								19.56							20.16		
South Acton		19.03				19.23	19/28		19.38	19/43						20.01	19.58							20.18		
ACTON CENTRAL		19.06				19.26			19.41							20.03	20.00							20.21		
ACTON YARD																R/R										
Acton Wells Jcn		19/08				19/28	19/36		19/43	19/53							20/02				20.10	20/14				
Old Oak Sidings										19/57											20.15					
WILLESDEN (HL)		19/11				19/31			19/46								20/07					20/17	20/23			
WILLESDEN (HL Sdgs)														20.00					20/15							
Kensal Green Jcn	19/05	19/12			19/25	19/32			19/47				19/56				20/08						20/25			
Kensal Rise		19.13				19.33			19.48								20.09							20.28		
Brondesbury Park		19.15				19.35			19.50								20.12							20.29		
Brondesbury		19.17				19.37			19.52								20.14							20.32		
West End Lane		19.19				19.39			19.54								20.16							20.34		
Finchley Road	19/13	19.21			19/32	19.41			19.56				20/01				20.18							20.36		
Hampstead Heath		19.23				19.43			19.58								20.20							20.38		
GOSPEL OAK	19/18	19.25			19/40	19.45			20.00				20/06				20.22							20.40		
Kentish Town West		19.27				19.47			20.02															20.42		
CAMDEN				19.35				19.53				20/04		20/12				20/24								
Primrose Hill				19.36				19/55				20.05		20/14				20/26								
CAMDEN ROAD	19/23	19.29		19.39	19/42	19.49		19/57	20.04			20/08	20/12	20/16			20.24	20/27	20/35					20.44		
Maiden Lane								20/01																		
St Pancras Sidings			19.35											20.20												
Caledonian Road				19.42					20.07			20.11					20.27		20.47							
Highbury				19.44					20.09			20.13					20.29		20.49							
Canonbury Jcn	19/29	19.36		19.46	19/49	19.56			20.11			20.15	20/17				20.31	20/33						20.51		
Dalston W. Jcn	19/31	19.37		19.47	19/51	19.57			20/12			20/16	20/19				20.32	20/35						20.52		
Dalston Jcn	19/33	19.39		19.49	19/53	19.59			20.14			20.18	20.21				20.34	20/37						20.54		
Broad St Goods	19/41				20/01								20.28					20/45								
BROAD STREET		19.45		19.54		20.06			20.20			20.24					20.40							21.00		
Kingsland			19.45																20/49	20.45		21/10				
Dalston E. Jcn			19.46																20/51	20/47						21/12
Graham Road																										
Hackney																										
Homerton																										
Hackney Wick																										
VICTORIA PARK			19.51										20/37						20/55						20/59	21/17
TEMPLE MILLS																				20.05	20.21					21.30
GOODMAYES																										
THAMES WHARF																										
VICTORIA DOCKS																										
Old Ford															20.21											
Tredegar Road																										
Fairfield Road											20.05															
TILBURY JCN			19.54										20/47		20/23			20/58	20.51						21/04	
PLAISTOW																										
RIPPLE LANE																										
Bow Junction			19.55								20/06				20/24				20.59						21/05	
Devons Road			19.59								20.10				20/27				21.03						21.10	
Devon's Rd Loco																										
POPLAR DOCKS																										
Destination																										

Notes: C7 (FEL 133) — "To Brent (M)". C14 (1B/94) St Pancras Sidings — "to St P."

WORKING TIMETABLE : 1953

	1	2	3	4	5	6	7	8	9	10	11	12	13	14	15	16	17	18	19	20	21	22	23	24	25
Train From		19.35 Brent(M)									19.15 Barking			19.47 Bow				20.05 St P						19.58 Stratford Fish	
Class	K	H	Light	J	H	Pass	Coupled	Pass	H	D	Pcls	Light	Light	J	ECS	D	Pass	Pcls	ECS	H	K	ECS	D	K	K
Engine	3F 0-6-0T	S15 4-6-0	4MT 2-6-0	3F 0-6-0T	J17 0-6-0	EMU	2F 0-6-0	EMU	J17 0-6-0	SMT 4-6-0	4MT 2-6-0	3F 0-6-0T	3F 0-6-0T	3F 0-6-0T	EMU	SMT 4-6-0	EMU	4MT 2-6-0	EMU	3F 0-6-0T	S15 4-6-0	EMU	4F 0-6-0	4MT 2-6-0	3F 0-6-0T
Shed	DR 4	FEL 114	DR 5	DR 13	SX 102	65/30	DR 38/40	28	SX 101	11A/262	DR 1	DR 4	DR 28	DR 13	53/14	1A/52	25	DR 23	29/56	DR 12	FEL 115	6	1A/147	DR 5	DR 3
POPLAR DOCKS			19.09				19.30																		
Devon's Rd Loco																									
Devons Road			19.11	19.20			19.38						19.47												
Bow Junction				19.25									19.48	19.52											
RIPPLE LANE																									
PLAISTOW																									
TILBURY JCN	19.12			R/R								19.50													
Fairfield Road	*Bow*											R/R		19.55											
Tredegar Road	*Gas*													R/R											
Old Ford	R.R											R.R													
VICTORIA DOCKS					18.45				19.00																
THAMES WHARF																									
GOODMAYES									19.20							19.50									
TEMPLE MILLS																19.53				19.53					
VICTORIA PARK			19.17		19.13				19.24		19.45									19.53				20.14	
Hackney Wick			R/R																						
Homerton																									
Hackney																									
Graham Road																									
Dalston E. Jcn			19.20						19.33							20.01				20.01				20.18	
Kingsland			19.22						19.35											20.03				20.19	
Kingsland											19.50					19.50									
BROAD STREET						19.21		19.28							19.45	19.42	19.58		20.07						
Broad St Goods	19.15									19.35						19.52			20.10						
Dalston Jcn	19.22					19.27		19.34		20.00					19.53	20.04	20.04		20.14						
Dalston W. Jcn	19.24				19.24	19.28		19.35	19.37	20.02	19.52				19.49	20.05	20.05			20.21			20.19		
Canonbury Jcn	19.25		19.26		19.26	19.29		19.36	19.39	20.04	19.53				19.50	20.06	20.06			20.07		20.22	20.21		
Highbury						19.31		19.38							19.52	20.08	20.08								
Caledonian Road						19.33		19.40							19.54	20.10	20.10								
St Pancras Sidings														20.00		20.14							20.33		
Maiden Lane									*Via T&H*										*ex Carr Sdg*						
CAMDEN RD	19.32					19.36		19.43	19.50	19.53	20.01	20.03	20.03		19.57	20.09	20.13	20.16	20.18	20.18		20.25		20.30	20.37
Primrose Hill						19.39				19.56	20.06	20.08	20.08		20.00	20.12		20.18	20.28	20.28					
CAMDEN						19.40				19.58	20.10	20.12	20.12		20.01	20.14		20.20		20.30					
Kentish Town West								19.45									20.15								
GOSPEL OAK					19.37			19.47	19.55		20.08			20.08			20.17		20.23			20.23		20.35	
Hampstead Heath								19.49									20.19								
FINCHLEY ROAD					19.40			19.51	20.00		20.13			20.13			20.21		20.25			20.25		20.40	
West End Lane								19.53									20.23								
Brondesbury								19.55									20.25								
Brondesbury Park								19.57																	
Kensal Rise								19.59									20.28		20.36						
Kensal Green Jcn					20.22			20.01	20.11					20.22			20.31		20.36	20.41		20.46	20.54		21.10
WILLESDEN (BRENT)		19.55																							21.10
WILLESDEN (HL)					20.13			20.02	20.13					20.24			20.32		20.38	20.43		20.48		20.51	
Old Oak Sidings									20.30												20.52				
Acton Wells Jcn		19.50			20.03			20.04									20.34		20.50		20.58	20.50		20.51	
ACTON YARD								20.18														20.55			
ACTON CENTRAL		19.55						20.07									20.37		20.39				21.04		
South Acton								20.09									20.39		20.42						
Gunnersbury								20.12									20.42		20.45						
Kew Gardens								20.15									20.45								
RICHMOND								20.18									20.48								
Bollo Lane																					21.04				
KEW EAST JCN	19.59																				21.08				
Destination	Feltham	Stratford		Watford											Watford				Camden	W'den	Mitre B			Plaistow	Feltham

Station	Pass EMU 28	K 3F 0-6-0T DR 31	Light 4-2-6-0 DR 1	Pass EMU 25	H 3F 0-6-0T DR 25	Light 3F 0-6-0T DR 16	ECS EMU 27	H J17 0-6-0 SX 102	Pass EMU 37/19	Light 3F 0-6-0T DR 51	K 3F 0-6-0T DR 4	H 3F 0-6-0T DR 12	H 4-2-6-0 DR 23	Pass EMU 31/66	C SXP 4-6-0 1A/1	Light 3F 0-6-0T DR 28	H J17 0-6-0 SX 101	H 8F 2-8-0 14A/153	Pass EMU 32	J 4F 0-6-0 14A/120	K 3F 0-6-0T DR 20	Pass EMU 25	J J52 0-6-0T HSY 11	H 3F 0-6-0T DR 26
Train			21.00			20.46				21.55		22.30			14.50			21.45		22.00			23.20	
From			W'den			Feltham				D.Road		Broad St			Wyre D			Feltham		B'sea			East Gds	
KEW EAST JCN — Bollo Lane						21/09												22/16		22/37				
RICHMOND	20.30			21.00					21.30					22.01					22.29			23.05		
Kew Gardens	20.33			21.03					21.33					22.04					22.32			23.08		
Gunnersbury	20.36			21.06					21.36					22.07					22.35			23.11		
South Acton	20.38			21.08		21/14			21.38					22.09		22/41		22/19	22.37			23.13		
ACTON CENTRAL	20.41			21.10					21.40					22.11					22.39			23.15		
ACTON YARD								21.23				21.45					22.15							
Acton Wells Jcn	20/43			21/12				21/28	21/42			21/53		22/13			22/22		22/41		22/47	23/17		
Old Oak Sidings																								
WILLESDEN (HL)	20.47			21.15		21/24		21/32	21.45			21/57		22.16			22/25		22.46			23.21		
WILLESDEN (HL Sdgs)		20.38									21.40		22/10		22/20		22/27				22.50			23.05
Kensal Green Jcn	20.48	20/51		21.16					21.46		21/50	21/59	22/08	22.17	22/24				22/47		23/07	23/22		23/25
Kensal Rise	20.49			21.17					21.47					22.18					22.48			23.23		
Brondesbury Park																								
Brondesbury	20.52			21.20					21.50					22.21					22.51			23.26		
West End Lane	20.54			21.22					21.52					22.23					22.53			23.28		
Finchley Road	20.56	21/05		21.24				21/43	21.54				22/17	22.25	22/32		22/35		22.55			23.30		
Hampstead Heath	20.58			21.26					21.56					22.27					22.57			23.32		
GOSPEL OAK	21.00	21/10		21.28				21/48	21.58		22/05	22/14	22/22	22.29	22/35	22/40	22/40		22.59			23.34		23/41
Kentish Town West	21.02			21.30					22.00					22.31					23.01			23.36		
CAMDEN		21/13					21/46				21.05					22.43								
Primrose Hill		21/15	21/15				21.47				21/08													
CAMDEN ROAD	21.04	21/15	21/20	21.32			21/50	21/53	22.02		22/10	22/19	22/27	22.33	22/38		22/45		23.03		23/28	23.38		23/46
Maiden Lane			21.40				21/54									22.43								
St Pancras Sidings											22.16					22.55								
Caledonian Road	21.07			21.35					22.05					22.36					23.06			23.41		
Highbury	21.09			21.37					22.07					22.38					23.08			23.43		
Canonbury Jcn	21.11	21/21		21.39					22.09				22/38	22.39	22/43		22/52		23.09			23.44		
Dalston W. Jcn	21/12	21/23		21/40					22/10				22/40	22/40	22/45		22/54		23/10			23/45		
Dalston Jcn	21.14			21.42					22.12					22.42	22/47				23.12			23.47		
Broad St Goods															22/55									
BROAD STREET	21.19			21.47					22.17					22.47					23.17			23.52		
Kingsland		21/25						22/04					22/42				22/56						23.45	
Dalston E. Jcn		21/27						22/06				22/29	22/44				22/58						00w03	
Graham Road																							00/06	
Hackney																								
Homerton																								
Hackney Wick																								
VICTORIA PARK		21/32						22/11				22/35	22/54				23/12						00/13	
TEMPLE MILLS								22/23																
GOODMAYES																								
THAMES WHARF																	23.32							
VICTORIA DOCKS																								
Old Ford																								
Tredegar Road																								
Fairfield Road					21.55																			
TILBURY JCN		21/35										22/37									23.00		00/17	
PLAISTOW					22.08																00/06			
RIPPLE LANE																					23.37			00.33
Bow Junction		21/36			22.02							22/38												
Devons Road		21/40			22.06							22/41												
Devon's Rd Loco			21/45																					
POPLAR DOCKS																								
Destination						To Brent(M)	via	T&H							F. Park			To Toton			R/R		Acton	Acton

28

WORKING TIMETABLE : 1953

Train / From															21.35 Brent(M)		20.30 F.Park					22.00 Brent(M)					22.20 Hendon
Class	D	Pass	EBV	ECS	K	Fish	H	ECS	D	Pass	Fish	H	D	Light	H	H	J	Pass	Light	D	ECS	J	H	Staff	Pass	Light	J
Engine	SXP4-6-0	EMU	J17 0-6-0	EMU	3F 0-6-0T	4MT 2-6-0	3F 0-6-0T	EMU	SMT 4-6-0	EMU	S15 4-6-0	3F 0-6-0T	SMT 4-6-0	J50 0-6-0T	700 0-6-0	3F 0-6-0T	J52 0-6-0T	EMU	3F 0-6-0T	4F 0-6-0	EMU	4F 0-6-0	J17 0-6-0	EMU	EMU	3F 0-6-0T	8F 2-8-0
Shed	5A/39	37/19	SX 101	59/23	DR 11	DR 5	DR 26	20/60	8B/1	66/31	FEL 108	DC2	1A/59	HSY 21	FEL 133	DR 28	HSY 10	32	DR 6	1B/58	27	14A/121	SX 100	27	25	DR 25	14A/125
POPLAR DOCKS																											
Devon's Rd Loco					20.02														20.44								21.35	
Devons Road					20.05														20/46								21/38	
Bow Junction					20/10		19.55																				21/40	
RIPPLE LANE																												
PLAISTOW																	21.03											
TILBURY JCN					20/11		20/30										21/13			20/47								21/42
Fairfield Road																												
Tredegar Road																				20.48								21.45
Old Ford													20.00							R/R								
VICTORIA DOCKS																												
THAMES WHARF																												
GOODMAYES																								20.55				
TEMPLE MILLS																												
VICTORIA PARK					20/18		20/34						20/37				21/17											
Hackney Wick																												
Homerton																												
Hackney																												
Graham Road																												
Dalston E. Jcn					20/30		20/40						20/47				21/22											
Kingsland					20w33		20w43						20w50				21/24											
Kingsland					20w38		20w47						20w57		21.18													
BROAD STREET		20.28		20.34				20.40		20.58									21.28							21.58		
Broad St Gds	20.23								20.53				21.08							21.33								
Dalston Jcn	20/30	20.34		20/40				20.48	21/00	21.04			21.15						21.34	21.40						22.04		
Dalston W. Jcn	20/32	20/35		20/41	20/41		20/50		21/02	21/05		21/00	21/17	21/20		21/26			21/35	21/42						22/05		
Canonbury Jcn	20/34	20/36		20/42	20/43		20/52		21/04	21/06		21/02	21/19	21/23		21/28			21/36	21/44						22/06		
Highbury		20/38								21/08									21/38							22/08		
Caledonian Road		20/40								21/10						21.34			21/40							22/10		
St Pancras Sidings							21/00															22.05						
Maiden Lane																		Via T&H						Via T&H				
CAMDEN RD	20/38	20/43		20/48	20/54				21/09	21/13		21/17	21/23						21/43	21/48	22/07			22/11	22/13		
Primrose Hill	20/41								21/12				21/26							21/51				22/13				
CAMDEN	20.43								21.14				21.28							21.53				22/14				
Kentish Town West	20.45									21.15									21.45						22.15			
GOSPEL OAK	20.47									21.17								21/33	21.47					21/49	22.17			
Hampstead Heath	20.49									21.19									21.49						22.19			
Finchley Road	20.51									21.21								21/39	21.51					21/54	22.21			
West End Lane	20.53									21.23									21.53						22.23			
Brondesbury	20.55									21.25									21.55						22.25			
Brondesbury Park																												
Kensal Rise	20.58									21.28									21.58						22.28			
Kensal Green Jcn	21/01				21/11		21/19			21/30		21/37						21/51	22/00					22/07				
WILLESDEN (BRENT)			21/06		21.25		21.30					21.39																
WILLESDEN (HL)	21.02									21.32								21.53	22.02							22.32		
Old Oak Sidings			21.02			21.15					21.30																	
Acton Wells Jc	21/04		21/07			21/18				21/34	21/38	21/45			21/50		21/57		22/04			22/19			22/34		22/48
ACTON YARD			21.12			21.23						21.50					22.02										
ACTON CENTRAL	21.07									21.37	21.44								22.07						22.37			
South Acton	21.09									21.39					21.56				22.09			22/25			22.39		22/54
Gunnersbury	21.12									21.43									22.12						22.44			
Kew Gardens	21.15									21.46									22.15						22.47			
RICHMOND	21.18									21.49									22.18						22.50			
Bollo Lane																												
KEW EAST JCN											21/47				21/59							22/28					22/57
Destination			Mitre B			Feltham					Feltham				Feltham		Acton		Plaistow			B'sea	Hither Green	Harrow			H. Green

29

WORKING TIMETABLE : 1953

From	22.15 Feltham		23.45 Plaistow			Pass	23.30 Feltham
Class	K	K	H	J	J52 0-6-0T	EMU	H
Engine	3F 0-6-0T	H16 4-6-2T	3F 0-6-0T	DR 3	HSY 10	19	70C 0-6-0
Shed	DR 11	FEL 144	DR 14				FE. 136
Bollo Lane			23/14				
KEW EAST JCN							
RICHMOND					23.43	23.43	
Kew Gardens					23.46		
Gunnersbury					23.49		
South Acton	23/18				23/50	23.52	
ACTON CENTRAL						23.52	
ACTON YARD			23.35				
Acton Wells Jcn	23/25		23/43		23/54		00/01 To B'ent/M)
Old Oak Sidings	23.31				23/55		
WILLESDEN (HL)	23.15		23/47		23/57	23.55	
WILLESDEN (HL Sdgs)	23.15		23.25				
Kensal Green Jcn	23/35		23/42	23/49	ECS		
Kensal Rise					to		
Brondesbury Park					Mitre		
Brondesbury					Bge CS		
West End Lane							
Finchley Road	23/46					23.55	
Hampstead Heath	23/51		00/00	00/05			
GOSPEL OAK				via			
Kentish Town West				T&H			
CAMDEN							
Primrose Hill							
CAMDEN ROAD	23/56		00/05				
Maiden Lane			00.06				
St Pancras Sidings							
Caledonian Road							
Highbury							
Canonbury Jcn	00.04		00/12				
Dalston W Jcn	00/06		00.14				
Dalston Jcn	00/08		00.14				
Broad St Goods							
BROAD STREET							
Kingsland			00/16				
Kingsland	00/08		00/18				
Dalston E. Jcn	00/10		00/18				
Graham Road							
Hackney							
Homerton							
Hackney Wick							
VICTORIA PARK	00.18		00/24				
Temple Mills							
Goodmayes							
Thames Wharf							
Victoria Docks							
Old Ford							
Tredegar Road							
Fairfield Road	00.30						
TILBURY JCN	00/21						
PLAISTOW							
Bow Junction	00/22						
Devons Road	00.26						
Devon's Rd Loco							
RIPPLE LANE							
POPLAR DOCKS							
Destination	F. Park						

ST PANCRAS SIDINGS (1953)

Train	Arr	Engine	Shed	Dep	Destination
Pilot		3F 0-6-0T	4	00.11	Highbury
		3F 0-6-0T	49	00.25	Light to Devons Rd Loco
00.15 Cricklewood (West End)	00.40	3F 0-6-0T	14B/41	(00.45)	
		3F 0-6-0T	14B/41	00.45	Light to Church Yard Sdgs
		3F 0-6-0T	14B/55	00.55	Somers Town
01.35 St Pancras Goods	01.45	3F 0-6-0T	14B/55	(02.10)	
		3F 0-6-0T	14B/55	02.10	Somers Town
02.20 Willesden	03.00	4F 0-6-0			
03.08 Camden	03.16	4F 0-6-0	1A/119	(03.30)	
03.15 St Pancras Goods	03.25	3F 0-6-0T	14B/55	(03.50)	
		4F 0-6-0	1A/119	03.30	Light to Maiden Lane
		3F 0-6-0T	14B/55	03.50	Somers Town
03.50 Goodmayes	04.52	J15 0-6-0	SD 113	05.44	Temple Mills
Light ex Devons Road Loco	05.30	3F 0-6-0T	9	06.05	Old Oak
		J15 0-6-0	SD 113		
06.25 Cambridge Street	06.35	3F 0-6-0T	14B/55	(07.05)	
06.42 Camden	06.52	3F 0-6-0T	1B/132	(07.09)	
		3F 0-6-0T	14B/55	07.05	Church Yard Sdgs
		3F 0-6-0T	1B/132	07.09	Camden
Pilot		3F 0-6-0T	18	08.10	Light to Broad Street
08.30 Kings Cross	08.50	J52 0-6-0	34A/NLP	09.20	Kings Cross
09.16 Broad Street ECS	09.33	3F 0-6-0T	18	(09.55)	
Light ex Devons Road Loco	09.52	3F 0-6-0T	10	(10.52)	
10.05 Camden	10.15	3F 0-6-0T	1B/103	(11.15)	
10.05 St Pancras Goods	10.15	3F 0-6-0T	14B/55	(10.30)	
		3F 0-6-0T	14B/55	10.30	Church Yard Sdgs
Light ex Devons Road Loco	10.56	3F 0-6-0T	43	(11.36)	
Light ex Maiden Lane	11.19	4F 0-6-0	1A/119	(11.47)	
11.28 Maiden Lane	11.38	3F 0-6-0T	10	(14.26)	
11.22 Plaistow	12.12	3F 0-6-0T	18	(12.53)	
		4F 0-6-0	1A/119	11.47	Broad Street
		3F 0-6-0T	18	11.15	Camden
		3F 0-6-0T	43	11.36	Plaistow
		3F 0-6-0T	18	12.53	Camden
12.40 Poplar	13.12	3F 0-6-0T	12	(13.40)	
		3F 0-6-0T	12	13.40	Acton
13.55 Camden	14.05	4F 0-6-0	1A/111	(14.47)	
		3F 0-6-0T	10	14.26	Maiden Lane
14.30 St Pancras Goods	14.40	3F 0-6-0T	14B/51	(15.00)	Broad Street
		4F 0-6-0	1A/111	14.47	Broad Street
		3F 0-6-0T	14B/51	15.00	Church Yard Sdgs
15.17 Maiden Lane	15.27	3F 0-6-0T	49	(15.52)	
15.10 Poplar	15.38	3F 0-6-0T	44	(16.22)	
15.30 Maiden Lane	15.40	3F 0-6-0T	10	(17.46)	
15.40 St Pancras Goods	15.50	3F 0-6-0T	14B/51	(16.30)	
		3F 0-6-0T	49	15.52	Light to Camden
		3F 0-6-0T	44	16.22	Kingsland
		3F 0-6-0T	14B/51	16.30	Church Yard Sdgs
		4F 0-6-0	1A/147	17.36	ECS Broad Street
		3F 0-6-0T	10	17.46	Light to Maiden Lane
17.39 Camden	17.49	3F 0-6-0T	49	Pilot	
17.40 St Pancras Goods	17.50	3F 0-6-0T	14B/55	(18.35)	
17.48 Willesden Pcls	18.03	4MT 2-6-(	23	(20.14)	
		3F 0-6-0T	14B/55	18.35	Church Yard Sdgs
18.10 Willesden	18.49	4F 0-6-0	15	(19.35)	
EBV ex St Pancras Goods	19.12	3F 0-6-0T	14B/55		
Light ex St Pancras	19.25	3F 0-6-0T	14B/41	(19.50)	
19.15 Broad Street	19.32	3F 0-6-0T	4	(20.00)	
		4F 0-6-0	15	19.35	Light to Devons Rd Loco
		3F 0-6-0T	14B/41	19.50	Church Yard Sdgs
		3F 0-6-0T	4	20.00	Light to Willesden
Light ex Camden	20.01	3F 0-6-0T	3	(20.33)	
20.00 St Pancras Pcls	20.10	3F 0-6-0T	14B/55	(20.22)	
		4MT 2-6-(	23	20.14	Willesden Pcls
20.05 Willesden Pcls	20.20	3F 0-6-0T	15		
		3F 0-6-0T	14B/55	20.22	St Pancras Pcls
		3F 0-6-0T	1B/94	20.30	Light to Camden
		3F 0-6-0T	3	20.33	Willesden
21.03 Plaistow	21.34	3F 0-6-0T	28	(22.17)	
21.05 Camden	21.35	3F 0-6-0T	16	(21.40)	
		3F 0-6-0T	16	21.40	Light to Devons Rd Loco
Light ex St Pancras	22.10	3F 0-6-0T	14B/55	(23.00)	
21.40 Willesden	22.16	3F 0-6-0T	4	(00.11)	
Light ex Maiden Lane	22.55	3F 0-6-0T	28	(23.34)	
		3F 0-6-0T	14B/55	23.00	Somers Town
23.20 Devons Road	23.47	3F 0-6-0T	28	23.34	Maiden Lane
23.45 St Pancras Goods	23.55	3F 0-6-0T	18	Pilot	
		3F 0-6-0T	14B/55	(00.55)	

One of the busiest locations on the North London was St Pancras Sidings which was the point of contact with the Midland which ran a regular service of trip workings to and from the yards in the vicinity of St Pancras. There was also a direct connection from Kings Cross Goods although traffic tended to be light with only one daily service in each direction. Work was continuous in the sidings with pilot engines being provided throughout the day not only to shunt the yards but to transfer traffic across the running lines to the adjacent Maiden Lane goods depot.

We believe that this is the first time that a complete (passenger, goods and trip) version of the North London WTT has been published since previous versions - LMS and BR - required three separate books which made it very difficult to see things in chronological order.

The detail of the table should be reasonably self-explanatory and we have kept notes to a bare minimum. Of those that do appear: 'w' indicates a stop for water, 'L' for crew relief and 'R/R' to indicate a movement that reverses direction or runs-round.

Some matter appears that was not included in the timetable such as the engine type and diagram for each service. Thus it can be seen without any further reference that, for example, 23.45 Temple Mills to Hither Green was booked to be worked by Stratford 104 J17 0-6-0. A glance through the timetable will reveal that the return working of Stratford 104 was the 03.50 Hither Green to Temple Mills. It can be added that the first thing most operating railwaymen did with their working timetables was to annotate them with the engine workings for easy reference.

For all their worth, timetables do not convey much about the state of line occupation and to make good the omission a set of line occupation graphs have been included on the following pages. These should leave no-one in any doubt about the contribution make by the North London. Although the timetable and graphs are those for 1953, they are generally representative of the period 1946-60.

Station	C / SMT 4-6-0 / 9A/57	H / 3F 0-6-0 / DR 6	K / 3F 0-6-0 / DR 28	Light / 3F 0-6-0 / DR 51	Light / 3F 0-6-0 / 51	Light / To Broad St	E / SMT 4-6-0 / 1B/67	Pass / EMU / 19/37	Light / 4MT 2-6-0 / DR 7	K / 4MT 2-6-0 / DR 7	F / 4F 0-6-0 / 1A/58	J (22.10 F. Park) / J6 0-6-0 / HSY 5	Pass / EMU / 66/31	H / 700 0-6-0 / FEL137	H / J17 0-6-0 / SX 104	Light / 3F 0-6-0 / DR 14	K / 3F 0-6-0 / DR 28	H / 3F 0-6-0 / DR 25	K / 3F 0-6-0 / DR 18	(23.20 E. Gds) / J52 0-6-0 / HSY 11	H / 3F 0-6-0 / DR 14
POPLAR DOCKS																					
Devon's Rd Loco				21.55					22.05							22.45		23.20			
Devons Road				22.04												22.49		23.24			
Bow Junction				22.09																	
RIPPLE LANE																					
PLAISTOW		21.38												22.58							23.45
TILBURY JCN		21.55		22.05					22.10							22.50 R/R	23.25	23.14		23.55	
Fairfield Road																	23.20				
Tredegar Road																	23.24				
Old Ford																					
VICTORIA DOCKS																					
THAMES WHARF																					
GOODMAYES																					
TEMPLE MILLS														22.30	22.45						
VICTORIA PARK		22.00		22.08					22.13					22.53	Via T&H		23.28	23.19			23.59
Hackney Wick																					
Homerton																					
Hackney																					
Graham Road																					
Dalston E. Jcn		22.07 / 22w09		22.15					22.19 / 22.21				23.13	22.58			23.36	23.24 / 23w27		23w32	00.03
Kingsland		22w14												23.00			23.38			23.55	
Kingsland																					
BROAD STREET	To Broad St				22.24			22.28					22.58								
Broad St Goods	22.02					22.20															
Dalston Jcn	22.09				22.30	22.27		22.34					23.04								
Dalston W. Jcn	22.11				22.32			22.35		22.43	22.50		23.05	23.02		23.50	23.40	23.35	23.58		23.47
Canonbury Jcn	22.13				22.34			22.36		22.45	22.52		23.06	23.04		23.55	23.42	23.37	00.01		
Highbury								22.37					23.07								
Caledonian Road								22.39					23.09						23.24		
St Pancras Sidings											Via T&H								23.34		
Maiden Lane																					
CAMDEN RD	22.17	22.27			22.36			22.43		22.53	22.58		23.13	23.19	23.45				00.08		
Primrose Hill	22.19				22.39						23.01										
CAMDEN	22.20				22.41						23.03										
Kentish Town West								22.45					23.15								
GOSPEL OAK		22.32						22.47		22.58		23.08	23.17	23.24	23.40	23.50			00.13		
Hampstead Heath								22.49					23.19								
Finchley Road		22.37						22.51		23.03		23.13	23.21	23.29	23.45	23.55			00.18		
West End Lane								22.53					23.23								
Brondesbury								22.55					23.25								
Brondesbury Park													23.25								
Kensal Rise								22.58					23.28								
Kensal Green Jcn		22.46						23.01		23.13	22.58	23.22	23.31	23.39	23.57	23.05			00.26		
WILLESDEN (BRENT)		22.48																			
WILLESDEN (HL)								23.02		23.15		23.24	23.32	23.42	23.59	23.07			00.28		
Old Oak Sidings										23.30											
Acton Wells Jcn		22.51										23.27	23.34	23.45		00.10			00.31		
ACTON YARD		22.55						23.04								00.15			00.38		
ACTON CENTRAL								23.07					23.37								
South Acton								23.09					23.39	23.52							
Gunnersbury								23.12					23.43								
Kew Gardens								23.15					23.46								
RICHMOND								23.18					23.49								
Bollo Lane																					
KEW EAST JCN														23.55							
Destination	Stockport	B. St	Devons Rd			Broad St	Watford					Feltham		Feltham	H. Green	Plaistow					Broad St

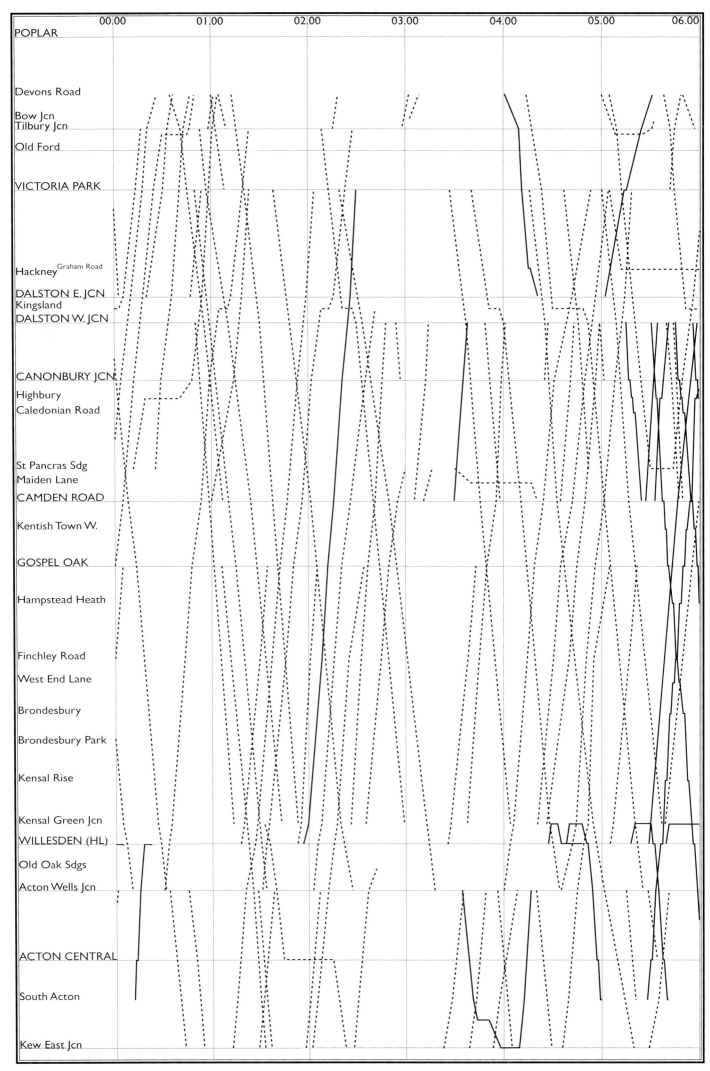

8F 2-8-0 48325 of Willesden approaches Tilbury Junction whilst running light from Willesden to Devons Road or Poplar on Sunday 12th August 1956. The photograph has been taken from Tredegar Road siding whilst, opposite, a train of oil tanks waits in Fairfield Road Sidings to be tripped down to the Esso sidings at Caspian Wharf, Bow. The network of railways in the area was impressive: the first overbridge ahead of the engine carries the Liverpool - Norwich main line over the North London whilst immediately beyond it is the bridge carrying the Bow Junction - Fenchurch Street branch of the Great Eastern. Beyond the second of these overbridges, the North London splits into three routes: to Plaistow and the LTSR on the left, to Bow Gas Works and Fenchurch Street on the right and, centre, straight on for Devons Road. (A E Bennet/transport treasury.co.uk).

A train of Oerlikon DC stock arrives at Broad Street with a service from Watford Junction circa 1953. These sets were unusual in that the accommodation was of the saloon type with a mix of conventional seats and 'settee' seats that faced inwards. The later 1927 and 1957 stock was of the compartment type; the Oerlikon sets being withdrawn between 1956 and 1959. The photograph clearly shows the dual nature of Broad Street, only the lines on one side of the station being electrified, platforms 1 to 4 having no third-rail and being reserved for steam services. (Photograph © 2010 - 53A Models of Hull Collection (the late John C Berry))

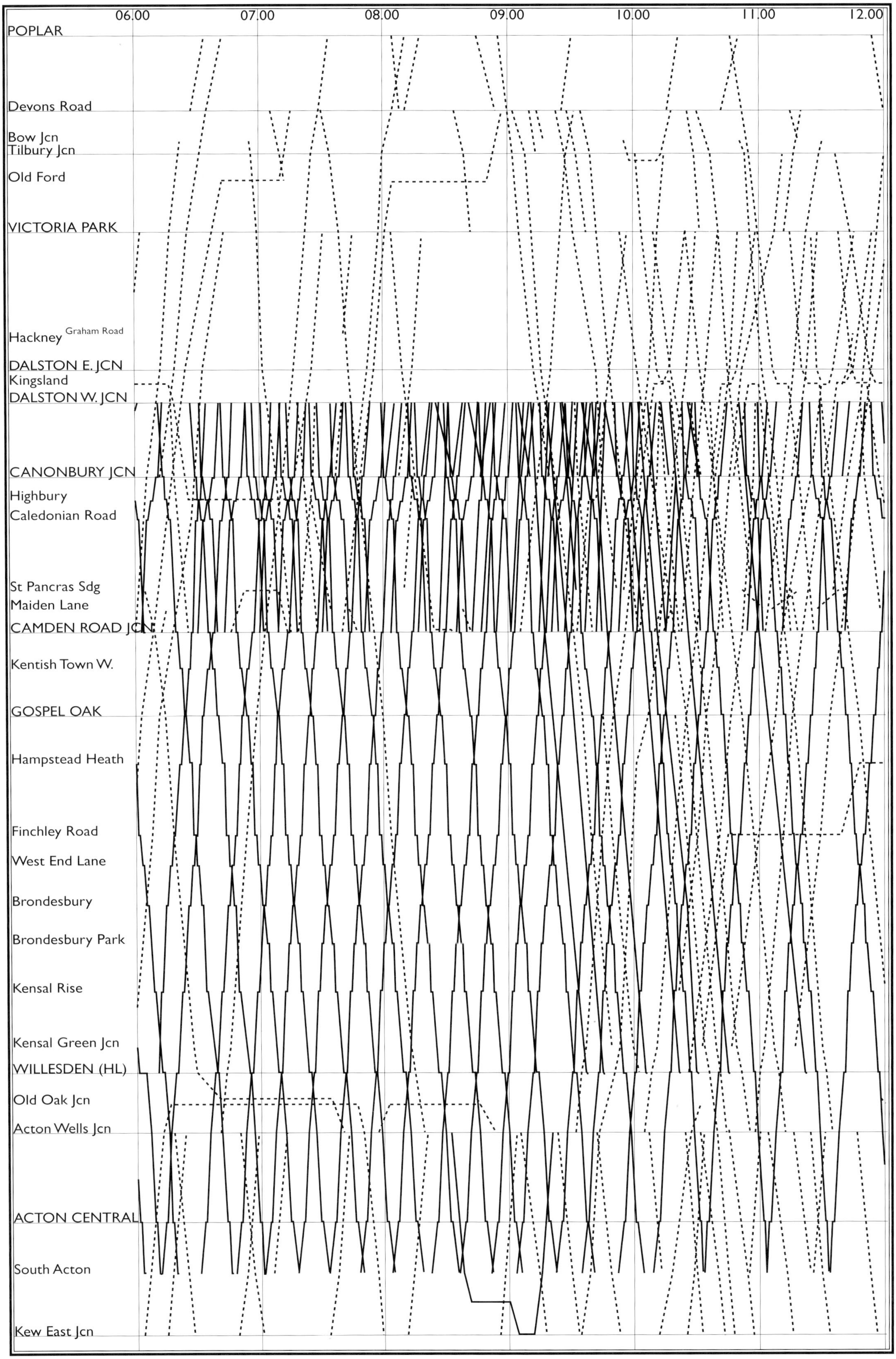

POPLAR

Devons Road

Bow Jcn
Tilbury Jcn

Old Ford

VICTORIA PARK

Hackney Graham Road

DALSTON E. JCN
Kingsland
DALSTON W. JCN

CANONBURY JCN

Highbury
Caledonian Road

St Pancras Sdg
Maiden Lane
CAMDEN ROAD JCN

Kentish Town W.

GOSPEL OAK

Hampstead Heath

Finchley Road

West End Lane

Brondesbury

Brondesbury Park

Kensal Rise

Kensal Green Jcn
WILLESDEN (HL)

Old Oak Jcn

Acton Wells Jcn

ACTON CENTRAL

South Acton

Kew East Jcn

06.00   07.00   08.00   09.00   10.00   11.00   12.00

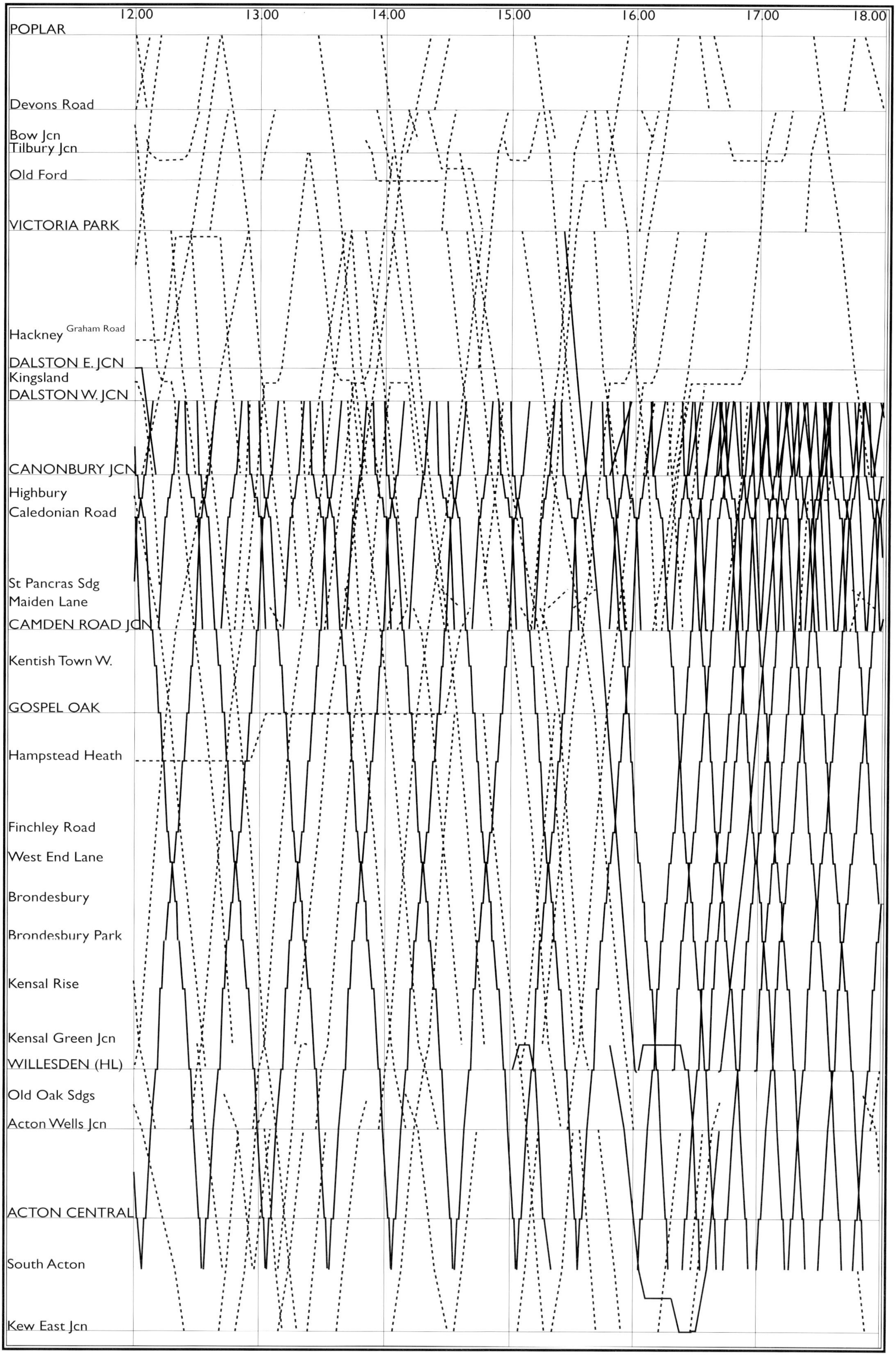

12.00 13.00 14.00 15.00 16.00 17.00 18.00

POPLAR

Devons Road

Bow Jcn
Tilbury Jcn

Old Ford

VICTORIA PARK

Hackney Graham Road
DALSTON E. JCN
Kingsland
DALSTON W. JCN

CANONBURY JCN
Highbury
Caledonian Road

St Pancras Sdg
Maiden Lane
CAMDEN ROAD JCN

Kentish Town W.

GOSPEL OAK

Hampstead Heath

Finchley Road

West End Lane

Brondesbury

Brondesbury Park

Kensal Rise

Kensal Green Jcn
WILLESDEN (HL)

Old Oak Sdgs

Acton Wells Jcn

ACTON CENTRAL

South Acton

Kew East Jcn

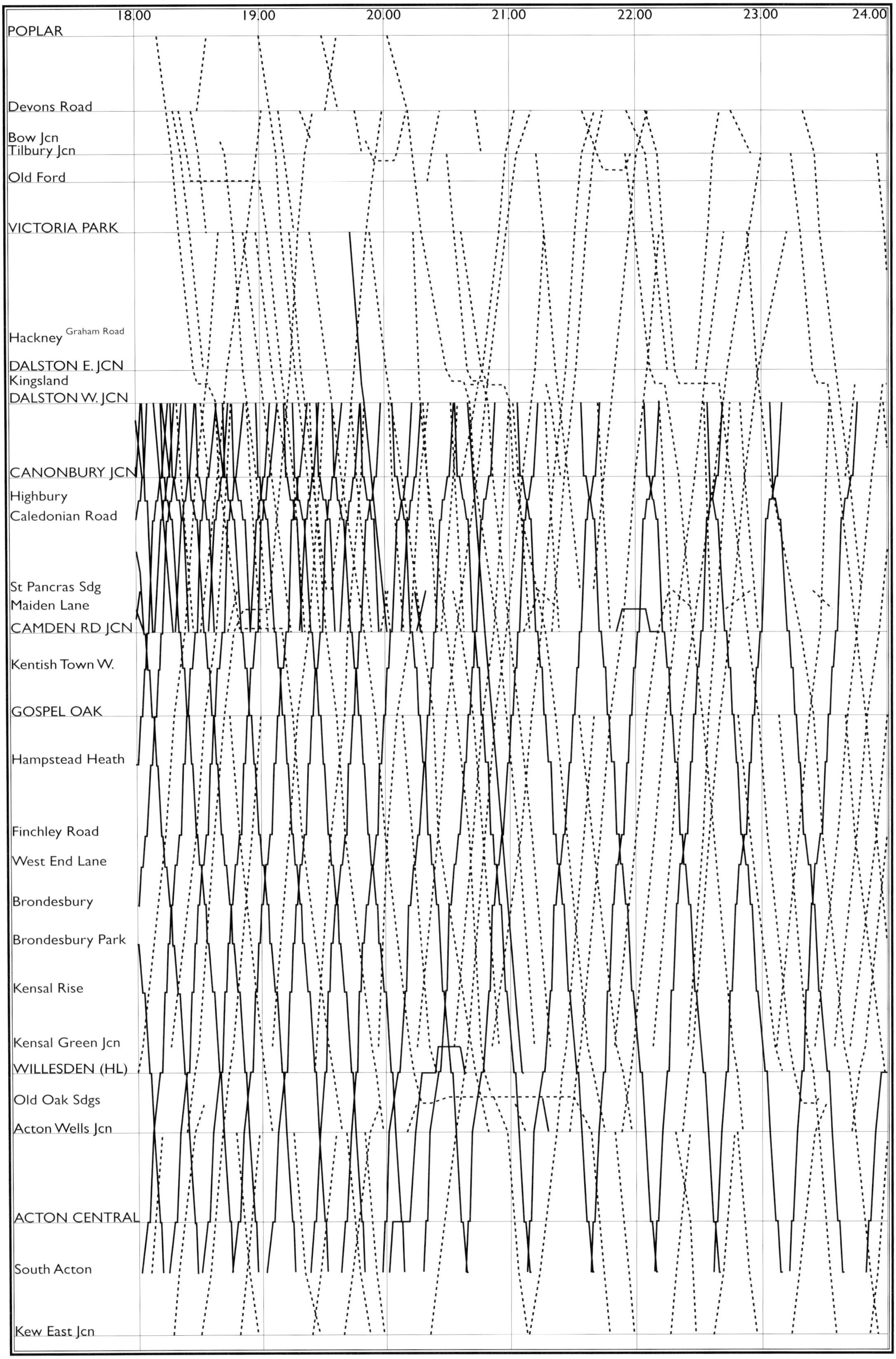

1
4MT 2-6-0

	Devons Road	15.33	Light
5.45	Barking	19.15	Pcls
0.20	Willesden	21.00	Light
1.45	Devons Road		

2
3F 0-6-0T

	Devons Rd	01.13	K
2.10	Willesden	05.25	K
6.41	Haydon Square	10.30	K
1.18	Camden	11.25	
1.30	Camden Loco	12.40	Coupled
3.05	Broad St	14.35	K
4.58	Devons Road	18.27	EBV
9.00	Vic Docks	20.00	H
1.50	Acton		
	Control Orders		
1.45	Devons Rd		

3
3F 0-6-0T

	Devons Rd	09.35	Light
0.05	Camden	10.58	K
1.55	Haydon Square	13.30	K
4.55	Camden	15.05	Light
5.36	Devons Rd	18.21	Light
8.27	Old Ford	19.00	K
9.25	Camden	19.53	Light
0.01	St Pancras Sdgs	20.33	K
1.19	Willesden	23.25	K
0.30	Fairfield Rd	00.45	Light
0.50	Devons Road		

4
3F 0-6-0T

	Devons Road	18.18	Light
8.41	Broad St	19.15	K
9.32	St Pancras Sdgs	20.00	Light
0.20	Willesden	21.40	K
2.16	St Pancras Sdgs	00.11	K
0.19	Barnsbury	00.40	EBV
1.07	Devons Road		

5
4MT 2-6-0

	Devons Road	19.09	Light
9.30	Stratford M	19.58	Fish
0.57	Old Oak	21.15	Fish
1.23	Acton		
	Control orders		

6
3F 0-6-0T

	Devons Road	20.44	Light
0.57	Plaistow	21.38	H
2.56	Acton	00.25	H
1.35	Plaistow	02.05	Light
2.19	Devons Rd		

7
4MT 2-6-0

	Devons Rd	22.05	Light
2.21	Kingsland	22.40	K
3.30	Old Oak	00.40	ECS
0.55	Kensington	01.45	Milk
2.33	Channelsea	02.57	Milk
3.10	Tredegar Rd	03.15	Light
3.20	Devons Road	04.00	Pass
4.20	Broad Street	04.55	Pass
5.16	Devons Rd		
5.25	Loco		

8
3F 0-6-0T

	Devons Rd	01.05	EBV
1.19	Plaistow	02.00	H
3.10	Willesden	05.30	K
6.42	Old Ford	07.10	Light
7.15	Devons Rd		

9
3F 0-6-0T

	Devons Rd	05.05	Light
05.30	St Pancras S.	06.05	K
06.40	Old Oak	07.35	K
07.46	Acton	10.50	H
12.11	T. Mills	12.15	Light
12.44	Devons Rd	17.40	Light
17.45	Poplar	18.10	K
19.45	Acton		
	Control Orders		
01.25	Devons Rd		

10
3F 0-6-0T

	Devons Rd	09.23	Light
09.52	St Pancras S	10.52	K
11.02	Maiden Lane	11.28	K
11.38	St Pancras Sdgs	14.26	K
14.36	Maiden Lane	15.30	K
15.40	St Pancras Sdgs	17.46	light
17.56	Maiden Lane	18.00	Pcls
18.07	Camden	18.28	Light
19.02	Devons Rd		

11
3F 0-6-0T

	Devons Rd	19.32	Light
19.37	Poplar	20.02	K
21.25	Willesden	23.15	K
00.26	Devons Road		

12
3F 0-6-0T

	Devons Rd	12.00	K
12.07	Poplar	12.40	K
13.12	St Pancras Sdgs	13.40	K
14.15	Acton	15.23	H
16.40	Temple Mills	19.30	
20.55	Acton	21.45	H
22.54	Temple Mills	00.20	H
01.40	Acton	03.55	H
05.08	Temple Mills	05.15	Light
05.49	Devons Rd		

13
3F 0-6-0T

	Devons Rd	09.14	K
09.27	Bow Gas	09.50	J
09.58	Fairfield Rd Sdgs	10.11	J
10.18	Devons Rd	11.15	J
11.26	Bow Gas	12.01	J
12.10	Fairfield Rd Sdgs	12.23	J
12.30	Devons Rd	14.10	J
14.22	Bow Gas	14.50	J
14.59	Fairfield Rd Sdgs	15.07	J
15.13	Devons Rd	16.02	J
16.14	Bow Gas	16.40	J
16.47	Fairfield Rd Sdgs	17.10	J
17.15	Devons Rd	19.20	J
19.32	Bow Gas	19.47	J
19.55	Fairfield Rd Sdgs	20.05	J
20.10	Devons Rd		

14
3F 0-6-0T

	Devons Rd	22.45	Light
22.59	Plaistow	23.45	H
00.14	Broad St	00.40	Light
01.04	Temple Mills	03.15	H
04.40	Acton	06.30	K
07.34	Poplar	08.05	Light
08.10	Devons Rd		

15
4F 0-6-0

	Devons Road	03.55	
04.20	T. Mills	04.30	H
05.50	Willesden	09.00	K
10.10	T. Mills	10.55	Coupled
11.20	Devons Rd	15.45	Light
16.30	Willesden	18.10	K
18.49	St Pancras Sdgs	19.35	Light
19.59	Devons Road		

16
3F 0-6-0T

	Devons Road	15.18	Light
15.34	Haydon Square	18.28	E
19.09	Camden	21.05	K
21.15	St Pancras Sdgs	21.40	Light
22.06	Devons Road		

17
3F 0-6-0T

	Devons Road	07.30	EBV
08.25	Acton	09.27	H
10.36	T. Mills	10.55	Coupled
11.20	Devons Rd		

18
3F 0-6-0T

	Devons Road	23.20	K
23.47	St Pancras Sdgs		Pilot
	St Pancras Sdgs	08.45	Light
09.00	Broad Street	09.16	ECS
09.30	St Pancras Sdgs	09.55	H
10.26	Plaistow	11.22	K
12.12	St Pancras Sdgs	12.53	K
13.00	Camden	15.10	K
15.35	Old Ford	15.45	K
15.55	Poplar	16.37	K
16.45	Devons Rd		

20
3F 0-6-0T

	Devons Road	18.30	Light
18.35	Poplar	19.00	K
19.34	Camden		K
	Willesden	22.50	K
23.45	Broad St	00.15	Light
00.37	Devons Rd		

21
3F 0-6-0T

	Devons Rd	05.00	Light
05.08	Fairfield Rd	05.25	K
05.49	Haydon Square	06.42	Light
07.20	Camden	07.36	H
08.05	Old Ford	08.50	K
08.57	Devons Rd	10.16	Light
10.21	Poplar	10.46	K
11.55	Willesden	13.00	J
14.11	Devons Rd		

22
3F 0-6-0T

	Devons Road	01.00	Light
01.24	T. Mills	01.55	H
03.25	Acton	05.46	H
07.00	T. Mills	09.35	H
10.50	Acton	11.52	H
13.07	T. Mills	14.05	Light
14.33	Devons Rd		

23
4MT 2-6-0

	Devons Rd	14.20	Light
14.25	Tredegar Rd	14.40	Milk
14.57	Channelsea	15.20	Milk
16.10	Shepherds Bush	16.49	Light
17.15	Willesden ML	17.48	Pcls
18.03	St Pancras Sdgs	20.14	Pcls
20.30	Willesden ML		
	Willesden	21.50	H
	R. Lane	00.25	H
01.55	Willesden	04.05	H
05.35	Vic Docks	07.35	H
08.38	Camden	09.02	Light
09.32	Devons Rd		

25
3F 0-6-0T

	Devons Rd	21.35	Light
21.45	Tredegar Rd	21.55	H
22.08	Plaistow	22.58	H
00.15	Acton	01.25	H
02.36	Plaistow	02.55	Light
03.12	Devons Rd		

26
3F 0-6-0T

	Devons Rd	09.03	J
10.05	Willesden	13.00	H
14.14	Plaistow	14.30	Light
14.25	Plaistow Loco	19.15	Light
19.35	R. Lane	19.55	H
21.30	Willesden	23.05	H
00.33	Plaistow	00.50	Light
01.02	Devons Road		

27
3F 0-6-0T

	Devons Rd Loco	09.18	Light
	Devons Rd	09.28	EBV
10.05	Vic Docks	10.25	H
12.50	Willesden	15.00	K
16.20	Poplar	16.30	Light
16.35	Devons Rd		

28
3F 0-6-0T

	Devons Rd	19.46	Light
20.02	Plaistow	21.03	H
21.34	St Pancras Sdgs	22.17	K
22.27	Maiden Lane	22.43	Light
22.53	St Pancras Sdgs	23.24	K
23.34	Maiden Lane		
	Control Orders		
03.16	Devons Rd		

30
3F 0-6-0T

	Devons Rd	04.14	EBV
04.30	Kingsland	04.49	J
05.30	Acton	07.50	K
08.03	Old Oak	08.45	EBV
08.58	Acton	10.00	H
11.25	Vic Docks	14.08	H
15.30	Acton	18.15	K
18.52	Maiden Lane	19.04	Light
19.26	Devons Rd		

31
3F 0-6-0T

	Devons Rd	08.35	EBV
09.10	Vic Docks	10.00	H
11.18	Acton	12.50	H
14.10	Vic Docks	18.15	H
19.18	Camden		
	Willesden	20.38	K
21.40	Devons Road		

36
3F 0-6-0T

	Devons Rd	10.25	Light
10.37	Channelsea	11.10	H
12.15	Acton	13.50	H
15.00	T. Mills	15.40	Light
16.10	Devons Rd		

37
3F 0-6-0T

	Devons Road	10.42	K
10.50	Poplar	11.54	37
13.05	Willesden		
	Camden	16.03	K
17.07	Devons Road		

38
2F 0-6-0T

	Devons Rd	06.27	K
06.32	Poplar	19.30	Light
19.38	Devons Road		

39
3F 0-6-0T

	Devons Rd	05.50	Light
06.15	Bow Midland		Pilot
	Bow Midland	17.05	
17.29	Devons Rd		

40
2F 0-6-0T

	Devons Rd	06.27	K
06.32	Poplar	12.00	
12.05	Devons Rd	12.30	
12.35	Poplar	19.30	
19.38	Devons Rd		

41
2F 0-6-0T

	Devons Rd	09.25	Light
09.30	Poplar	17.50	Light
18.00	Devons Rd		

42
3F 0-6-0T

	Devons Rd	00.01	Light
	Pilot		
23.59	Devons Rd		

43
3F 0-6-0T

	Devons Rd	08.10	K
08.18	Poplar	08.45	K
08.54	Devons Rd	10.30	Light
10.56	St Pancras Sdgs	11.36	43
12.14	Plaistow	13.05	H
14.30	Acton		
	Control Orders		
16.00	Devons Rd		

44
3F 0-6-0T

	Devons Road	14.15	K
14.22	Poplar	15.10	K
15.38	St Pancras Sdgs	16.22	EBV
16.33	Kingsland	20.45	J
21.03	Devons Road		

45
3F 0-6-0T

	Devons Road	09.10	Light
09.30	Plaistow	09.50	H
11.02	Acton	12.20	H
13.34	Plaistow	13.57	Light
14.15	Devons Road		

48
3F 0-6-0T

	Devons Rd	07.06	Light
07.12	Old Ford		Light
	Pilot		
	Old Ford	13.00	Light
13.06	Devons Rd	13.55	K
14.02	Old Ford		
	Pilot		
	Old Ford	20.21	Light
20.27	Devons Rd		

49
3F 0-6-0T

	Devons Rd	05.38	EBV
05.52	Kingsland	06.16	J
06.25	Highbury	07.25	K
07.35	Maiden Lane	08.38	Light
08.46	Camden		
	Willesden	10.30	H
12.04	T. Mills	13.30	H
14.10	Maiden Lane	15.17	K
15.27	St Pancras Sdgs	16.00	
	Camden	17.39	K
17.49	St Pancras Sdgs		Pilot
	St Pancras Sdgs	00.25	Light
00.47	Devons Road		

51
3F 0-6-0T

	Devons Rd	21.55	Light
22.20	Broad St		Pilot
	Broad St	22.20	Light
22.41	Devons Rd		

Viewed from the brakevan, an 8F 2-8-0 working a special of tanks takes the West Hampstead road at Camden Road Junction on 12th August 1956. (A E Bennet/ transporttreasury.co.uk)

							ALLOCATION AND TRANSFERS : DEVONS ROAD MPD					
Loco	Class	Aug-50	Sep-50	Oct-50	Nov-50	Dec-50	Jan-51	Feb-51	Mar-51	Apr-51	May-51	Jun-51	Jul-51
43000	4MT 2-6-0 (1947)	X	X	X	X	X	Ex Bletchley						
43001	4MT 2-6-0 (1947)	X	X	X	X	X	Ex Cambridge						
43020	4MT 2-6-0 (1947)	X	X	X	X	X	Ex Nuneaton						
43021	4MT 2-6-0 (1947)	X	X	X	X	X	Ex Nuneaton						
43022	4MT 2-6-0 (1947)	X	X	X	X	X	Ex Nuneaton						
43024	4MT 2-6-0 (1947)	X	X	X	X	X	Ex Nuneaton						
44348	4F 0-6-0 (1924)												
44370	4F 0-6-0 (1924)									To Willesden	X	X	X
44372	4F 0-6-0 (1924)	X	X	X	X	X	X	X	X	Ex Willesden			
47302	3F 0-6-0T (1924)												
47304	3F 0-6-0T (1924)												
47306	3F 0-6-0T (1924)								To Plaistow	X	X	X	X
47307	3F 0-6-0T (1924)												
47310	3F 0-6-0T (1924)												
47312	3F 0-6-0T (1924)								To Plaistow	X	X	X	X
47314	3F 0-6-0T (1924)												
47315	3F 0-6-0T (1924)												
47348	3F 0-6-0T (1924)												
47349	3F 0-6-0T (1924)												
47350	3F 0-6-0T (1924)												
47411	3F 0-6-0T (1924)						To Edge Hill	X	X	X	X	X	X
47482	3F 0-6-0T (1924)												
47483	3F 0-6-0T (1924)												
47486	3F 0-6-0T (1924)												
47487	3F 0-6-0T (1924)						To Edge Hill	X	X	X	X	X	X
47488	3F 0-6-0T (1924)												
47489	3F 0-6-0T (1924)						To Edge Hill	X	X	X	X	X	X
47490	3F 0-6-0T (1924)												
47492	3F 0-6-0T (1924)												
47493	3F 0-6-0T (1924)												
47494	3F 0-6-0T (1924)												
47495	3F 0-6-0T (1924)												
47497	3F 0-6-0T (1924)												
47498	3F 0-6-0T (1924)						To Edge Hill	X	X	X	X	X	X
47499	3F 0-6-0T (1924)												
47500	3F 0-6-0T (1924)												
47501	3F 0-6-0T (1924)												
47506	3F 0-6-0T (1924)												
47511	3F 0-6-0T (1924)												
47514	3F 0-6-0T (1924)												
47515	3F 0-6-0T (1924)												
47516	3F 0-6-0T (1924)												
47517	3F 0-6-0T (1924)												
47518	3F 0-6-0T (1924)												
47558	3F 0-6-0T (1924)												
47559	3F 0-6-0T (1924)												
47560	3F 0-6-0T (1924)												
47561	3F 0-6-0T (1924)												
47564	3F 0-6-0T (1924)												
58852	2F 0-6-0T (1879)												
58853	2F 0-6-0T (1879)												
58855	2F 0-6-0T (1879)												
58858	2F 0-6-0T (1879)												
58859	2F 0-6-0T (1879)												
58865	0F: Crane 0-4-2ST (1858)						W/D	X	X	X	X	X	X

Western Junction, Dalston looking East with the route for Victoria Park and Poplar - known as the Pound - straight ahead, that for Dalston Junction and Broad Street curving to the right. The electrified pair of rails were designated as No.2 up and down with the slow lines being named No.1 up and down. Only the No.2 lines were electrified but the No.1 pair carried the Great Northern suburban service in addition to goods workings. (R E Vincent/transporttreasury.co.uk)

Loco	Class	Aug-51	Sep-51	Oct-51	Nov-51	Dec-51	Jan-52	Feb-52	Mar-52	Apr-52	May-52	Jun-52	Jul-52
	ALLOCATION AND TRANSFERS : DEVONS ROAD MPD												
43000	4MT 2-6-0 (1947)												
43001	4MT 2-6-0 (1947)												
43020	4MT 2-6-0 (1947)												
43021	4MT 2-6-0 (1947)												
43022	4MT 2-6-0 (1947)												
43024	4MT 2-6-0 (1947)												
44348	4F 0-6-0 (1924)												
44372	4F 0-6-0 (1924)												
44441	4F 0-6-0 (1924)	X	X	X	X	X	X	Ex Watford					
47302	3F 0-6-0T (1924)												
47304	3F 0-6-0T (1924)												
47307	3F 0-6-0T (1924)												
47310	3F 0-6-0T (1924)												
47314	3F 0-6-0T (1924)												
47315	3F 0-6-0T (1924)												
47348	3F 0-6-0T (1924)												
47349	3F 0-6-0T (1924)												
47350	3F 0-6-0T (1924)												
47482	3F 0-6-0T (1924)												
47483	3F 0-6-0T (1924)												
47486	3F 0-6-0T (1924)												
47488	3F 0-6-0T (1924)												
47490	3F 0-6-0T (1924)												
47492	3F 0-6-0T (1924)												
47493	3F 0-6-0T (1924)												
47494	3F 0-6-0T (1924)												
47495	3F 0-6-0T (1924)												
47497	3F 0-6-0T (1924)												
47499	3F 0-6-0T (1924)												
47500	3F 0-6-0T (1924)												
47501	3F 0-6-0T (1924)												
47506	3F 0-6-0T (1924)												
47511	3F 0-6-0T (1924)												
47514	3F 0-6-0T (1924)												
47515	3F 0-6-0T (1924)												
47516	3F 0-6-0T (1924)												
47517	3F 0-6-0T (1924)												
47518	3F 0-6-0T (1924)												
47558	3F 0-6-0T (1924)												
47559	3F 0-6-0T (1924)												
47560	3F 0-6-0T (1924)												
47561	3F 0-6-0T (1924)												
47564	3F 0-6-0T (1924)												
58852	2F 0-6-0T (1879)												
58853	2F 0-6-0T (1879)												
58855	2F 0-6-0T (1879)												
58858	2F 0-6-0T (1879)												
58859	2F 0-6-0T (1879)												

Devons Road's allocation was interesting rather than exciting, the bulk of the engine complement consisting of LMS Standard 3F 0-6-0 tanks the haulage powers of which were about equal to the rather restricted loading limits imposed by the North London operating authorities. The 3F tanks could haul 58 wagons of goods - quite adequate on most North London routes - at class H speed and it was only on coal trains that they were at a disadvantage; their limit being around thirty wagons.

In an attempt to circumvent this problem a small number of 4F 0-6-0's and 4MT 2-6-0's were sent to the shed but received something of a hostile reception. The 4F's were notoriously poor steamers whilst the 2-6-0's were said to be 'Jerry-built': heavy on coal and rough riding. The fact that engines could not be turned at Acton, which was the terminating point for many North London workings, did not help.

Several of the lines within the Dock Area at Poplar were barred to all but the lightest engines and for this reason Devons Road retained a small number of NLR outside cylinder 0-6-0T's which were the only BR engines allowed to work these sections. Attempts were made to replace the NLR tanks - 47007 and 47164 were tried but met with only partial success - and it was not until the arrival of a pair of 0-4-0 diesel shunters in April 1958 that the 1879 engines were taken out of traffic.

In spite of the considerable work done by the Devons Road Loco - an engine came off shed every thirty minutes on average - much of its light lay hidden under a bushel: of those who had heard of it, perhaps a quarter could find it on a map yet in mid-1957 it hit the headlines when it was announced that it would become the first all-diesel depot in the country.

The change came swiftly. Four new English Electric type 1 (later class 20) diesels arrived in July 1957 and by August 1958 the last of the steam allocation was transferred away.

Ironically traffic levels that had remained high until the late 1950's, simply evaporated as soon as the diesels had settled in and within a few years of steam departing it became clear that Devons Road Loco could not survive. In early 1964 the depot closed with all traffic being worked from Willesden shed.

Loco	Class	Aug-52	Sep-52	Oct-52	Nov-52	Dec-52	Jan-53	Feb-53	Mar-53	Apr-53	May-53	Jun-53	Jul-53
43000	4MT 2-6-0 (1947)												
43001	4MT 2-6-0 (1947)												
43020	4MT 2-6-0 (1947)												
43021	4MT 2-6-0 (1947)												
43022	4MT 2-6-0 (1947)												
43024	4MT 2-6-0 (1947)												
44348	4F 0-6-0 (1924)												
44372	4F 0-6-0 (1924)											W/D	X
44441	4F 0-6-0 (1924)												
47302	3F 0-6-0T (1924)												
47304	3F 0-6-0T (1924)												
47307	3F 0-6-0T (1924)												
47310	3F 0-6-0T (1924)												
47314	3F 0-6-0T (1924)												
47315	3F 0-6-0T (1924)												
47348	3F 0-6-0T (1924)												
47349	3F 0-6-0T (1924)												
47350	3F 0-6-0T (1924)										To Willesden	X	X
47482	3F 0-6-0T (1924)												
47483	3F 0-6-0T (1924)												
47486	3F 0-6-0T (1924)												
47488	3F 0-6-0T (1924)												
47490	3F 0-6-0T (1924)												
47492	3F 0-6-0T (1924)										To Willesden	X	X
47493	3F 0-6-0T (1924)												
47494	3F 0-6-0T (1924)												
47495	3F 0-6-0T (1924)												
47497	3F 0-6-0T (1924)												
47499	3F 0-6-0T (1924)												
47500	3F 0-6-0T (1924)												
47501	3F 0-6-0T (1924)												
47506	3F 0-6-0T (1924)												
47511	3F 0-6-0T (1924)												
47514	3F 0-6-0T (1924)												
47515	3F 0-6-0T (1924)												
47516	3F 0-6-0T (1924)												
47517	3F 0-6-0T (1924)												
47518	3F 0-6-0T (1924)												
47558	3F 0-6-0T (1924)												
47559	3F 0-6-0T (1924)												
47560	3F 0-6-0T (1924)												
47561	3F 0-6-0T (1924)												
47564	3F 0-6-0T (1924)												
58851	2F 0-6-0T (1879)	X	X	X	Ex Birkenhead								
58852	2F 0-6-0T (1879)												
58853	2F 0-6-0T (1879)												
58854	2F 0-6-0T (1879)	X	X	Ex Birkenhead									
58855	2F 0-6-0T (1879)												
58857	2F 0-6-0T (1879)	X	X	Ex Birkenhead									Crewe Wks
58858	2F 0-6-0T (1879)										W/D	X	X
58859	2F 0-6-0T (1879)												
58863	2F 0-6-0T (1879)	X	X	Ex Birkenhead		W/D	X	X	X	X	X	X	X

ALLOCATION AND TRANSFERS : DEVONS ROAD MPD

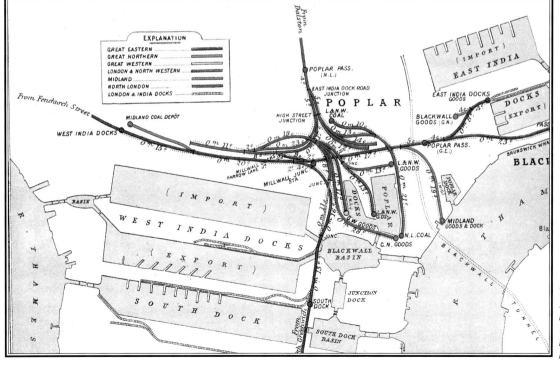

The Railway Clearing House Maps give an indication of the routes within the Poplar and West India Docks area although the mileage of sidings can only be guessed at.

Loco	Class	Aug-53	Sep-53	Oct-53	Nov-53	Dec-53	Jan-54	Feb-54	Mar-54	Apr-54	May-54	Jun-54	Jul-54
43000	4MT 2-6-0 (1947)												
43001	4MT 2-6-0 (1947)												
43020	4MT 2-6-0 (1947)												
43021	4MT 2-6-0 (1947)												
43022	4MT 2-6-0 (1947)												
43024	4MT 2-6-0 (1947)												
44348	4F 0-6-0 (1924)												
44441	4F 0-6-0 (1924)												
47302	3F 0-6-0T (1924)												
47304	3F 0-6-0T (1924)												
47307	3F 0-6-0T (1924)												
47310	3F 0-6-0T (1924)												
47314	3F 0-6-0T (1924)												
47315	3F 0-6-0T (1924)												
47348	3F 0-6-0T (1924)												
47349	3F 0-6-0T (1924)												
47482	3F 0-6-0T (1924)												
47483	3F 0-6-0T (1924)												
47486	3F 0-6-0T (1924)												
47488	3F 0-6-0T (1924)												
47490	3F 0-6-0T (1924)		To Speke Jcn	X	X	X	X	X	X	X	X	X	X
47493	3F 0-6-0T (1924)												
47494	3F 0-6-0T (1924)												
47495	3F 0-6-0T (1924)												
47497	3F 0-6-0T (1924)												
47499	3F 0-6-0T (1924)												
47500	3F 0-6-0T (1924)								To Bletchley	X	X	X	X
47501	3F 0-6-0T (1924)												
47506	3F 0-6-0T (1924)										To Gloucester	X	X
47511	3F 0-6-0T (1924)												
47514	3F 0-6-0T (1924)												
47515	3F 0-6-0T (1924)												
47516	3F 0-6-0T (1924)		To Speke Jcn	X	X	X	X	X	X	X	X	X	X
47517	3F 0-6-0T (1924)												
47518	3F 0-6-0T (1924)												
47558	3F 0-6-0T (1924)												
47559	3F 0-6-0T (1924)												
47560	3F 0-6-0T (1924)												
47561	3F 0-6-0T (1924)												
47564	3F 0-6-0T (1924)												
58851	2F 0-6-0T (1879)												
58852	2F 0-6-0T (1879)												
58853	2F 0-6-0T (1879)												
58854	2F 0-6-0T (1879)												
58855	2F 0-6-0T (1879)												
58857	2F 0-6-0T (1879)	Ex Crewe Wks											
58859	2F 0-6-0T (1879)												
47007	0F 0-4-0ST (1953)	X	X	X	X	X	X	X	X	X	X	Ex Birkenhead	

POPLAR (1953)

Train	Arr	Engine	Shed	Dep	Destination	Train	Arr	Engine	Shed	Dep	Destination
06.27 Devons Road	06.34	2F 0-6-0T	1D/38		Pilot	11.57 East Goods	12.40	J50 0-6-0T	34B/21		GN Yard Pilot
06.27 Devons Road	06.34	2F 0-6-0T	1D/40		Pilot	GN Yard Pilot		J50 0-6-0T	34B/22	13.27	Ferme Park
06.05 East Goods	06.42	J50 0-6-0T	34B/20					4F 0-6-0	1A/121	13.57	Willesden
06.30 Acton	07.34	3F 0-6-0T	1D/14			14.15 Devons Road	14.22	3F 0-6-0T	1D/44		
		3F 0-6-0T	1D/14	08.05	Light to Loco			3F 0-6-0T	1D/44	15.10	St Pancras Sdgs
07.38 East Goods	08.10	J50 0-6-0T	34B/22		GN Yard Pilot	15.03 Camden	15.55	3F 0-6-0T	1D/18		
08.10 Devons Road	08.18	3F 0-6-0T	1D/43			15.00 Willesden	16.20	3F 0-6-0T	1D/27		
		3F 0-6-0T	1D/43	08.45	Devons Road			3F 0-6-0T	1D/27	16.30	Light to Loco
		J50 0-6-0T	34B/20	08.55	Clarence Yard			3F 0-6-0T	1D/18	16.37	Light to Loco
Light ex Loco	09.30	2F 0-6-0T	1D/41		Pilot	GN Yard Pilot		J50 0-6-0T	34B/21	17.25	Clarence Yard
Light ex Loco	10.21	3F 0-6-0T	1D/21			Light ex Loco	17.45	3F 0-6-0T	1D/9		
		3F 0-6-0T	1D/21	10.46	Willesden	Pilot		2F 0-6-0T	1D/41	17.50	Light to Loco
10.42 Devons Road	10.50	3F 0-6-0T	1D/37					3F 0-6-0T	1D/9	18.10	Acton
		3F 0-6-0T	1D/37	11.54	Willesden	Light ex Loco	18.35	3F 0-6-0T	1D/20		
		2F 0-6-0T	1D/40	12.00	Loco			3F 0-6-0T	1D/20	19.00	Camden
12.00 Devons Road	12.07	3F 0-6-0T	1D/12			Pilot		2F 0-6-0T	1D/38	19.30	Light to Loco
11.00 Willesden	12.12	4F 0-6-0	1A/121			Pilot		2F 0-6-0T	1D/40	19.30	Light to Loco
Light ex Loco	12.35	2F 0-6-0T	1D/40		Pilot	Light ex Loco	19.37	3F 0-6-0T	1D/11		
		3F 0-6-0T	1D/12	12.40	St Pancras Sdgs			3F 0-6-0T	1D/11	20.02	Willesden

Docks traffic was difficult to arrange train services for since activity was determined by the arrival of ships and therefore neither the volume or frequency of goods was constant. The railway therefore timetabled what it hoped was sufficient for most needs and relied on special trains organised by the Controller for the rest. The apportionment of services was interesting with five going to the LNW (Willesden or Camden), three going to the GN (Clarence Yard and Ferme Park) and two for the Midland via St Pancras Sidings. The balance was made up by one train to the GWR (Acton) and one local service.

Loco	Class	Aug-54	Sep-54	Oct-54	Nov-54	Dec-54	Jan-55	Feb-55	Mar-55	Apr-55	May-55	Jun-55	Jul-55
ALLOCATION AND TRANSFERS : DEVONS ROAD MPD													
43000	4MT 2-6-0 (1947)												
43001	4MT 2-6-0 (1947)												
43020	4MT 2-6-0 (1947)												
43021	4MT 2-6-0 (1947)												
43022	4MT 2-6-0 (1947)												
43024	4MT 2-6-0 (1947)												
44348	4F 0-6-0 (1924)												
44441	4F 0-6-0 (1924)												
47302	3F 0-6-0T (1924)												
47304	3F 0-6-0T (1924)												
47307	3F 0-6-0T (1924)												
47310	3F 0-6-0T (1924)												
47314	3F 0-6-0T (1924)												
47315	3F 0-6-0T (1924)												
47348	3F 0-6-0T (1924)												
47349	3F 0-6-0T (1924)												
47482	3F 0-6-0T (1924)												
47483	3F 0-6-0T (1924)				To Speke Jn	X	X	X	X	X	X	X	X
47486	3F 0-6-0T (1924)												
47488	3F 0-6-0T (1924)												
47493	3F 0-6-0T (1924)												
47494	3F 0-6-0T (1924)												
47495	3F 0-6-0T (1924)												
47497	3F 0-6-0T (1924)												
47499	3F 0-6-0T (1924)												
47501	3F 0-6-0T (1924)												
47511	3F 0-6-0T (1924)												
47514	3F 0-6-0T (1924)												
47515	3F 0-6-0T (1924)												
47517	3F 0-6-0T (1924)												
47518	3F 0-6-0T (1924)												
47558	3F 0-6-0T (1924)												
47559	3F 0-6-0T (1924)												
47560	3F 0-6-0T (1924)												
47561	3F 0-6-0T (1924)												
47564	3F 0-6-0T (1924)												
58851	2F 0-6-0T (1879)							W/D	X	X	X	X	X
58852	2F 0-6-0T (1879)											W/D	X
58853	2F 0-6-0T (1879)			W/D	X	X	X	X	X	X	X	X	X
58854	2F 0-6-0T (1879)											To Bletchley	X
58855	2F 0-6-0T (1879)												
58857	2F 0-6-0T (1879)												
58859	2F 0-6-0T (1879)												
47007	0F 0-4-0ST (1953) To Birkenhead	X	X	X	X	X	X	X	X	X	X	X	X

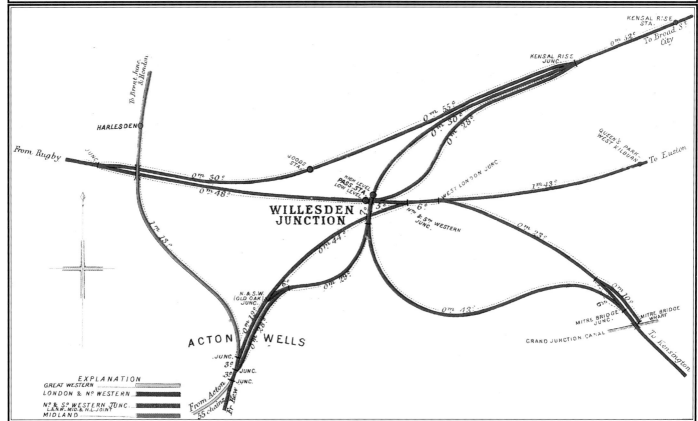

The extraordinary complexity of track in the Willesden area. The principal elements are the London & North Western from Euston to the North, the North London from Broad Street to Richmond, the West London to Kensington and, joining the North London at Acton Wells Junction, the Midland line from Cricklewood. The plethora of lines did not eliminate some of the more awkward moves that had to be made: engines arriving in Old Oak Yard, for example, and needing to turn had to run to Mitre Bridge via West London Junction, reverse over the spur to High Level Junction and then change direction again to regain the yard via Old Oak Junction.

Loco	Class	Aug-55	Sep-55	Oct-55	Nov-55	Dec-55	Jan-56	Feb-56	Mar-56	Apr-56	May-56	Jun-56	Jul-56
43000	4MT 2-6-0 (1947)												
43001	4MT 2-6-0 (1947)												
43020	4MT 2-6-0 (1947)												
43021	4MT 2-6-0 (1947)												
43022	4MT 2-6-0 (1947)												
43024	4MT 2-6-0 (1947)												
44348	4F 0-6-0 (1924)												
44381	4F 0-6-0 (1924)	X	X	X	X	X	X	X	X	X	X	Ex Willesden	
44441	4F 0-6-0 (1924)												
47302	3F 0-6-0T (1924)												
47304	3F 0-6-0T (1924)												
47307	3F 0-6-0T (1924)												
47310	3F 0-6-0T (1924)												
47314	3F 0-6-0T (1924)												
47315	3F 0-6-0T (1924)												
47348	3F 0-6-0T (1924)												
47349	3F 0-6-0T (1924)												
47482	3F 0-6-0T (1924)												
47483	3F 0-6-0T (1924)												
47486	3F 0-6-0T (1924)												
47488	3F 0-6-0T (1924)												
47494	3F 0-6-0T (1924)												
47495	3F 0-6-0T (1924)												
47497	3F 0-6-0T (1924)												
47499	3F 0-6-0T (1924)												
47501	3F 0-6-0T (1924)												
47511	3F 0-6-0T (1924)												
47514	3F 0-6-0T (1924)												
47515	3F 0-6-0T (1924)												
47517	3F 0-6-0T (1924)												
47518	3F 0-6-0T (1924)												
47558	3F 0-6-0T (1924)												
47559	3F 0-6-0T (1924)												
47560	3F 0-6-0T (1924)												
47561	3F 0-6-0T (1924)												
47564	3F 0-6-0T (1924)												
47164	2F 0-6-0T (1928)	X	X	X	X	X	X	X	X	X	X	X	Ex Bidston
58854	2F 0-6-0T (1879)	X	X	X	X	X	X	X	X	X	X	X	Ex Bletchley
58855	2F 0-6-0T (1879)												W/D
58857	2F 0-6-0T (1879)												
58859	2F 0-6-0T (1879)												
47007	0F 0-4-0ST (1953)	X	X	X	X	X	X	X	X	X	X	X	Ex Birkenhead

ALLOCATION AND TRANSFERS : DEVONS ROAD MPD

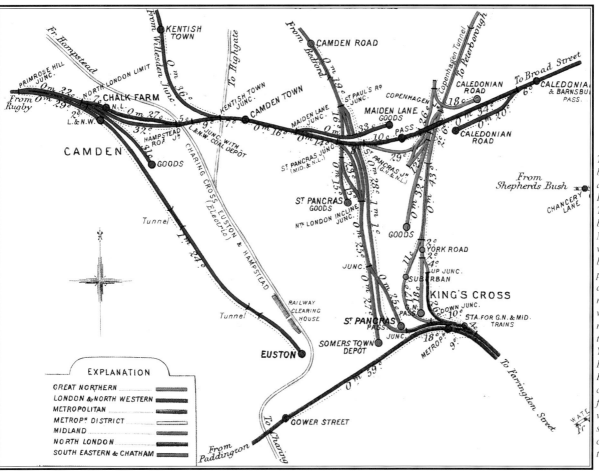

The relationship between the NLR and Kings Cross, St Pancras and Euston. The connection between the Great Northern and the NLR was not greatly used because the main point of exchange was at Finsbury Park, two miles to the north, where goods and mineral traffics were taken to Clarence Yard and Ferme Park respectively. However the Midland connection to and from Kentish Town was heavily used since it was the only connection between the two systems.

NORTH LONDON GOODS TRAIN LOADINGS

From	To	Route	Comments	Class 3 engine Min (J)	Class 3 engine Goods (H)	Class 4 engine Min (J)	Class 4 engine Goods (H)	Class 7 engine Min (J)	Class 7 engine Goods (H)	Class 8 engine Min (J)	Class 8 engine Goods (H)	Line Max
Acton	Maiden Lane		00.00 - 08.00	24	34	29	34	34	34			34
Acton	Maiden Lane		08.00 - 00.00	24	50	29	50	39	50	43	50	50
Acton	St Pancras Sdgs/Poplar			24	50	29	50	39	50	43	50	50
Acton	Ferme Park	T&H		24	50	29	50	39	50	43	50	50
Acton	Broad St		00.01 - 05.40	24	50	29	50	39	50	43	50	50
Acton	Broad St		05.40- 14.30	24	40	29	40	39	40	40	40	40
Acton	Broad St		14.30 - 22.20	24	24	24	24	24	24			24
Acton	Broad St		22.20 - 00.01	24	40	29	40	39	40	40	40	40
Acton	Temple Mills	Both Routes		24	45	29	45	39	45	43	45	45
Acton	Victoria Docks/T. Wharf			24	50	29	50	39	50	43	50	50
Acton	Plaistow/Ripple Lane			24	35	29	35	35	35			35
Acton	Clarence Yard	Kingsland		24	38	29	38	38	38			38
Battersea	Brent (M)	Barnes		29	44	35	44	44	44	44	44	44
Bow Common	Devons Rd/Poplar			22	22							22
Brent (M)	Feltham			27	50	33	50	44	50	48	50	50
Brent (M)	Battersea			48	50	50	50	50	50	50	50	50
Brent (M)	Hither Green	Barnes		26	50	31	50	41	50	46	50	50
Brent (M)	West Kensington			26	50							50
Brent (M)	Kensington (H. St)			18	18							18
Broad St	St Pancras Sdgs/Willesden/Camden	Both Routes		27	35	33	35	35	35			35
Camden	St Pancras Sdgs/Miden Lane	Primrose Hill		42	50	50	50					50
Camden	Temple Mills	Primrose Hill		36	45	43	45	45	45			45
Camden	Victoria Docks	Primrose Hill		36	50	43	50	50	50			50
Camden	Broad St		00.01 - 05.40	24	50	29	50	39	50	43	50	50
Camden	Broad St		05.40- 14.30	24	40	29	40	39	40			40
Camden	Broad St		14.30 - 22.20	24	24							24
Camden	Broad St		22.20 - 00.01	24	40	29	40	39	40			40
Camden	Haydon Square			27	27							27
Camden	Plaistow			24	35	29	35	35	35			35
Camden	Poplar			36	50	43	50	50	50			50
Devons Rd	Bow Common			19	19							19
East Goods	Temple Mills			27	45	33	45					45
East Goods	Victoria Docks/T. Wharf			24	45	29	45					45
East Goods	Acton	Kingsland (R/R)		27	38	33	38					38
Feltham	Brent (M)			17	29	21	36	28	49	31	50	50
Feltham	Toton (etc)	Cricklewood Jcn		17	29	21	36	28	70	31	70	70
Feltham	Neasden			17	29	21	36	28	49	31	54	55
Feltham	Temple Mills	Both Routes		36	45	43	45	45	45			45
Ferme Park	Willesden	T&H		27	50	33	50					50
Ferme Park	Acton	T&H		27	49	33	49					49
Haydon Square	Bow Junction			24	30	29	30					30
Hither Green	Brent (M)	Barnes		33	44	40	44					44
Neasden	Feltham			27	50	33	50	44	50	48	50	50
Old Oak	Maiden Lane		00.00 - 08.00	24	34	29	34	34	34			34
Old Oak	Maiden Lane		08.00 - 00.00	24	50	29	50	39	50	43	50	50
Old Oak	Poplar/St P. Sdgs/Ferme Pk (T&H)			24	50	29	50	39	50	43	50	50
Old Oak	Broad St		00.01 - 05.40	24	50	29	50	39	50	43	50	50
Old Oak	Broad St		05.40- 14.30/22.20-00.0	24	40	29	40	39	40	40	40	40
Old Oak	Broad St		14.30 - 22.20	24	24							24
Old Oak	Temple Mills	Both Routes		24	45	29	45	39	45	43	45	45
Old Oak	Victoria Docks/T. Wharf			24	50	29	50	39	50	43	50	50
Old Oak	Plaistow/Ripple Lane			24	35	29	35	35	35			35
Old Oak	Clarence Yard	Kingsland		24	38	29	38	38	38			38
Plaistow/Ripple Lane	Acton/Camden/Willesden/St Pancras Sdgs/Maiden Lane			27	45	33	45	44	45	45	45	45
Poplar	Camden			27	50	33	50	44	50	48	50	50
Poplar	Willesden	Both Routes		27	58	33	60	44	60	48	60	60
Poplar	Acton			27	49	33	49	44	49	48	49	49
Poplar	Old Oak			77	48	33	48	44	48	48	48	48
Poplar	Bow Common			19	19							19
Temple Mills	Camden			27	50	33	50	44	50	48	50	50
Temple Mills	Willesden	Both Routes		27	50	33	50	44	50	48	50	50
Temple Mills	Clarence Yard			27	45	33	45	44	45	45	45	45
Temple Mills	Acton			27	49	33	49	44	49	48	49	49
Temple Mills	Old Oak			27	48	33	48	44	48	48	48	48
Victoria Dock	Camden/Willesden/St Pancras Sdgs	Both Routes		24	50	29	50	39	50	43	50	50
Victoria Dock	Acton			24	49	29	49	39	49	43	49	49
Victoria Dock	Old Oak			24	48	29	48	39	48	43	48	48
Victoria Dock	Clarence Yard			24	45	29	45	39	45	43	45	45
Willesden	Maiden Lane	Primrose Hill	00.00 - 08.00	34	34							34
Willesden	Maiden Lane	Primrose Hill	08.00 - 00.00	42	60	50	60	60	60			60
Willesden	St Pancras Sdgs	Primrose Hill		42	60	50	60	60	60			60
Willesden	Poplar/Kingsland	Primrose Hill		36	50	43	50	50	50			50
Willesden	Temple Mills	Primrose Hill		36	45	43	45	45	45			45
Willesden	Haydon Square	Primrose Hill		27	27							27

Train loading was an exact and complex science, each train varying according to the type of traffic conveyed, the route, the speed of the train and the type of engine. The table above shows the loadings for most of the important North London traffic flows - the list is not exhaustive - for Mineral (Class J) and Goods (class H) services. J and K class trains were (more or less) the same thing on the North London, the chief difference being that a class K service generally conveyed a mix of goods and mineral traffic. The table also shows the length limit in standard wagons for each route and all trains had to be loaded within this figure. Much of the traffic conveyed on the North London was goods (as opposed to mineral) traffic and this, coupled with the 45/50 wagon trains that were typical of the system, meant that for most purposes the Standard 3F 0-6-0 tank locomotive was quite adequate. A class H train worked by a 3F 0-6-0T could take as many as 58 wagons of goods and since this was in excess of most North London runs, it can be seen why Devons Road placed so much reliance on the class.

Black Five 4-6-0 44774 (Cricklewood) enters South Acton with a train of empties from Feltham to Brent (Midland) on Thursday 9th August 1956. Generally 8F 2-8-0's were preferred for these duties since they were the only engines that could take a full train of fifty loaded wagons of coal on the outward working whilst 5MT 4-6-0's were limited to thirty-six. Traffic between Brent and Feltham was extremely heavy and not infrequently special trains had to be run, using whatever motive power happened to be available. An interesting feature of the return workings from Feltham was that if trains were conveying a full load of empties for Wellingborough or Toton (etc), then the normal limit of fifty wagons could be increased to seventy. The line to the left is the electrified branch to Richmond (A E Bennet/transporttreasury.co.uk)

One of the great attractions of the North London and its extension to Kew was that one never knew what the next train was going to produce. Devons Road engines did not work west of Acton but a wide variety of engines from Feltham, Hornsey, Cricklewood and Stratford more than made up for the loss. Southern Q1 0-6-0 33006 approaches South Acton with the 14.10 Old Oak to Feltham on Thursday 9th August 1956. (A E Bennet/transporttreasury.co.uk)

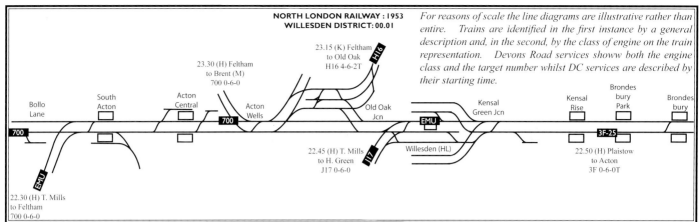

NORTH LONDON RAILWAY : 1953
WILLESDEN DISTRICT: 00.01

For reasons of scale the line diagrams are illustrative rather than entire. Trains are identified in the first instance by a general description and, in the second, by the class of engine on the train representation. Devons Road services showw both the engine class and the target number whilst DC services are described by their starting time.

CONTROLLER'S LOG: One often comes across references in the railway press to the extraordinary volume of cross-London traffic but few of these reports give any details of the trains involved: the yards they run from and to and the engines and men that work them. In fact it is difficult to describe in words the activity of the North London Railway and the only way to see it clearly is to sit for twenty-four hours with the District Controller whose job it is to superintend the engines, trains and

A third Southern engine - one of the massive H16 4-6-2 tanks - shunts the 23.15 from Feltham into the sidings at Old Oak Yard prior to taking up its back working, the 01.25 Old Oak to Feltham.

Another foreigner - a Great Eastern J17 0-6-0 - skirts the Acton area as it takes the junction at Willesden High Level and crosses over to the West London Railway with the 22.45 Temple Mills to Hither Green.

Another hallmark of the North London is

to gain the agreement of the Western to accept the train and then has to come, cap in hand, to the North London for an engine and crew to work the train.

Varied as the goods service is, it is rare for supply and demand to coincide and to provide a degree of flexibility, several workings to Acton are left without specific return workings and have enough time in hand to work a special to either Temple Mills or Plaistow. One of these trains is approaching Caledonian Road

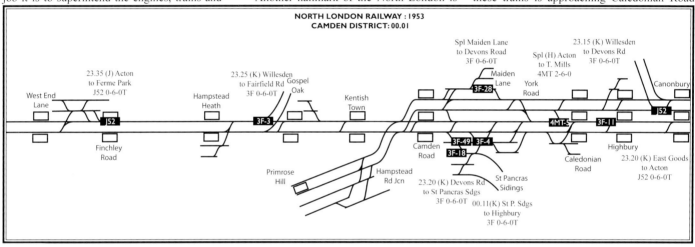

NORTH LONDON RAILWAY : 1953
CAMDEN DISTRICT: 00.01

traffic of the system.

One hallmark of the system is the volume of traffic, another is the variety of motive power that makes the North London one of the most cosmopolitan in Britain. Whilst the workhorse of the line is the Standard LMS 3F 0-6-0T, engines from all four railways except the Great Western are regular visitors as can be seen in the Willesden District where a pair of Feltham 700 0-6-0's can be seen: one leaving the North London with a through train from Temple Mills whilst another approaches Acton Wells with a train of empties from Feltham to Cricklewood.

the fact that there is no focal point for traffic and trains therefore run through from starting to finishing points without any intermediate remarshalling. Thus instead of there being a frequent service of trains from Temple Mills and Plaistow to a central marshalling yard at somewhere like Kingsland, trains run through from a variety of starting points to a wide range of destinations. Complicating matters is the fact that many of these trains are powered by Devons Road engines and men and if the Southend District, for example, wants to run a special from Plaistow to Acton, it first of all has

with a load for the Great Eastern. On paper the crew have ample time to get to Temple Mills and return light engine to Devons Road without incurring overtime but in anticipation of delays on the Great Eastern plus the fact the crew on the engine will be fed to the back teeth with tender-first running - the turn is booked to a 4MT 2-6-0 and there is no provision for turning an engine at Acton - a spare set of men will be despatched to Victoria Park to relieve the train and finish the diagram. Another of these special workings will leave Maiden Lane for Devons Road in a few minutes time.

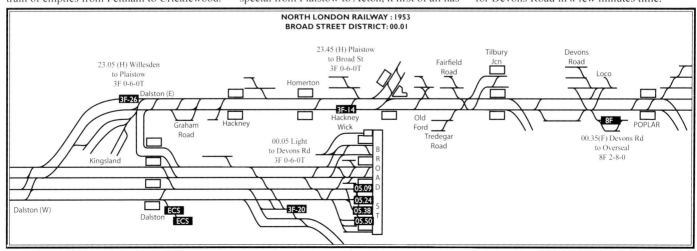

NORTH LONDON RAILWAY : 1953
BROAD STREET DISTRICT: 00.01

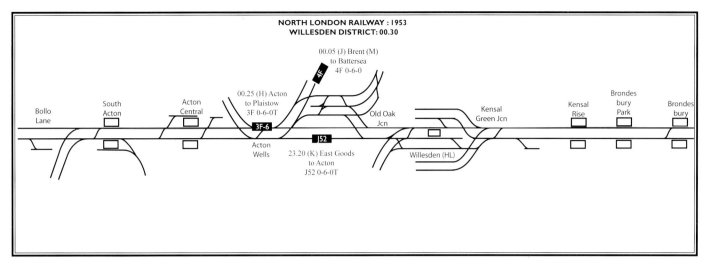

NORTH LONDON RAILWAY : 1953
WILLESDEN DISTRICT: 00.30

CONTROLLER'S LOG: Eight-coupled engines are a regular sight west of Acton Wells where 8F 2-8-0's work much of the Midland traffic between Brent (Cricklewood) and the Southern but they are less common on the North London proper, being largely confined to a few Super D 0-8-0's which work some of the trips between Camden and Broad Street. Standard 8F 2-8-0's are quite uncommon and have in fact

to be remembered that whilst a 3F 0-6-0T can manage 60 empty wagons without difficulty, it would be severely handicapped when returning with a loaded train).

The cluster of trains that congregated around Maiden Lane and Caledonian Road half an hour ago has dispersed and all that remains for the moment is target 18 which works as the pilot for the next eight hours. Much of its work

less use than the Midland spur. A J52 can bring in 23 goods and return with 37 empties, inward services having to have a brakevan at each end of the train; the leading brake being vacuum fitted whilst the trailing brake has to be at least a 20-tonner.

At the west end of the district, life is made interesting for the Acton Wells signalman with the approach of a Midland train from Brent to

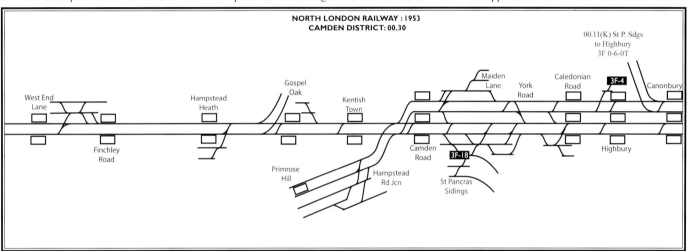

NORTH LONDON RAILWAY : 1953
CAMDEN DISTRICT: 00.30

only one booked working which is the 00.35 Devons Road to Overseal; a through service to the South Derbyshire coalfield designed to accelerate the return of empty wagons. Since the maximum load between Poplar and Willesden (either route) is 60 wagons, the use of a 2-8-0 is rather excessive since a Standard 3F tank could handle a full load. However, the 8F engine is justified by the fact that it works through to Overseal while the train is made up to seventy wagons at Willesden. (It has

consists of shunting out traffic brought in from St Pancras by the Midland trips and preparing trains for their return workings. The branch from Kentish Town is a steeply graded single line worked by electric token; the Standard 3F tanks used on the dozen or so daily services bringing in a maximum of 16 wagons of coal or 28 of goods from the Midland and returning with up to 50 empties.

There is also a corresponding connection from Kings Cross Goods although it sees much

Battersea and a GN service from East Goods to Acton. An Acton - Plaistow train is heaving itself up the bank and so the box is instructed to give the two Acton trains preference and let the Midland come third. One has to be cogniscent of the fact that a second Midland train - a Brent - Feltham working - is not far behind the Battersea service.

The two specials make their way slowly towards Victoria Park where a set of men have arrived to take over the 2-6-0 from Acton.

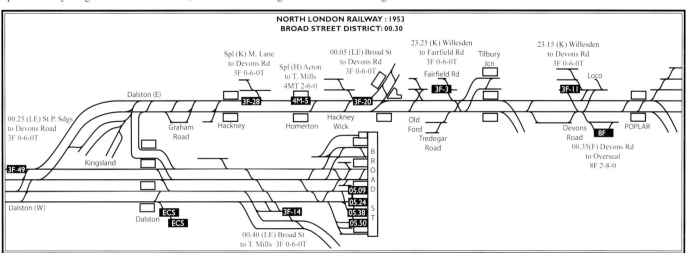

NORTH LONDON RAILWAY : 1953
BROAD STREET DISTRICT: 00.30

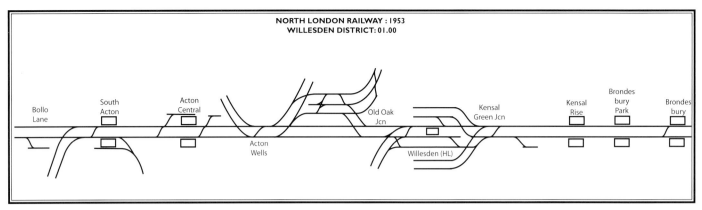

NORTH LONDON RAILWAY : 1953
WILLESDEN DISTRICT: 01.00

DISTRICT CONTROLLER'S LOG: Although distances are short on the North London - Temple Mills to Acton is barely twenty miles - it should not be thought that its goods trains are any less in status from those operating on the trunk lines radiating from London. One sometimes hears the expression 'transfer freight' used in connection with North London workings but the phrase is both inaccurate and misleading. A transfer freight is simply a shunt that takes wagons from one

the Controller at Stratford agreeing with his opposite number at Reading the type of traffic each train should take. Half an hour later we, the North London, will contact Stratford and ask him if he will be running the two trains: if the answer is in the affirmative, then the engine will be sent as booked.

The entire transaction is conducted by a few short sentences on the telephone with nothing in writing.

Stratford: *"Hello, Reading? 00.20 with*

come on the circuit. *"Hello, North London. 00.20 Feltham to Temple Mills, 33007, Feltham eleven-forty, forty-five pools equal forty-five. 01.00 Feltham to Brent, 30838, Feltham twelve thirty-five, sixty-two equal sixty-two pools, Toton. Both right time."*

This - known as wiring on - is the formal advice that two trains are approaching Kew Bridge. Pools are a synonym for empty mineral wagons whilst the 'equal' refers to the length of the train: the basic unit being one four-wheeled

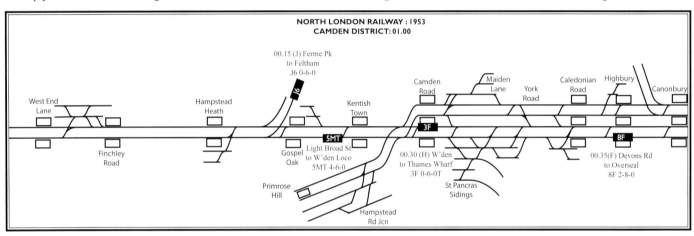

NORTH LONDON RAILWAY : 1953
CAMDEN DISTRICT: 01.00

side of a marshalling yard to another whilst North London workings are as much main line services as those operating between Kings Cross and Peterborough. The formalities of arranging goods trains on the North London are actually slightly more complicated than those pertaining at, say Kings Cross, since North London trains travel from one railway to another with the engines and men being provided by a third party! There are for example, two services (00.20 and 01.55) on the run between Temple Mills and Acton, both of which would have been arranged (agreed) at about 22.00 by

empties and the 01.55 with two cattle Bath and Acton roughs made up with empties."

Reading : *"Right you are."*

Stratford: *"Hello, North London? 12 and 22 as booked."*

North London: *"Right, I'll send the engines and men."*

With a few short words the destinies of two trains their crews and more than fifty wagons are determined. A model of administration!

The acceptance of trains by one Controller from another is similarly informal and a few minutes after 1 am the Woking Controller will

wagon. Feltham eleven-forty, in the case of the first train, simply refers to the home station of the men working the train and the time they took duty. The classification of the train is taken as read unless it has been changed.

The Brent train is an interesting service since trains for Cricklewood are normally limited to fifty wagons unless they are taking a full load of empties for the north in which case the limit is extended to seventy. The engine is a Southern S15 4-6-0 - hence the shortfall of eight wagons - which will be replaced at Brent No.1 by an LMS 8F 2-8-0.

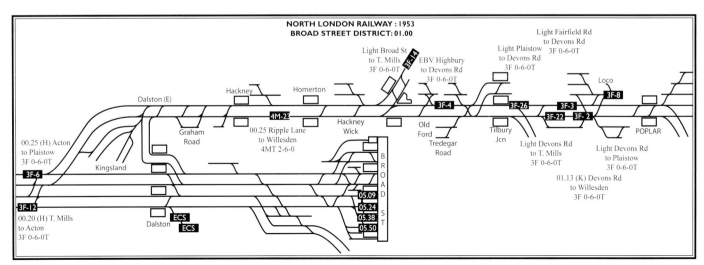

NORTH LONDON RAILWAY : 1953
BROAD STREET DISTRICT: 01.00

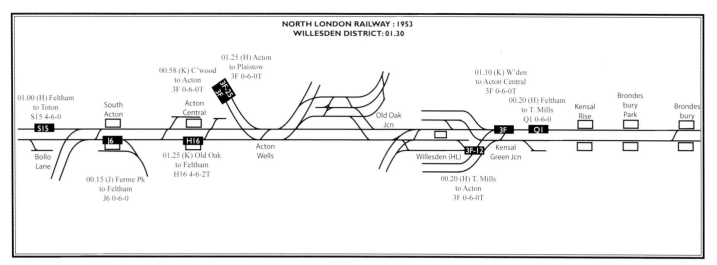

NORTH LONDON RAILWAY : 1953
WILLESDEN DISTRICT: 01.30

CONTROLLER'S LOG: The speed at which trains come and go on the North London has to be seen to be believed. A short time ago the section between Kew and Gospel Oak was completely devoid of trains whilst now they are like like flies round a jam pot! With them, the trains bring a cheering variety of engines from all parts of BR except the Great Western. A Q1 0-6-0 attacks the climb to Hampstead with a Feltham - Temple Mills service whilst

engaged with the 01.10 Willesden to Acton Central; one engine at each end of the train. This is because the train starts from Willesden High Level yard and therefore has to reverse at Kensal Green Junction but instead of blocking the main line whilst the engine runs round, a trip engine is used to haul the train from the High Level Yard to Kensal Green with the train engine trailing.

Further up the line a Great Eastern J17

dealt with by the shed could be handled by a class 3 engine whilst the majority of modern classes were considerably more powerful than any calls the North London could have placed on them. A few 4F 0-6-0's - not the most free-steaming engines in the Kingdom - were drafted in to be joined by half a dozen 4MT 2-6-0's in late 1951.

It was expected that these engines with their all-round cabs and reserve of power would have

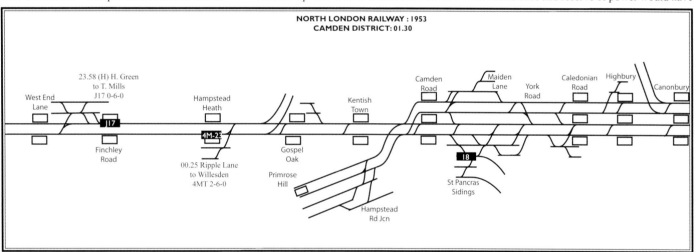

NORTH LONDON RAILWAY : 1953
CAMDEN DISTRICT: 01.30

an S15 4-6-0 approaches South Acton with a block load of empty wagons for Toton. In the opposite direction, one of the massive H16 tanks passes Acton Central with a train from Old Oak sidings.

The LNER is represented by a Great Northern J6 0-6-0 at South Acton with a Ferme Park to Feltham service whilst the LMS sports a quintet of Standard 3F tanks at and around Acton Wells Junction. Two of the latter are

0-6-0 wakes half London as it heaves its forty wagons over the steepest part of Hampstead bank. This train will leave the North London at Gospel Oak and transfer to the Tottenham & Hampstead.

Approaching the J17 from the East is a Ripple Lane to Willesden service, an reminder of the attempt in 1951 to modernise the allocation of Devons Road. This initiative was made difficult by the fact that almost every train

been welcomed with open arms yet the precise opposite proved to be the case with complaints of rough-riding and heavy coal consumption heading the agendas of many LDC meetings. The fact that the engines cannot be turned at Acton does not help and although they remain at Devons Road they make little impact on the work done by the Standard 0-6-0T's, being used mainly on parcels workings and special trains to the West Coast main line.

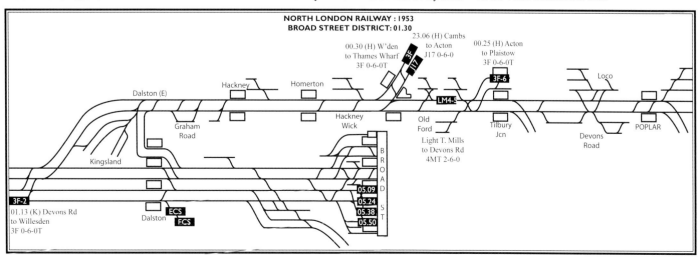

NORTH LONDON RAILWAY : 1953
BROAD STREET DISTRICT: 01.30

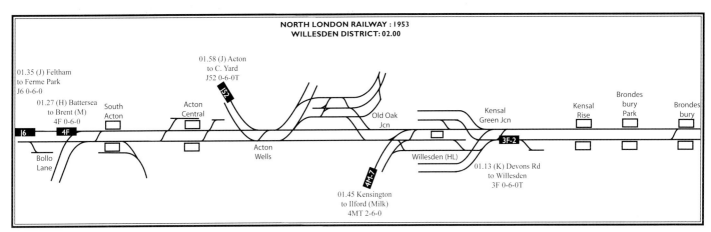

CONTROLLER'S LOG: A reminder that there is more to North London life than coal and goods is given by the appearance of the 01.45 Kensington Milk which comes off the West London line at North Pole Junction to join the North London at Willesden HL Junction. The Devons Road engine will work the train as far as Channelsea Junction, Stratford from where the Great Eastern will take over.

It is an important train and the need for a clear run should need no stressing yet its appearance on the North London is preceded

empties from Feltham to Ferme Park and a J50 0-6-0 pannier tank pulling away from Acton Yard with a train of goods for Clarence Yard (Finsbury Park). The two services will travel via different routes; the J50 running round its train at Kingsland whilst the J6 will leave the North London at Gospel Oak and run via the Tottenham & Hampstead.

It may seem strange that trains heading for destinations only a couple of miles apart should take different routes but Great Northern goods traffic has to terminate at Clarence Yard where

- about a dozen engines are in continuous use simply for tripping traffic between the yards and sidings between Ferme Park and Kings Cross - that such an experiment would probably delay the wagons by a week.

The 23.06 Cambridge to Acton, seen approaching Camden Road behind a Great Eastern J17 0-6-0, is actually a conventional Temple Mills - Acton service, differing only that it re-engines the 23.05 ex Cambridge at Temple Mills. East Anglia generates quite a respectable amount of through traffic for the

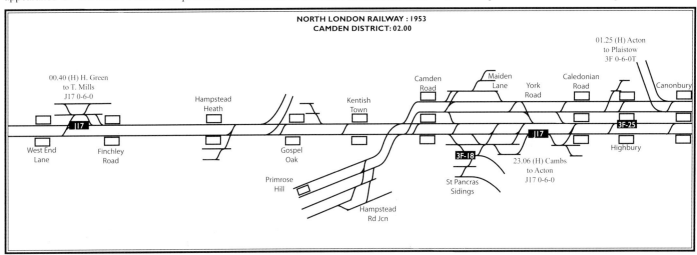

by a J17 0-6-0 with the 00.40 Hither Green - Temple Mills running on a five minute margin; a state of affairs that condemns the Ilford Milk to crawl miserably all the way to Gospel Oak from which point the J17 and its train take the Tottenham & Hampstead route.

Whilst the balance of power around Acton has reverted in favour of the LMS, there are still a pair of Great Northern engines in evidence: a J6 0-6-0 working the 01.35 mineral

it can connect with a series of express goods services to the North whilst Ferme Park deals predominately with empty wagons. One could try to send a train of goods via Ferme Park but the result would be a howl of protest from Kings Cross and a sheaf of correspondence whilst the wagons would have to go from the down side to the up side at Ferme Park before being tripped to Clarence Yard via East Goods or Holloway. Congestion on the GN is of such proportions

West of England and it has proved possible to concentrate much of it on Cambridge; the 23.05 loading with a London & South Western section (detached at Temple Mills for the 04.00 to Feltham) on the engine; the remainder being Great Western traffic for Acton. The arrangement accelerates the traffic appreciably since there is no shunting (and, ergo, no delay) to be done at Temple Mills. This, however, is an isolated example of such working.

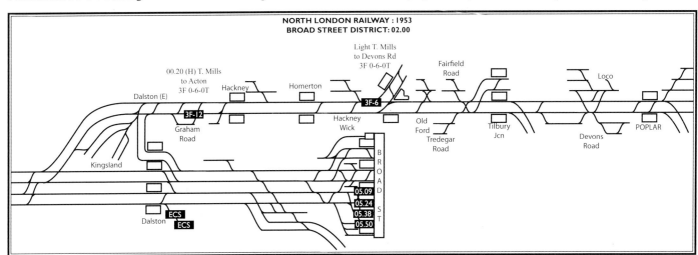

Standing in for the booked Feltham S15 4-6-0, H15 4-6-0 30846 of Nine Elms passes Kew East Junction with the 11.58 Old Oak to Feltham goods on Monday 21st May 1956. Normally the only time an H15 paid a visit to Kew was with the Lowestoft to Feltham fish train. Being a goods-only line, the section between South Acton and Kew East attracted very little attention which is rather a shame since it presented the spectator with an average of one train every sixteen minutes worked by no less than eleven classes of engine from three regions of British Railways. There were few stretches of track that could compete with such variety and the actual daily tally came to: J6 0-6-0 (10), Q1 0-6-0 (14), '700' 0-6-0 (10), S15 4-6-0 (14), H15 4-6-0 (2), H16 4-6-2T (4), 8F 2-8-0 (12), 7F 0-8-0 (2), 4F 0-6-0 (14), 3P 2-6-2T (2) and 3F 0-6-0T (2).

One of the principal signalboxes on the system was Acton Wells Junction which signalled several junctions between Willesden and Acton Central. The pair of lines to the left are the Midland route to Neasden and Cricklewood, the lines in the centre are the goods lines to Old Oak Junction and Old Oak Yard whilst the electric lines to Broad Street run straight ahead. Immediately behind the photographer is the Junction of the Acton and Richmond lines. (R E Vincent/transporttreasury.co.uk)

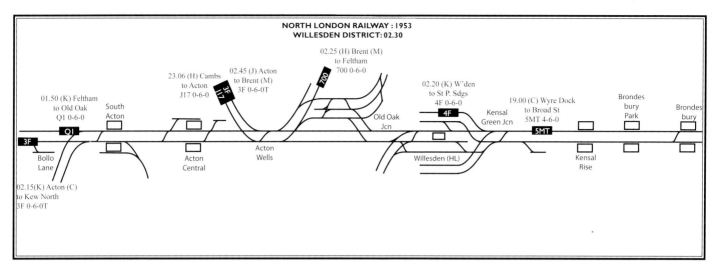

CONTROLLER'S LOG: In addition to its role as a passenger terminus, Broad Street is one of the principal LM London goods stations and is served by thirteen inwards trains and eighteen departures. Several of the former run through from West Coast destinations; one being the 19.00 ex Wyre Dock (Fleetwood) which joins the North London at Kensal Green Junction and arrives in Broad Street at 02.57. Coming from

in others main line 4-6-0's from Willesden or Camden are used before heading northward down the LNW main line. These services bring quite a degree of colour to the North London since taper-boiler express 4-6-0's not infrequently deputise for Black 5's whilst the mid-day goods from Broad Street to Camden (actually a through working to Glasgow, Buchanan Street) is booked to a parallel-boiler

is a problem then the reversal can be made on the up main line between Canonbury and Dalston East.

The cosmopolitan air of the western end of the district has a new dimension added as a venerable LSWR 700 0-6-0 approaches Acton Wells with a Brent (Midland) to Feltham goods. Only a class 3 engine, the 700's have to be used with some care since heavy coal trains

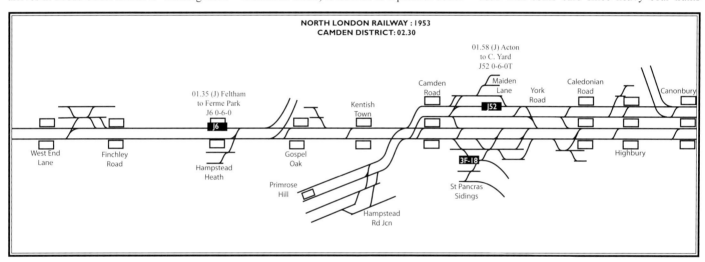

Fleetwood, fish naturally forms a large part of the train's traffic although not exclusively since at Crewe a large consignment of biscuits for Willesden is attached. After removing its Willesden traffic in the High Level sidings, it proceeds onto the North London, still behind the engine which has worked it into Willesden, with the remnants of its load.

The method of working trains between Camden or Willesden and Broad Street varies: in some cases local trip engines are used whilst

2-6-0 which later works a business train from Euston to Bletchley.

The formalities for dealing with the Wyre Dock are no different to those for any other train: details of the train being received from the West Coast Controller before being passed forward to the Inspector at Broad Street Goods.

The 01.58 Acton to Ferme Park has passed Camden Road and it is time to check that Kingsland is able to accept the train whilst its J52 runs round and reverses direction. If there

predominate on the Brent - Feltham route and the 700's are limited to 27 of coal. The 02.25 from Brent, however, is a goods train and the 700 is quite equal to the line maximum of 50 wagons of the lighter traffic. As a contrast, one of the modern Q1 0-6-0's approaches South Acton with sixty mineral empties for Old Oak Yard, Willesden where they will remain until called for by the LNW. The Q1 will return to the Southern with the 03.58 Old Oak to Feltham, taking 53 loaded coal.

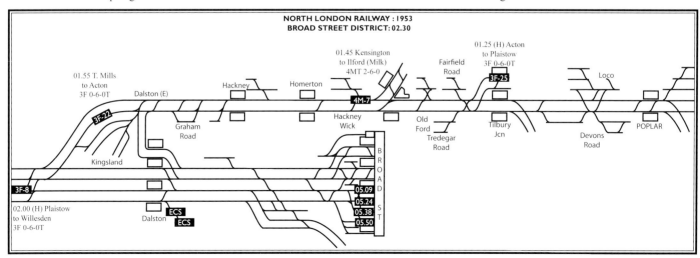

56

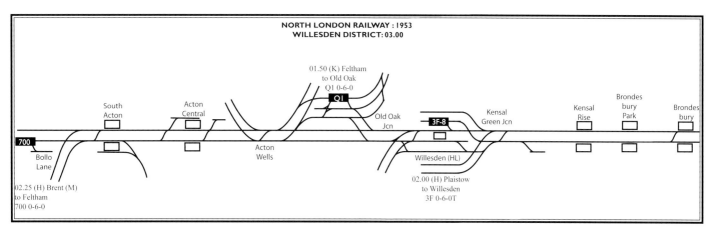

NORTH LONDON RAILWAY : 1953
WILLESDEN DISTRICT: 03.00

CONTROLLER'S LOG: One item of nomenclature that invites confusion is the name 'Brent'; not the least of the problem being the fact that North London trains work to and from two entirely separate marshalling yards, both named Brent! One of these is located near Cricklewood on the Midland main line (and to aid the confusion further is subdivided into several other yards known as Brent Up Sidings, Brent South Sidings and Brent Empty Sidings).

The other Brent Yard is at Willesden and line, most of which is brought in on local trip workings. Shortly after three o'clock a pair of trains leaves Camden for Broad Street and St Pancras Sidings respectively whilst right behind them will be the overnight Fish from Perth which will run through to Broad Street behind the 4-6-0 that has brought it up from the North. Finally a fourth and fifth train will run from Camden and Willesden respectively for Broad Street, collectively sweeping up the last of the overnight North London traffic.

Ahead of all this a Willesden 4F arrives at St Pancras Junction with a train from Willesden via Hampstead and galvanises the yard pilot - target 18 - into action. As soon as it has been released, the 4F will run light to Camden for the 04.10 to Broad Street. Keeping in mind the time limit on trains into Broad Street, a close watch is kept on this working.

Elsewhere, the flow of traffic has diminished considerably. A pair of engines, their day's work over, make their way light towards Devons

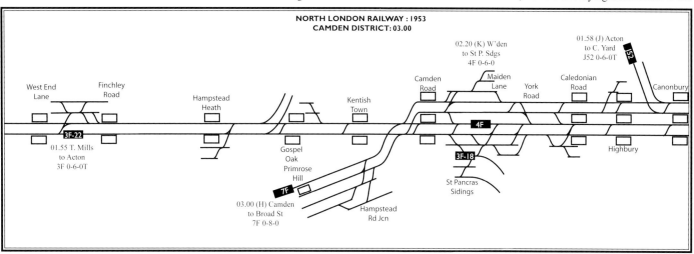

NORTH LONDON RAILWAY : 1953
CAMDEN DISTRICT: 03.00

deals with most of the northbound traffic for the West Coast main line. Since there is a heavy flow of North London traffic into both Brent yards, it goes without saying that one has to be on one's guard to avoid dubiety. The Midland yard is usually referred to in writing as Brent (M).

So far, the movement of trains has been fairly general but this is about to change since the emphasis for the next hour or so is going to focus on traffic from the West Coast main

There is something of a race against time with these trains since the normal limit of forty wagons per train is extended to fifty between midnight and 05.40 and the volume of traffic is usually such that it is unthinkable that any train should be required to shed a fifth of its load simply because of delay.

The first of these trains can be seen approaching Primrose Hill behind a Super-D 0-8-0 whilst the second waits to leave Camden behind another of the same class.

Road Loco whilst Target 22 eases its way downhill towards West End Lane and Acton. A Q1 0-6-0 at Old Oak gets ready to turn on the angle at Mitre Bridge before working back to Feltham.

The 01.45 Kensington Milk has reappeared at Victoria Park after running to Channelsea (Stratford) where the Ilford vehicles were handed over to a Great Eastern engine. The 2-6-0's will take the remaining tanks to Tredegar Road and then retire to Devons Road Loco.

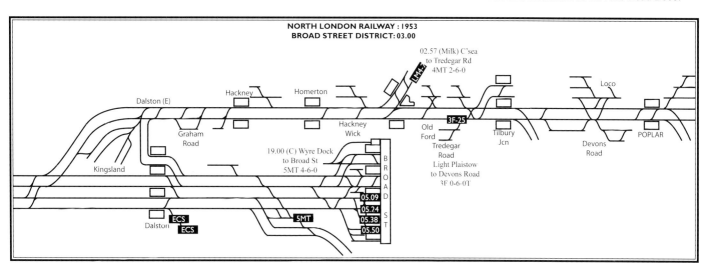

NORTH LONDON RAILWAY : 1953
BROAD STREET DISTRICT: 03.00

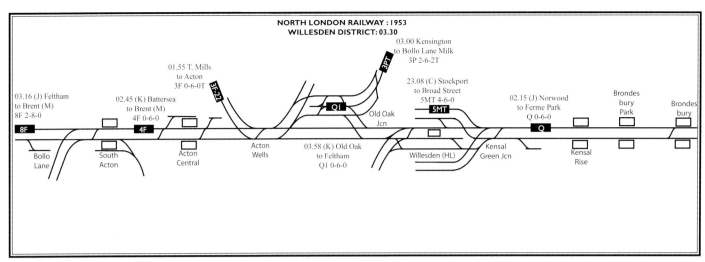

NORTH LONDON RAILWAY : 1953
WILLESDEN DISTRICT: 03.30

CONTROLLER'S LOG: Class C trains - the aristocrats of express goods - are not especially plentiful on the North London but at the moment no less than two can be seen: one, the Perth Fish now passing Camden Road and the other, the 23.08 Stockport - Broad Street which is approaching Kensal Green Junction and conveys a full train of fifty conflats and containers.

Another noteworthy train is the 03.00

that is heading towards Kensal Rise: the only diagrammed instance of a Southern engine working through to the Great Northern - a working that, presumably because of the time of day, receives little or no public attention.

Worked by a Norwood Junction Q 0-6-0, the train runs to Ferme Park via Gospel Oak and the Tottenham & Hampstead but for some extraordinary reason - probably in the hope that Norwood Junction men will eventually sign the

Ferme Park. Nowadays there is an even chance that the crew might get to Harringay without calling for someone to hold their hand although not infrequently a set of conductors have to be sent to Gospel Oak to bring the train in. Sometimes the engine returns via Canonbury but more often not the GN will send it back the way it has come.

The working is really a remnant of the war when it was deemed prudent to have an

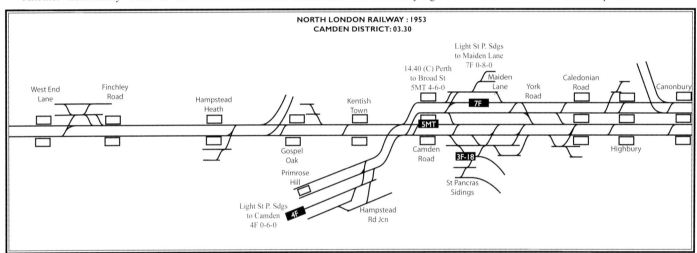

NORTH LONDON RAILWAY : 1953
CAMDEN DISTRICT: 03.30

Kensington to Cricklewood Milk, worked by a Willesden 3P 2-6-2T, which follows an extremely circuitous route involving the West London to Willesden and the connection via Old Oak to Acton Wells, detaching parts of its load at Bollo Lane before running round in Kew Yard and continuing on to Cricklewood via Acton Wells and Dudding Hill.

Interesting as these trains are, none compares in terms of novelty with the working

road - the engine returns light via Finsbury Park and Canonbury Junction, reversing at the latter.

The present routing is a fairly recent alteration and previously the service ran via Camden Road and Kingsland with the farcical result that the Norwood men - who never worked the turn often enough to sign the road - would need a set of North London pilotmen to take them from Canonbury to Finsbury Park and a second set for the last couple of miles to

alternative to the Widened Lines route.

Although the 03.00 Thames Wharf to Willesden - approaching Hackney - does not appear to be anything out of the ordinary with its everyday 3F Standard tank, it is a unique working since it is the only Willesden diagram to work over the Victoria Park branch. This is a working that has only recently been introduced and some are wondering whether it has some long-term significance for Devons Road.

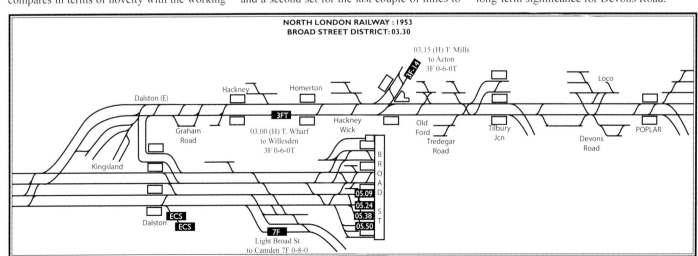

NORTH LONDON RAILWAY : 1953
BROAD STREET DISTRICT: 03.30

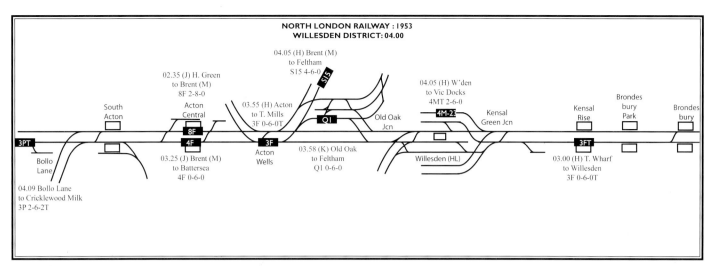

NORTH LONDON RAILWAY : 1953
WILLESDEN DISTRICT: 04.00

CONTROLLER'S LOG: There was a time when a passenger service operated between Poplar and Broad Street; indeed in the latter days of the North London trains had run at fifteen minutes intervals from around four in the morning until almost midnight. Alas, the service did not flourish and by the late thirties had been reduced to only half a dozen trains in each direction; a state of affairs that petered out completely in May 1944 when the service was discontinued. As it happened the extinction was not quite complete and for many years afterwards an unadvertised staff train made up of an elderly LNWR Brake Third and a 4MT 2-6-0 ran at 04.00 from Devons Road to Broad Street each morning, returning to Poplar at 04.55.

Following the passenger will be Target 30 which runs engine and brake to Kingsland to take over the 04.18 GN train from East Goods to Acton.

Maiden Lane, one of the North London's major goods stations, comes to life as a 7F 0-8-0 crosses over from St Pancras Sidings to work the 04.17 goods to Willesden via Camden.

Having circumnavigated the Richmond hinterland the 03.00 Kensington to Cricklewood Milk - now described as the 03.55 from Bollo Lane - reappears at Kew East Junction and makes its way up the North London as far as Acton Wells where it will take the Dudding Hill route to the Midland.

The running of the 04.00 Devons Road - Broad Street is a timely reminder to have a word with the Broad Street Inspector to confirm that he has the electric multiple-units needed to start the suburban service off from the London end of the line in just over an hour's time.

In an ideal world eleven 3-car units finish their day at Broad Street (five being stabled at Dalston Junction) and are automatically positioned for their workings the next day. Occasionally things go wrong and one or two six car sets will actually finish their workings as three car sets which of course means that some trains will be short of stock the next morning. Since multiple units are not positively controlled in the way that locomotives are, a physical check in the dead of night is the surest way of discovering shortages. Rectifying any shortages that come to light is usually done by sending the units required as a train of special empty stock from Croxley Green.

After backing its train into the Express Dairies siding at Bollo Lane, the Milk continues forward to Cricklewood, its 3P 2-6-2T running-round at Kew East Junction. Because of the volume of traffic on the Dudding Hill route, the Milk is allowed fifteen minutes for the four miles between Acton Wells and Cricklewood.

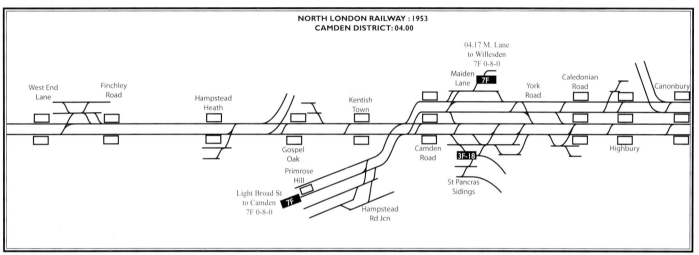

NORTH LONDON RAILWAY : 1953
CAMDEN DISTRICT: 04.00

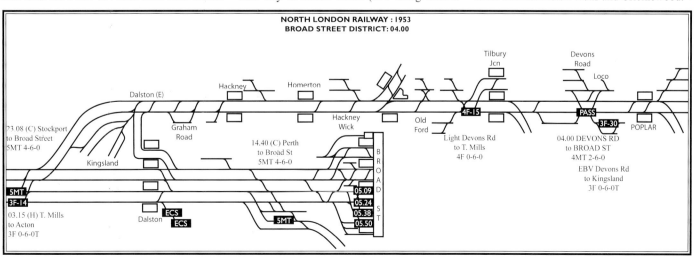

NORTH LONDON RAILWAY : 1953
BROAD STREET DISTRICT: 04.00

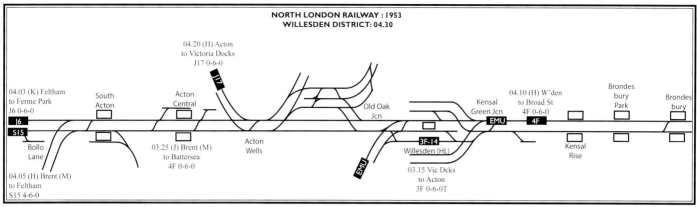

NORTH LONDON RAILWAY : 1953
WILLESDEN DISTRICT: 04.30

CONTROLLER'S LOG: The first signs of passenger traffic appear with the departure of two sets of electric stock from Mitre Bridge depot. Both run via Willesden High Level station and reverse at Kensal Green Junction; the first set forming the 04.48 Willesden Junction to Broad Street and the second, the 04.52 Willesden to Richmond.

The time is also approaching when the manner in which trains are run between Camden Road and Dalston has to be changed. Up to

Even so the general rule is that only one goods train can be sandwiched between successive passenger trains over this section. A clear run by a goods train during daylight hours is uncommon because passenger trains call at all stations which means that any following goods train either runs on adverse signals throughout or else the driver holds back in the early stages in order to let the passenger get well ahead but in so doing, risks delaying any following trains.

The other service is the 04.18 East Goods (Finsbury Park) to Acton which arrives behind a Hornsey J50 but goes forward behind Target 30; a 3F 0-6-0T which runs out with its brakevan from Devons Road to Kingsland. This is an unusual method of working but the J50 is required back at Finsbury Park for the 06.05 East Goods to Poplar, leaving the North London with no option but to work the traffic forward themselves.

A Southern Q1 0-6-0 rattles the 04.00

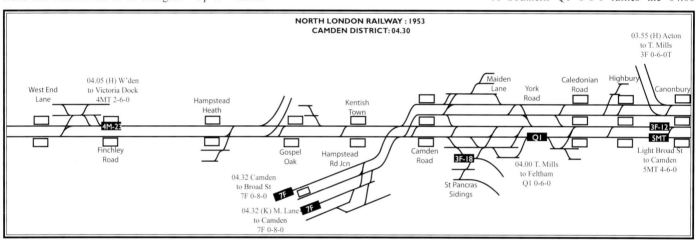

NORTH LONDON RAILWAY : 1953
CAMDEN DISTRICT: 04.30

the present there has been no reason why goods trains should not run on the fast lines of the four-track section but with the passenger service in operation, most goods trains have to be directed along the goods lines, leaving the southernmost set of rails free for passenger traffic. However, trains to and from St Pancras Sidings have to use the fast lines whilst goods trains for Broad Street are regulated individually.

The lengthy two-line section West of Camden Road also provides its share of regulating headaches although it must be one of the few instances in the country where passenger and goods trains have the same running times.

The eastern end of the district has only two trains at the moment but both are of interest since they involve foreign motive power. One is the 03.50 from Goodmayes to St Pancras Sidings and is a reminder that Temple Mills is not the only marshalling yard on the Great Eastern. Goodmayes yard is located between Romford and Ilford and deals with traffic arriving from the Norwich main line (as opposed to Temple Mills which handles traffic from the North of England). The train loads with rough North London traffic and the J15 0-6-0 return to the Great Eastern with the 05.44 St Pancras Sidings to Temple Mills.

Temple Mills to Feltham past the sidings at Maiden Lane, the Camden Road signalman watching anxiously for it to clear the junction so that the road can be set for the Broad Street trip that has just left Camden. In the opposite direction Target 12 passes Canonbury with an Acton - Temple Mills trains whilst one of the Devons Road 4MT 2-6-0's passes Finchley Road on its way from Willesden to Victoria Docks.

With three of BR's four components being visible within a few miles of each other, no-one can accuse the North London of lacking variety!

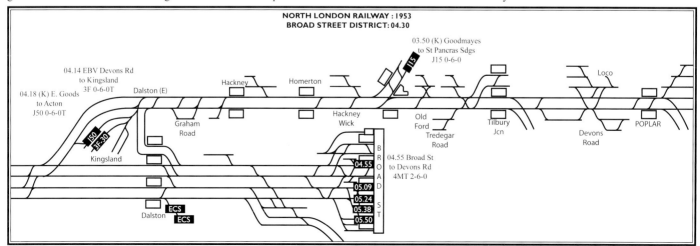

NORTH LONDON RAILWAY : 1953
BROAD STREET DISTRICT: 04.30

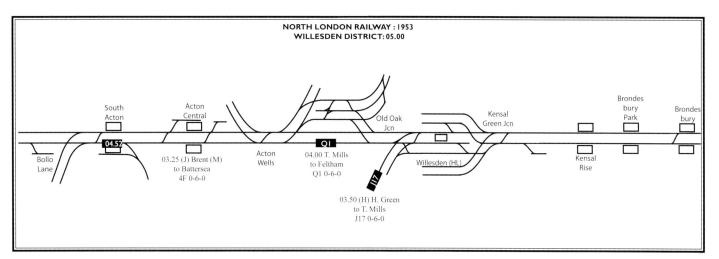

CONTROLLER'S LOG: There was a time when the line from Broad Street to Poplar played host to quite an intensive service of passenger trains. Many, alas, disappeared as a result of tramcar and underground competition during the Edwardian years; the service being withdrawn, apart from one working, in 1942.

The survivor is known to very few outside the North London clan and is a one coach staff train that leaves Devons Road for Broad Street at 04.00 and returns from Broad Street

still handled by steam!

The electric service has also started: the first train being the 04.52 Willesden (HL) - Richmond.

Broad Street's service consists of frequent trains to Watford Junction via Primrose Hill and to Richmond via Finchley Road although its first departure is an unadvertised staff service which runs only a far as Camden Road before returning to form the 06.05 to Richmond.

The goods service remains as heavy and

located immediately outside Fenchurch Street passenger terminus.

Another North London interest on the Bow branch is Bow Common Gas Works which has five workings a day from Devons Road, taking in coal and bringing empties out. The first of these workings, however, is some time off.

As Target 9 leaves to do battle in the heart of Great Eastern country, so two local Great Eastern trips arrive on the North London: one being the 03.50 Goodmayes to St Pancras

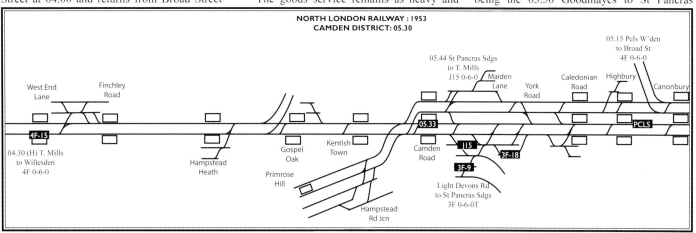

at 04.55. Formed of an LNW brake-third, the service is one of numerous mystery trains that abound in London; trains that have formed the basis of several scholarly works on the capital's railway system. A particular point of interest is that the up service calls at Bow and Homerton whilst the return service runs non-stop between Dalston and Devons Road.

It is pleasing to note that of a service consisting of hundreds, perhaps thousands, of electric trains, the first working of the day is

varied as ever; indeed a spectator at Highbury might have difficulty in believing that he was on the former LMS given the profusion of foreign engines in the vicinity.

Target 9 rings off Devons Road Loco and is a reminder that the North London has interests off the beaten track, the engine running initially to Fairfield Road to attach traffic left by the 23.35 ex Willesden and to work it via the Bow Junction branch to Haydon Square goods station; one of a cluster of goods depots

Sidings and the other being the 04.45 Temple Mills to Graham Road, a group of sidings a short distance west of Hackney.

Business is still brisk at Broad Street Goods. The 04.32 trip from Camden has arrived behind a Super-D 0-8-0 and is closely followed by a 4F 0-6-0 with the 04.10 from Willesden. Both trains convey traffic that has arrived overnight on West Coast services. The 4F will return light to Camden after half an hour but the 0-8-0 will remain to work the 06.07 Camden Goods.

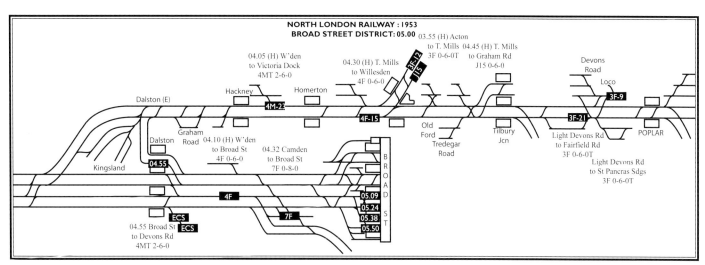

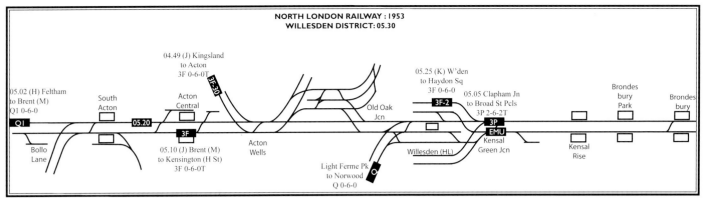

NORTH LONDON RAILWAY : 1953
WILLESDEN DISTRICT: 05.30

CONTROLLER'S LOG: The first up electric - the 05.20 Richmond to Broad Street - can be seen approaching Acton Central whilst the empty stock for the 05.33 Willesden - Richmond reverses at Kensal Green after arriving from Mitre Bridge carriage sidings. The latter has to be rather deftly crossed from the up to down main to avoid delaying the Clapham Junction - Broad Street Parcels: a one-van affair worked by a 3P 2-6-2T and said, by those with experience of the engines, to be just within the capabilities of the class. Some

2 which will follow the 05.30 electric from Richmond from Kensal Green.

Maiden Lane is about to receive the attentions of Target 49 which is on the point of running engine and brake from Devons Road to Kingsland to pick any local traffic that is on hand, taking it to Maiden Lane where the engine will position wagons for unloading before working a local trip to Highbury and back.

For the moment most of the foreign engines have left the Camden and Poplar areas and the only visitors remaining are a pair of Great

running over the District line of the LTE from Chiswick Park.

Understandably, London Transport are less than keen on the idea of long main line goods trains playing havoc with their tube services and accordingly a limit of eighteen wagons (plus a 20-ton brake) is imposed, a limit that coincidentally tallies nicely with the limit of eighteen loaded mineral wagons for a 3F 0-6-0T.

Normally one train a day is sufficient for the needs of Kensington although provision exists

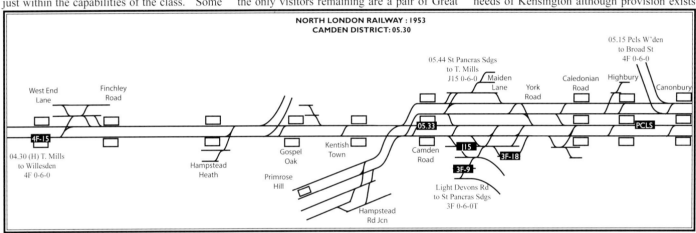

NORTH LONDON RAILWAY : 1953
CAMDEN DISTRICT: 05.30

distance ahead of it, another parcels train - the 05.15 ex Willesden - also heads for Broad Street.

Goods traffic is the stuff of the moment and although Broad Street goods has seen a fair degree of activity in the last few hours, the early turn brings Haydon Square (Fenchurch Street) and Maiden Lane to life; both awaiting goods traffic that has come into the district during the night.

Haydon Square traffic is being dealt with by two services: one being Target 21 which has just left Fairfield Road and is about to take the branch at Bow Junction, the other being Target

Eastern J15 0-6-0's: one at St Pancras Sidings and the other at Graham Road. Two other strangers can be seen at the western end of the district where a Q1 crosses the Kew East boundary with a Feltham - Cricklewood train of goods traffic and where a Q class 0-6-0 takes its leave of the North London at Willesden, en route light from Ferme Park to Norwood.

Incursions by main line engines over the Underground are rare but one of the exceptions - now passing Acton Central - is the 05.10 Brent to Kensington service. This working is another remnant of pregrouping times and serves the Midland coal depot at Kensington High Street,

for a second service should the need arise.

The Midland also had (has) a goods and coal depot at West Kensington, the services to which also use part of the District line. In the down direction trains can load up to fifty wagons (thirty-six in the up) with the booked Cricklewood 3F 0-6-0T being allowed to take either twenty-six loaded mineral wagons or the full fifty wagon limit of goods. Most trains consist of a mix of traffic and average about thirty-five wagons. There are normally three daily services to West Kensington, all booked to 3F 0-6-0T's which are amongst the very few classes permitted on the route.

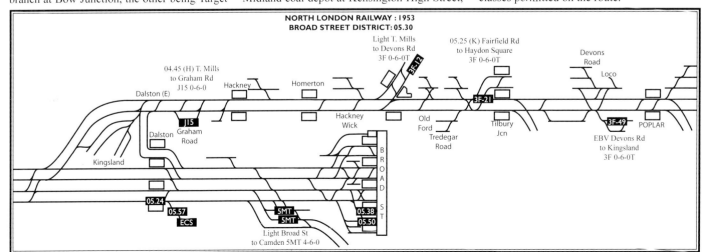

NORTH LONDON RAILWAY : 1953
BROAD STREET DISTRICT: 05.30

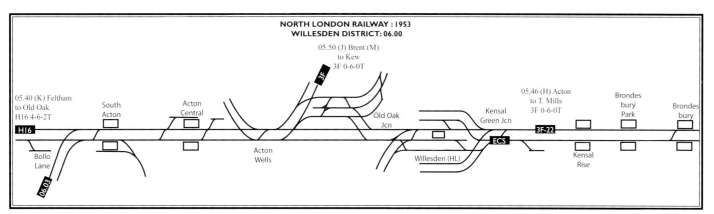

CONTROLLER'S LOG: The time is fast approaching when we have to bat very carefully! Although the peak service does not start for another hour and a half, steps have to be taken to ensure that both the Broad Street area or the adjacent district to which North London trains run, are free from slow moving trains and to this end, a series of embargoes are placed on goods workings. Almost no goods trains, for example, are allowed to leave the Great Eastern for the North London between 06.10 and 09.50 whilst a ban in the opposite direction

Thus much of the next hour is spent in anticipating which goods workings are going to clear the embargo and which are not, chivvying up the laggards as necessary. Because of the vagaries of working - fog, for instance, is a particular problem in London - it is by no means unusual to find a queue of trains on the down goods at Camden Road waiting, on the block, for the peak service to finish.

Of the two Great Eastern services currently on the district, one - running to beat the embargo - is passing Hackney en route to Temple Mills

Temple Mills. The price of any intransigence by Stratford will be the loss of the 09.35 Temple Mills to Acton!

The list of railway locations unfamiliar to enthusiasts will almost certainly include Old Ford; the destination of Target 8 which is approaching Hampstead Heath. Old Ford is the LNW goods depot at Bow and is still - like so many other locations - serviced as though the grouping had never taken place!

Another little-known location is Old Oak (not to be confused with the GWR location) a

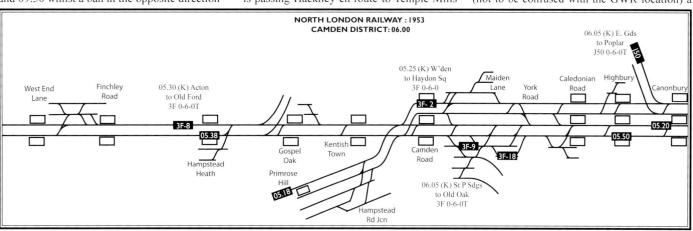

applies from 07.00 to 09.40. The demands of goods traffic, however, are heavy and in order to prevent congestion building up either side of the North London, one or two exceptions are made.

The restrictions are not simply a matter of goods trains clogging the system up - bad though that would be - but the fact that a train at the wrong time from, say, Temple Mills to Acton might sit on the goods line at Camden Road for so long that the return working might be lost due to the crew throwing in the towel upon reaching Acton.

and passing its running mate which is shunting in the yard at Graham Road. The latter is an embargo exception and will return to Temple Mills at 07.40. The 05.46 Acton - Temple Mills is a service that will have to be watched carefully since it is due to pass Victoria Park only seventeen minutes before the shutters come down and in the event of its losing time it will be necessary to plead - quite literally - with the Controller at Stratford and ask him to bend the rules a little. If he refuses then the train will be cancelled at somewhere like Hackney Wick and the engine sent back to Acton for the 11.52 to

little to the west of Willesden and which acts largely as an exchange yard for traffic between the LNW and the LSW.

The attraction of Old Oak so far as the observer is concerned is the variety of motive power that arrives on services from Feltham; workings being booked to S15 4-6-0's Q1 0-6-0's and the rather strange H15 4-6-2T's. An evening visit to the yard often produces the unusual sight of a Great Eastern J17 0-6-0 rubbing shoulders with a Southern S15 4-6-0. Other daily visitors vary from commonplace Devon Road types to an LNWR G2a 0-8-0.

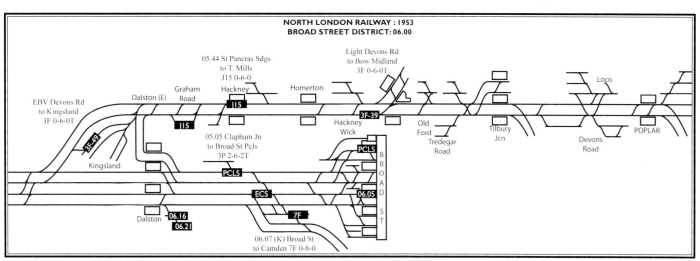

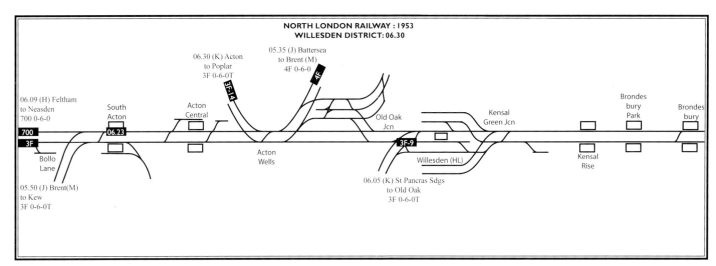

CONTROLLER'S LOG: The distinctive North London outside-cylinder 0-6-0T's continue in traffic although their present day duties are confined to Poplar where three of the class still shunt daily. Two of the class have just left Devons Road for Poplar whilst the third will come off shed in an hour and a half's time. The reason for the retention of these engines is because the Standard 3F 0-6-0 tanks are barred

service started, the number of goods trains between Broad Street and South Acton has diminished considerably, as well it might with six electrics in the up direction and three on the down.

East of Dalston, Poplar and Old Ford boxes have opened and a train to each is on its way. That to Poplar is a Great Northern service conveying goods that have arrived in Finsbury

less, quite an element of goods activity remains. LMS types predominate but the approach of a LSWR 700 0-6-0 with forty-seven wagons of goods (the capacity of the class is a frustrating three wagons less than the fifty wagon limit) for the Great Central adds a splash of colour.

The train to keep an eye on the 06.30 Acton to Poplar which may need some careful guidance between Acton Wells and Camden Road. If all

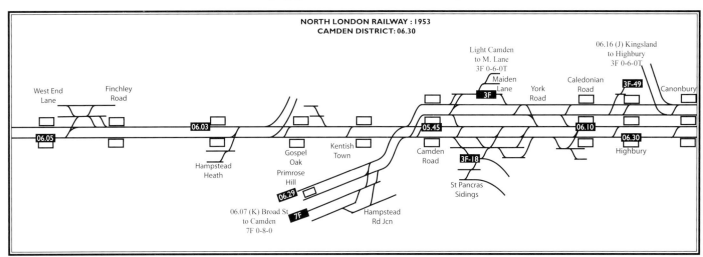

from working between Poplar Central and Preston Road and to the West India Docks. One should not speak of these engines in the past tense just yet since their potential exceeds by a considerable margin the expectation of their designer since in addition to the five engines at Devons Road, another five are allocated to far-off Birkenhead whilst four of the class are based at Rowsley for working over the Cromford & High Peak line.

It is noticeable that since the passenger

Park during the night from points on the East Coast route and is preceded by the pair of 2F pilots which will descend on the train as soon as it arrives.

The Old Ford service has just passed Hackney and behind it is an Acton - Temple Mills train which will be the last North London train before the Great Eastern embargo comes into play.

At the western end, where the danger of inflicting delays upon the passenger service is

goes to plan, it will follow the 06.23 Richmond - Broad Street to Kentish Town West and then dash onto the goods line at Camden Road as soon as the 06.14 Watford - Broad Street has cleared the Junction. However, the best laid plans of mice and men.................. if the 3F should start steaming badly (and the North London is plagued with poor coal) on the way to Hampstead or has to stop at Kentish Town to blow up, then the effects will probably reverberate for the rest of the peak.

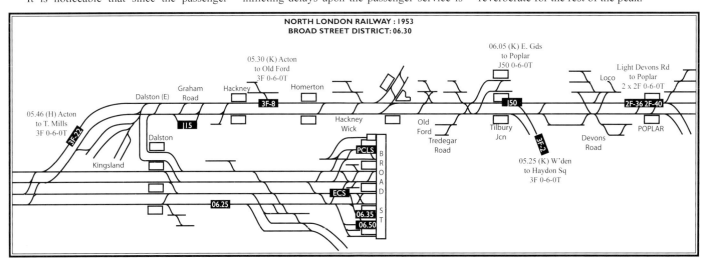

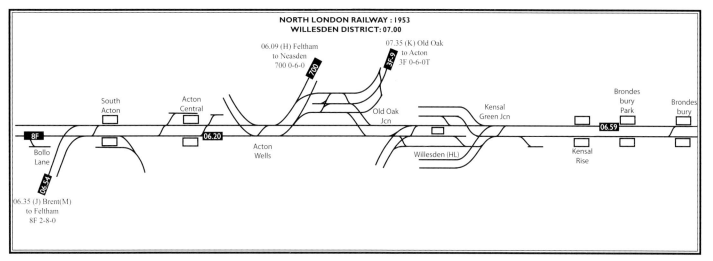

NORTH LONDON RAILWAY : 1953
WILLESDEN DISTRICT: 07.00

CONTROLLER'S LOG: The morning peak can be said to start now and - tongue in cheek - is held to run in three waves with shop assistants arriving in London between seven and eight, clerks between eight and nine and the Quality between nine and ten. There are already quite a number of trains on their way into London: one arriving in Broad Street, another at Caledonian Road, a third at Camden Road with a Watford train fast approaching

before the 06.26 Watford - Broad Street shows its face. Given the 20 mph restriction from Kentish Town to the York Road side of the Junction plus the inherent uncertainties of 3F tanks on indifferent coal, the regulation of such movements is often as much an art as it is a science.

Equal nicety of judgement has to be exercised in the opposite direction with the 07.09 goods from St Pancras Sidings which has

Also to be born in mind is the question of the 07.43 Maiden Lane to Camden and a light engine - the engine that brought in the Stockport containers - from Broad Street to Camden. Running at much the same speed as an electric but without the station stops, the Black 5 can probably be run down the main between the 07.07 and 07.18 electrics from Broad Street.

Away from the worries of suburban passenger trains, Old Ford yard comes to life as

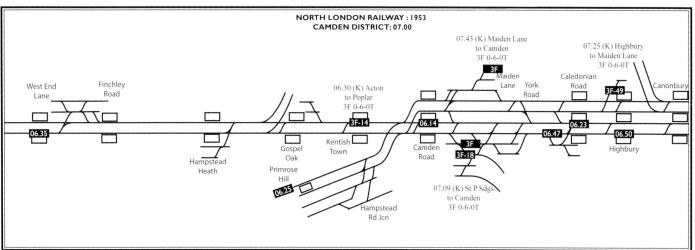

NORTH LONDON RAILWAY : 1953
CAMDEN DISTRICT: 07.00

Camden Road Junction. Traffic is also brisk in the opposite direction and although the numbers do not compare with the army of arrivals, the number of night-shifts in London results in quite a respectable counter-flow.

One can also see - and admire - the deftness with which Camden Road Junction has to be worked as target 14 with its 3F 0-6-0T and 42 wagons of goods drops down from Kentish Town and has to be swung onto the slow line

drawn its 35 wagons out onto the departure road and ought to get a run to Camden between the 06.54 and 07.06 electrics from Broad Street. Target 21, en route from Haydon Square, may well arrive on the slow line as the 3F leaves with the Camden goods and might be packed in between the goods and the 07.06 electric. One has to confer first with Camden to make sure they can take both trains without upsetting the passenger working.

the first of its trains backs in; the engine running to shed and being replaced by another 3F which will act as yard pilot for most of the day.

A Great Eastern J15 0-6-0 shunts the yard at Graham Road, Hackney; making up at the same time, the 07.40 goods to Temple Mills.

The Western section of the line is much quieter than the rest and the only goods activity at the moment feature an LMS 2-8-0 and a 700 0-6-0, both heading away from the area.

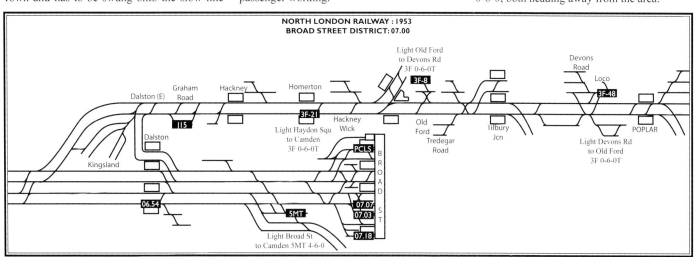

NORTH LONDON RAILWAY : 1953
BROAD STREET DISTRICT: 07.00

One could hardly produce a book on the North London Railway without some attention being given to the long-lived outside-cylinder class 75 0-6-0T's that were very much a hallmark of the line. Introduced in 1879 and numbering thirty engines, withdrawals began in the 1930's as the Standard 3F 0-6-0T's took over their duties. The latter, however, were prohibited from certain parts of Poplar Docks and as a result five of the North London engines were retained at Devons Road, the last not leaving until April 1958 when its duties were taken over by a diesel shunter. It was not just the longevity of the class that made them remarkable since they proved ideal for duties in parts of England far removed from the East end of London. By the early 1950's four of the class were employed on the Cromford & High Peak Railway with another five working on the docks at Birkenhead. In the view above, one of the class shunts at Broad Street whilst working Target 43 in August 1929. (Dr Ian C Allen/ transporttreasury.co.uk).

The great majority of the four hundred and seventeen Standard LMS 3F 0-6-0's - sometimes referred to as Jinties or Jocko's - seldom strayed far from shunting duties and rarely came to public notice. The exceptions were the Devons Road allocation which were main line engines within the meaning of the act, working scheduled goods trains from Plaistow and Temple Mills in the East to Acton in the West. Although of modest proportions and power classification, the class could handle very respectable tonnages of goods traffic and on the Poplar to Willesden run could take within two wagons of the 60-wagon line limit. The majority of workings on the North London were restricted to much shorter trains which were well within the compass of a 3F. The class was at something of a disadvantage with coal traffic and were limited to about 24 wagons on the hilly route between Camden Road and Acton Wells. On the relatively level route from Willesden to Maiden Lane a 3F could take as many as forty-two loaded mineral wagons. 47501 was for many years a Devons Road engine, remaining there until December 1957 when dieselisation saw its removal to Willesden. It is seen, above, working one of the Willesden carriage pilot turns on 7th October 1958. (Alec Swain/www.transporttreasury.co.uk)

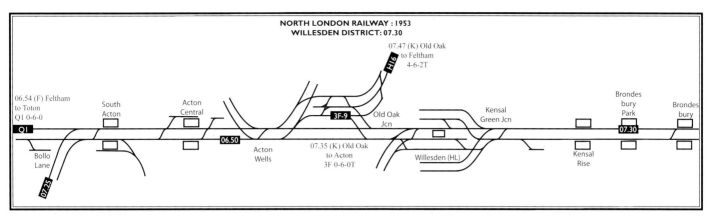

NORTH LONDON RAILWAY : 1953
WILLESDEN DISTRICT: 07.30

CONTROLLER'S LOG: Until the last war the North London used to operate passenger trains to a number of inner-suburban stations on the Great Northern and although these trains continue to run, they are now operated by Kings Cross engines and men using, with one exception, N2 'Met Tank' 0-6-2T's. The exception is an outer suburban service which is worked by a B1 4-6-0. The method of operation is relatively simple and starts with a light engine - now approaching Canonbury Junction - which takes the empty stock of the first GN arrival back to Finsbury Park. The

little used outside the hours of the peak, and platforms 5 to 9 which are used by the LM DC electrics.

Although the embargo on goods trains from the Great Northern to the North London runs from 07.00 until 09.45, an exception is made for the 07.10 East Goods to Poplar, the grounds being that it works forward urgent traffic that has come up the main line overnight and which should not be delayed any further than absolutely necessary.

In point of fact goods trains from the Great Northern only occupy passenger lines over the

limit on Feltham - Brent empty trains is a mere forty-four wagons but to clear more quickly the large number of empties that accumulate at Feltham, it has been agreed that through trains from Feltham to Toton (etc) can convey a maximum of seventy.

What is the result? Instead of arranging the working so that an 8F 2-8-0 handles the train throughout, the Southern somehow end up working the first part of the journey and are able to provide nothing better than a Q1 0-6-0 which has a limit of 63 wagons at class F speed!

Seven wagons may not sound much but on

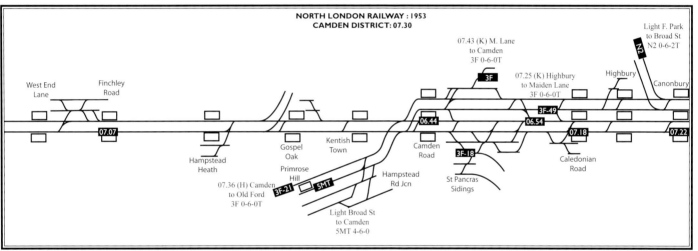

NORTH LONDON RAILWAY : 1953
CAMDEN DISTRICT: 07.30

engine thus released then takes back the stock of the second arrival and so on until all eight trains have been dealt with. The only variation is that the coaches of the seventh train to arrive remains at Broad Street until the evening peak, its engine returning light to Kings Cross coupled to the engine of the last arrival.

During the rush hour service, one realises that Broad Street is in fact two stations: one, platforms 1 to 4, being non-electrified and

short distance between Canonbury and Dalston West Junctions and some feel that the embargo is rather more rigid that it need be. The present arrangement, however, assures a clear path and an acceptable level of punctuality for passenger trains from the Great Northern.

The interesting visitor in the shape of a Q1 0-6-0 arrives on the section at Kew East with a Feltham - Toton service heralds a good example of left and right hand thinking. The normal

the Midland the underloading of a train comes almost as close to a capital crime as murder and the gap could easily be closed by the Southern diagramming an H16 4-6-2T to the working. At Cricklewood the train will be made up to 84 wagons which is the full load for a class F train down the Midland main line. If demand for empties in the north is excessive, then the train might be downgraded to class J at Cricklewood and made up to a full one hundred empties.

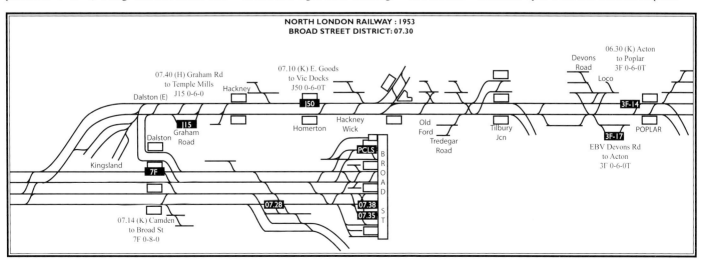

NORTH LONDON RAILWAY : 1953
BROAD STREET DISTRICT: 07.30

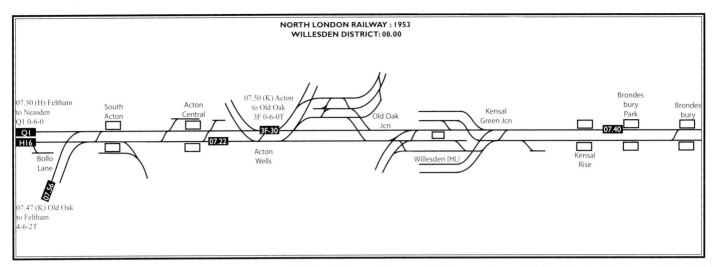

NORTH LONDON RAILWAY : 1953
WILLESDEN DISTRICT: 08.00

CONTROLLER'S LOG: The appearance of so many LNER engines in Broad Street is still regarded as something of a novelty by older hands since until the war the Great Northern workings used to be covered by North London engines and men; Standard 3F tanks being used for many years until being replaced in the late 1930's by 3P 2-6-2T's.

The nature of the service has changed considerably and whereas the pre-war empty, at 08.20, to Western Sidings at Finsbury Park. The inward engine will then run to the engine road and wait to dispose of the 07.30 from Hertford North in similar fashion.

The number of goods trains between Dalston and Acton Wells has decreased to a single engine and brakevan which is en route from Devons Road to Acton to work the 09.27 to Temple Mills.

A word from the Stratford Controller warns also require Camden Goods to be notified of all approaching trains in order to give him time to set his stall before they reach Camden Road.

Goods trains, however, do not run direct to Camden goods but are turned onto one of two goods arrival lines at Hampstead Road Junction where they can wait until the yard is ready to deal with them.

Having a pair of arrival roads which can hold at least two full-length trains gives a

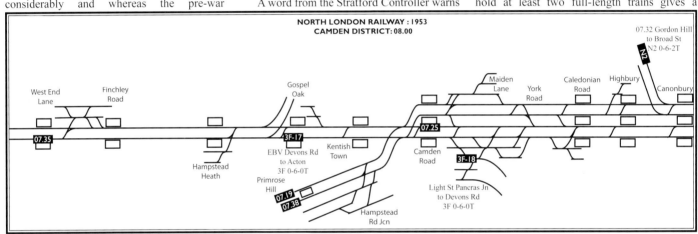

NORTH LONDON RAILWAY : 1953
CAMDEN DISTRICT: 08.00

arrangement extended no further than Potters Bar on the main line and Cuffley on the New Line, the present service sees trains running to Hertford North and Welwyn Garden City with one train going as far as Royston. This expansion has been matched by a contraction in the hours of operation to the morning and evening rush-hours only.

The first GN train, the 07.32 ex Gordon Hill can be seen entering the system at Canonbury and is due in Broad Street at 08.12 where the waiting N2 will back onto the stock and take it us that a Victoria Dock to Camden train is on its way - this is one of the trains that has an exemption from the embargo - and we wait anxiously for Victoria Park to report the passing of the train so that some idea of its likely progress can be made.

When Victoria Park announces the arrival of the train on the district - "*Camden goods at oh eight*" - we note that it has a clear run as far as Dalston West and should then trickle down the slow road to Camden Road before following the 08.06 Broad Street - Watford. Standing orders welcome measure of elasticity in the event of acceptance problems at Camden.

Services from the Southern are also subject to an embargo; no goods train being allowed to approach South Acton between 07.30 and 09.30 except for services running to Old Oak, Brent or the Great Central. The Q1 that is poking its nose over the boundary with a Feltham - Neasden working is not therefore affected by the peak service although careful attention will have to be given to its passage between South Acton Junction and Acton Wells.

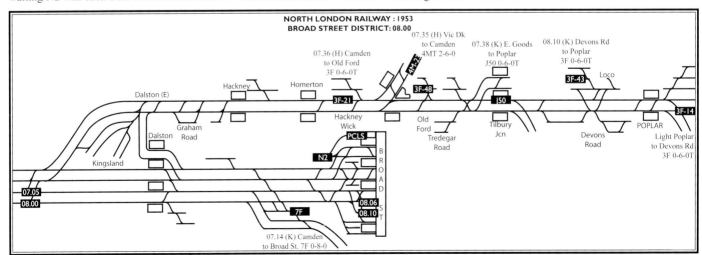

NORTH LONDON RAILWAY : 1953
BROAD STREET DISTRICT: 08.00

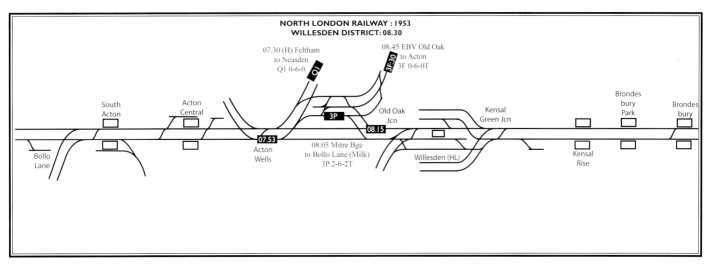

CONTROLLER'S LOG: *"Camden? Target 23. Engine 43020, 50 equal 50. 1 Green Arrow Warrington, 49 roughs. Engine and men light to Devons Road loco. Stale. Unless you can persuade them to work back......"*

"Old Oak? Bring me up to date with the stock, will you."

"Sixty-three London South Western. One hundred and twenty-four empty pools - 13 and

"Reading.......... Reading........."

"Target 23 is on its way down. What are your wishes?"

" Camden goods."

"Acton Wells. Up Passenger at 28. The down will be by me at 30. I've got the Bollo Lane warned. Is he as booked?"

"What's this goods warned from the GN?"

"Milk as booked."

enough when he finds a mystery train on his doorstep."

"Target 30, 42 empties for Acton. Right you are."

"Target 23 to Camden at thirty-five."

"Reading...... Hello. Reading."

"I can hear you."

"GN stock from Broad Street at 35."

"Target 30. 47511 49 equal 49 pool empties.

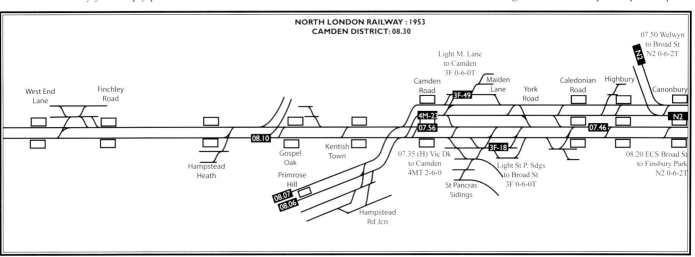

16 ton mixed."

"You're a bit over the top with pools. Is Target 30 in sight?"

"Engine four seventy-five eleven? It's just brought in twenty vans from Acton. You'd better add them to the list."

"Target 30 is booked engine and brake back to Acton. Don't let him go until I come back to you."

"Right."

"Watford passenger up No.2 at 27"

"Right away Hackney Wick."

"I'll cross 23 over as soon as the 07.56 Richmond has gone down."

"Right. Reading........... Hello, Reading. For God's sake say something if it's only -"

"Old Oak. I've got Target 30 guard with me,"

"Up Richmond passenger at 30."

"Well, I can't raise the Great Bloody Western..... Give Target 30 a full load, forty-nine pools, for Acton. Reading'll come on fast

Engine and men for 10.00 Acton - Vic Docks. Just leaving Old Oak."

"You're supposed to agree these loads - not just send them across."

"Try answering the line, then. Good morning to you."

"Harrow passenger up at 36."

"Target 21 from Old Ford at 40. 47315, 16 empty vans for Devons Road. The guard wants to know what he does next?"

"Shunt Devons Road and trip to Poplar."

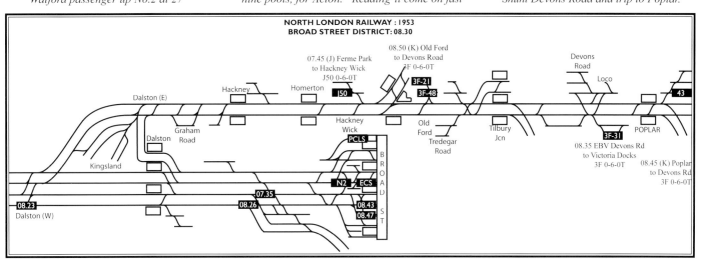

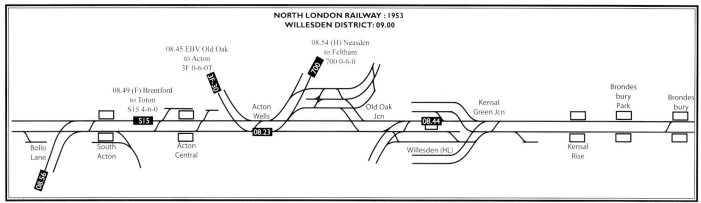

NORTH LONDON RAILWAY : 1953
WILLESDEN DISTRICT: 09.00

CONTROLLER'S LOG: For the moment steam has been all but banished from the system west of Dalston as the peak reaches its climax, the principal exception being the 07.50 from Tring which is a few minutes away from Broad Street. Running alongside is Target 18 which will take the empty stock to St Pancras Sidings where it will berth until forming the 18.02 Broad Street to Tring. The engine is a Watford 2-6-4T which, when released, will run light to Camden Loco. One might have thought that as the LNW's city terminus, Broad Street might line diesels are permitted to work into Broad Street.

Even when things are going like clockwork, superintending the peak is a fascinating experience as one watches over a large number of trains, making sure that nothing impedes their progress. It is also a rather wearing job since at the back of one's mind is the possibility that at any moment something will go wrong and that the solution - whatever it might be - will be the subject of close scrutiny at the post-mortem a day or two hence. It is no bad thing to mentally probably mean putting in single line working between Gospel Oak and Willesden High Level and operating shuttle services from Richmond to Willesden, Willesden to Gospel Oak and Gospel Oak to Broad Street. A triple service sounds cumbersome but is probably preferable to running trains through and undergoing single line working en route.

While electrics rule the roost over most of the railway, east of Dalston a number of steam workings mass, waiting for the moment the embargo can be lifted. The most striking of

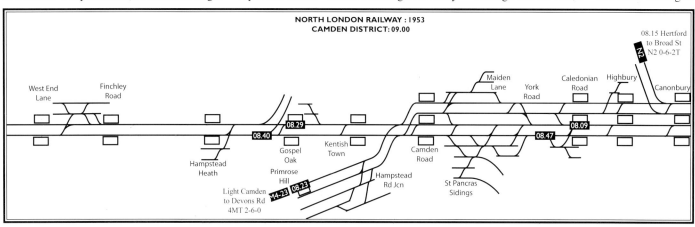

NORTH LONDON RAILWAY : 1953
CAMDEN DISTRICT: 09.00

have been given a few main line workings but it appears that travellers from stations north of Tring are happy (always supposing they are aware of Broad Street's existence) to complete their journeys at Euston. In 1910 a Birmingham - Broad Street business express was introduced but patronage was disappointing and the train did not operate for long. Since that time LNW traffic has been catered for by the DC electrics plus a pair of steam-worked services from Tring. In the (highly unlikely) event of main line trains being reintroduced, a close review of motive power would have to be exercised since neither the LMS Pacifics nor most of the main rehearse the actions to be taken in the event of trouble even though the inherent inflexibility of electric railways tends to limit the available options. A blockage of the line at Primrose Hill would be an interesting exercise since it would mean the diversion of all Watford trains via Finchley Road, Kensal Green Junction and the City Loop at Willesden where their normal route would be regained. The greatest problem would be to ensure that pilotmen were located at Camden Road and Willesden in sufficient numbers to keep trains moving. A less attractive scenario would be the blockage of a line at somewhere like Finchley Road which would these is a Great Northern service, the 08.50 Poplar to Clarence Yard (Finsbury Park) formed of a J50 0-6-0T with 45 vans many of which will connect into the 13.30 Clarence Yard - Niddrie express goods. Clarence Yard is a small but highly important marshalling yard about half a mile south of Finsbury Park and is the point at which most North London traffic is fed into the Great Northern system. Its counterpart for incoming traffic is the adjacent East Goods.

The J50 is not the only one of its class in the vicinity since another of the Hornsey collection can be seen shunting the yard at Hackney Wick, having arrived with a train from Ferme Park.

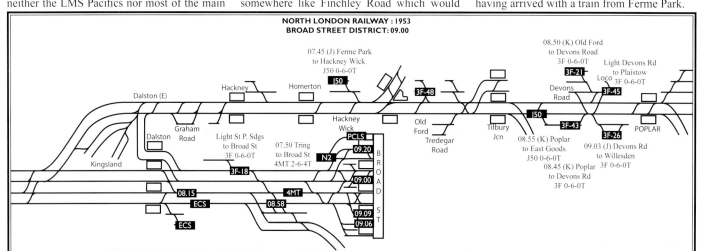

NORTH LONDON RAILWAY : 1953
BROAD STREET DISTRICT: 09.00

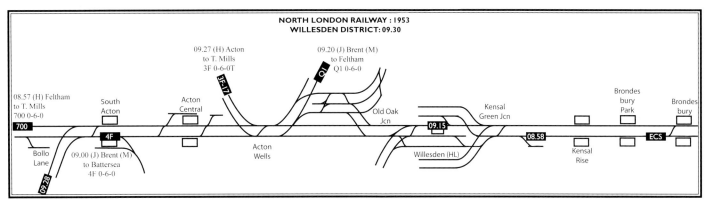

NORTH LONDON RAILWAY : 1953
WILLESDEN DISTRICT: 09.30

CONTROLLER'S LOG: If the electric railway has one depressing aspect, it lies in the drab uniformity of its services. In order to maximise track occupation and make the best use of rolling stock, all trains must run at exactly the same pace, calling at the same stations at the same interval of time each hour. Pity then the poor Watford passenger who has the choice of a meagre selection of relatively fast steam services or the more frequent but much slower electric service. Fortunately the timing office has noted the plight of its farther

One of the problems of running a suburban service is that a high proportion of the fleet has no work to do outside the rush hours; evidence of this being manifest by the several trains of empty stock which are en route from Broad Street to Mitre Bridge carriage sheds.

In anticipation of normal working, steam services in the vicinity of Devons Road are preparing to recapture the system and already a train of mineral empties from Devons Road to Willesden has managed to penetrate as far West as Camden Road and will get a clear run,

The makings of a conflict can be seen with the 08.57 Feltham - Temple Mills and 09.27 Acton - Temple Mills; the former passing Kew East behind an LSWR 700 0-6-0 whilst the latter approaches Acton Wells, worked by Target 17 3F 0-6-0T.

Hopefully the 3F will be waiting for the road at Acton Wells as the 09.15 Richmond - Broad Street passes, the 3F then pulling out onto the main line to follow the electric and heave its 24 wagons of coal up the bank to Hampstead and inside clear at Camden Road without delaying

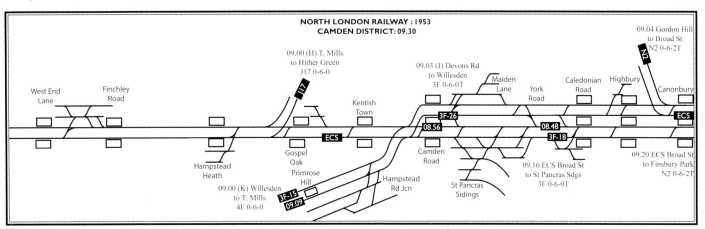

NORTH LONDON RAILWAY : 1953
CAMDEN DISTRICT: 09.30

flung passengers and to a very limited extent has waived the uniformity rule by running one or two of the DC electrics as expresses, one instance being the 08.48 ex Watford which can be seen approaching Caledonian Road. This service makes the normal stops as far as Stonebridge Park before running non-stop to Dalston Junction and arrives in Broad Street having shaved about eight minutes off the normal running time. Whilst the saving in time is important to the passenger, the chief benefit is the reduction in the number of tiresome station stops. If romance is to be found on a DC system, the 08.48 from Watford is probably its source.

ahead of the 09.23 Broad Street - Richmond, to Kensal Green Junction. Account will have to be taken of the 09.00 Temple Mills to Hither Green which is approaching Gospel Oak from the Tottenham direction and in all probability it will be held back to follow the 09.23 Broad Street - Richmond.

Before the rush-hour started goods trains had the system to themselves and there were few constraints on their movements. Now the position is entirely different and even though the rush hour is coming to an end, goods services have to negotiate their way through what is still a significant mass of passenger traffic and the scope for trouble is considerable.

the 09.28 Broad Street - Richmond.

The 700 0-6-0, which has 36 wagons of goods behind the tender, will drop down to South Acton to follow the 09.28 Richmond passenger up the hill and to the sanctuary of the slow line at Camden Road. The two trains will pass South Acton with only three minutes between then but the gap will gradually widen to eleven minutes at Camden Road - assuming that the 700, its coal and fireman are in a reasonable condition.

A crucial factor in the running of the electrics is that the Richmond trains have only nine minutes at Broad Street to turn-round and that leaves very little room for error.

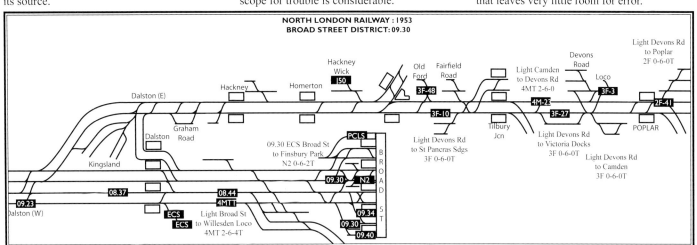

NORTH LONDON RAILWAY : 1953
BROAD STREET DISTRICT: 09.30

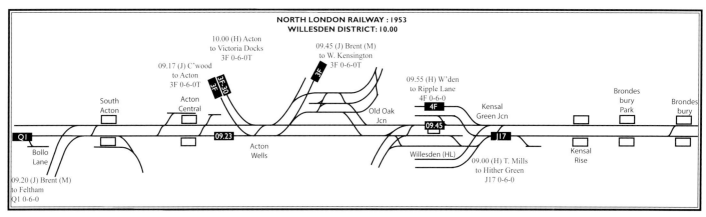

CONTROLLER'S LOG: The North London could well be described as begetter of surprises. Very few of us have not been surprised at the sight of a J17 in the heart of Southern suburban territory or espied a Q1 0-6-0 from the window of a Great Eastern express as it passes through the Stratford area and we have all wondered how such strange manifestations come to pass. The key is, of course, the North London and its service of trains that connect the various railways in Greater London. There are several examples on the run at the moment - a Great Eastern J17 at Kensal Green on its way to

to take forty-five wagons of goods or twenty-six of coal.

On the central part of the District, the more homely 3F 0-6-0T's are out in force and making up for time denied by the peak service. Target 18 which earlier broke its spell as the St Pancras Sidings pilot to work a train of empty stock from Broad Street, is on its way to Plaistow with a train from St Pancras Sidings whilst Target 10 has come light from Devons Road to take over as pilot; a job that during the day involves several transfer trips across the road to Maiden Lane. Eastbound trains from St Pancras

both worked by Standard 3F tanks, make their way towards Camden Road for Broad Street and St Pancras Sidings respectively. The first will be diverted to the up slow at Camden Road whilst the second will run up the main line to York Road where it will back into the arrival road.

The Great Northern service at Broad Street finishes with something of a flourish as the last train of the rush hour arrives behind a B1 4-6-0 instead of the usual 0-6-2T. The reason is that the train comes from Hitchin which is a little beyond the range of the smaller engines.

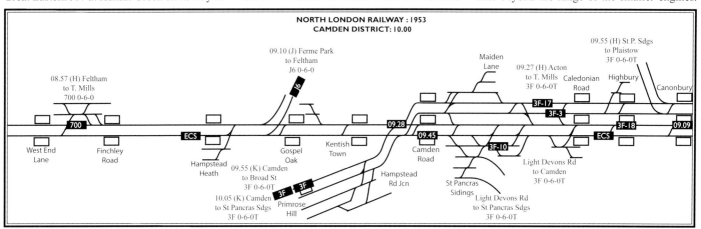

Hither Green, a Great Northern J6 approaching Gospel Oak with a train for Feltham and a LSWR 700 0-6-0 climbing Hampstead bank with a service for Temple Mills - but perhaps the quaintest is the West Kensington train that is approaching Acton Wells; fascinating because it will push deep into London Transport country and raise many an eyebrow on the District line. Unlike Kensington High Street which imposes severe load constraints on goods trains, West Kensington is far more liberal and the Standard 3F 0-6-0T's which work the trains are permitted

Sidings have to be regulated with some care at York Road since they have no direct access to the slow lines and have to use the fast lines as far as Dalston West. Departing trains have to be positioned on the departure road to wait for a gap in both up and down electric services before being allowed to leave. The worst thing that can happen is to have a train unable to leave the departure road because of traffic on the fast lines whilst a train for St Pancras Sidings approaches from the Camden direction!

On the Camden Road, a pair of goods trains,

After being released by the engine that brought in the 09.04 from Gordon Hill, the N2 and B1 are coupled together before setting off light for Kings Cross loco. Unlike the other GN arrivals which all return to their native section, the stock of the 09.04 Gordon Hill remains in Broad Street until forming the 18.06 to Hertford North.

Whilst the B1 is being released, the LMS 3P 2-6-2T that arrived at 06.08 with the Clapham Junction parcels pulls away with empty parcel vans for Willesden Junction via Camden .

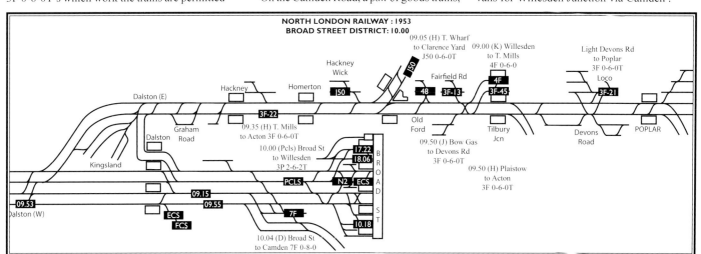

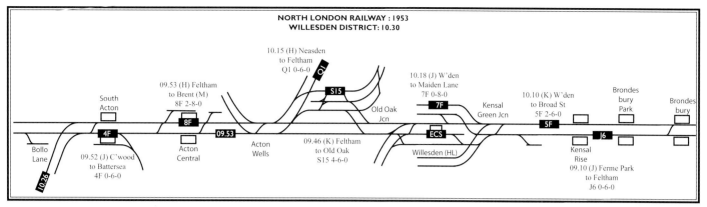

CONTROLLER'S LOG: Mention has been made - perhaps several times - of instances where pregrouping practices continue thirty years after the grouping (and long may they do so since history is the firmest foundation upon which we can choose to stand) and an example can be seen at the Great Northern yard at Hackney Wick which, appropriately, is being shunted by the J50 0-6-0T that arrived with the 07.48 goods from Ferme Park. The engine shunts the yard until 11.25 when it will propel its brake van to Kingsland where it will make up a train of Hackney and Hackney Wick

seven wagons.

Great Northern J50's make numerous appearances on the eastern part of the North London since they are used for most of the trip workings based at Ferme Park and East Goods. Another of the class is passing Ashburton Grove on the approach to Finsbury Park with the 09.05 Thames Wharf to Clarence Yard whilst a third member of the class leaves Finsbury Park to work the 11.40 Thames Wharf to Ferme Park.

Balancing the books in the area, as it were, was Target 13 which was covered by a Standard 3F 0-6-0T that spent all day working between

Road Yard with the brakevan next to the engine so that the engine simply has to run-round the train when it reverses. When the train leaves Bow Gas, the brakevan is next to the engine and in the correct position for the Fairfield - Devons Row leg. The possibility of allowing target 13 to propel its train from Devons Row to Fairfield Road and from Bow Gas to Fairfield Road has been examined but rejected although up to ten wagons may be propelled from Devons Road to Tilbury Junction.

Looking west, an unusual type of engine can be seen approaching Kensal Rise with the

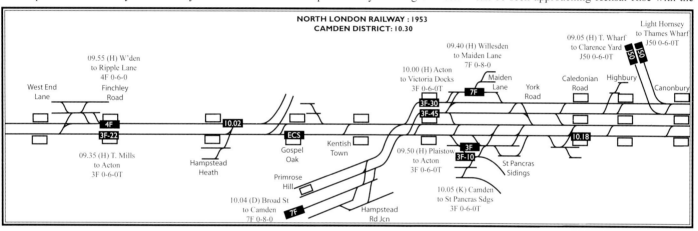

traffic, leaving Kingsland at 11.40. When the J50 arrives back at Hackney Wick, it will position the traffic it has brought down from Kingsland, shunt out the yard for a final time before departing with the 12.40 goods to Ferme Park. Much of the traffic worked by the trip is coal and a J50 can take either 27 wagons of coal or 35 wagons of goods. Space is a problem at Hackney Wick - the longest siding can only accommodate eighteen wagons - and trains have to be worked by a tank engine. Trains leaving Hackney Wick are limited to twenty-

Devons Road and Bow Common Gas Works; a labour of Sisyphus thanks to the fact that only twenty-two wagons and a brake van are permitted on each trip.

Bow Gas is located on the branch from Bow Junction to Fenchurch Street and each trip therefore has to reverse at Fairfield Road sidings or, if the sidings are blocked by traffic, on the main line at Bow Junction. To save having to reposition the brakevan every time the trip visits Fairfield Road, a concession has been agreed whereby the train can leave Devons

10.10 Willesden - Broad Street goods. This service is worked by one of Willesden's small batch of parallel-boilered 'Crab' 5MT 2-6-0's which on reaching Broad Street will work back with the 13.10 Scotch goods, taking the train as far as Camden where it will hand over to a 5XP 4-6-0. Later in the day the 2-6-0 will work the 16.30 Euston - Bletchley passenger working.

Following the 2-6-0 is a Super-D 0-8-0 on the 10.18 local goods from Willesden to Maiden Lane which serves many of the local stations via Finchley Road.

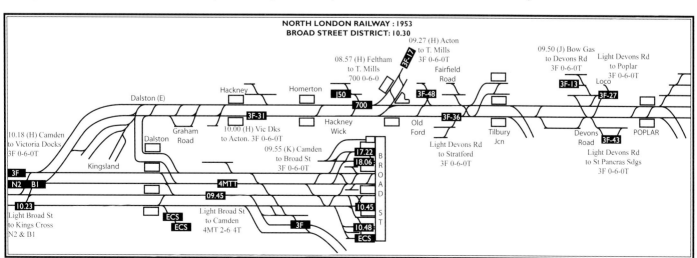

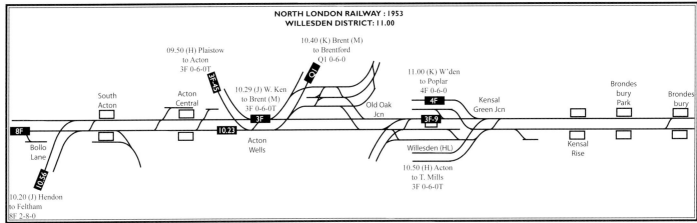

NORTH LONDON RAILWAY : 1953
WILLESDEN DISTRICT : 11.00

CONTROLLER'S LOG: the post-peak explosion of trains that could be seen on the line diagrams half an hour ago has settled down a little although the system is probably still the most concentrated network of trains in the country. The location of the moment is St Pancras Sidings which is attracting trains like flies round a jam-pot! Target 10 has just drawn away with a trip for Maiden Lane whilst another 3F tank has drawn out onto the departure road with a working for Camden. At the same time a third 0-6-0T, Target 43, arrives light

without delaying anything else requires skill and intelligence is an understatement of some magnitude.

Finally, a Willesden 7F 0-8-0 waits to run light from Maiden Lane to St Pancras Sidings to work the 11.47 Broad Street Goods.

Services between Ferme Park and Acton normally travel via Harringay Junction and Gospel Oak but there are exceptions such as the 10.00 from Ferme Park which attaches traffic at East Goods and therefore runs via Kingsland where the J52 0-6-0T runs round. Normally

inward journeys.

On the goods side of affairs at Broad Street, the 10.10 from Willesden with its 5MT 2-6-0 approaches Dalston Junction whilst a Camden 0-6-0T busies itself in putting together the 11.40 goods for Maiden Lane.

The remainder of the trains on the system are the usual miscellany of services that forms the staple diet of North London activity: a Q1 0-6-0 approaching Acton Wells with a Brent to Brentford train, an LMS 8F 2-8-0 with a Hendon - Feltham working and any number of Standard

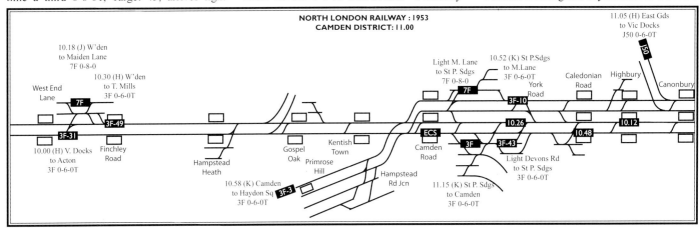

NORTH LONDON RAILWAY : 1953
CAMDEN DISTRICT : 11.00

from Devons Road to work the 11.36 goods to Plaistow. No peace for the shunters!

Although St Pancras Sidings and Maiden Lane face each other across the four running lines, trip working between the two of them is quite a rigmarole. Allowed to take up to twenty wagons without a brake van, Target 10 draws onto No.2 down at the Maiden Lane end of the yard, propels through the crossover to No.2 up, reverses again onto No.1 down, draws clear of the crossover and then backs into Maiden Lane Yard.

To say that signalling one of these trips

trains from the GN to Kingsland are limited to a mere 28 wagons but in the case of the 10.00 this is extended to 38 wagons of goods provided the train has a brakevan at each end of the train.

After its rush-hour exertions, Broad Street is now back to quiet normality, the only trains in the station being the stock for two evening departures, one LNW and one Great Northern, and a pair of DC units for the 13.18 and 15.18 Willesden and Watford trains. The next passenger departures, the 11.18 to Willesden Junction and the 11.23 to Richmond are at Highbury and York Road respectively on their

3F 0-6-0T's at work between Poplar and Acton. One train worth a moment's attention is the 10.18 Willesden to Maiden Lane which services the local yards at Finchley Road, Hampstead Heath and Gospel Oak. These stations are all situated too close to the trunk lines to deal in much beyond peripheral flows of traffic and much of what is dealt with is domestic coal from the collieries served by the ex-LNWR and worked into London via Willesden.

The use of an 0-8-0 seems rather an extravagance but being able to take 60 wagons of coal, they can cope with any surprises.

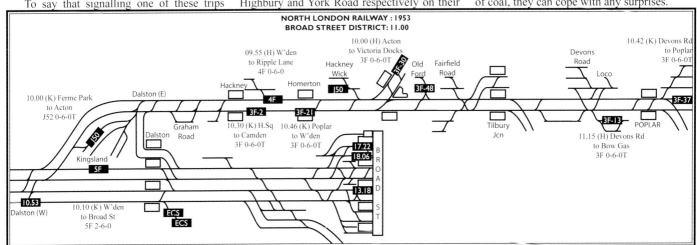

NORTH LONDON RAILWAY : 1953
BROAD STREET DISTRICT : 11.00

74

The North London was selected for the distinction of being the first system in Britain to go from steam to diesel traction, Devons Road receiving its first diesels in July 1957 with its last steam engine being transferred away in August 1958. Whether the change was a profitable one is open to debate since the arrival of diesels was unaccompanied by any changes in operating practices that might have produced benefits. Prior to 1958 the normal load for a Standard 3F 0-6-0T from Willesden to Poplar (for example) was thirty-six loaded 13-ton mineral wagons. After 1958 the limit for a Type 1 diesel was twenty-eight: a reduction of 22%! English Electric Type 1, D8015 passes Willesden Goods depot on its way to Kensal Green Junction on Tuesday 1 September 1959 with a service from Willesden High Level Sidings to the North London. The bridge crossing the LNWR main line in the distant background carries the Midland connection from Acton Wells to Cricklewood. (L Nicolson/ transporttreasury.co.uk)

Watching trains at South Acton was invariably an interesting pastime because of the variety of traffic that passed through the station. If any of these trains could be regarded as special then it was Willesden Target 92: a Super D 0-8-0 turn which served the Hammersmith & Chiswick branch. The working was complicated by the fact the train had to reverse at South Acton and to facilitate matters the train engine ran light from Willesden to South Acton to await its train which arrived behind another 0-8-0. The train engine then backed onto the rear of the train and worked it down the Hammersmith branch, serving the busy Acton coal depot on the way. The return service did not reverse at South Acton but continued westward to Kew Yard where the engine ran round its train and collected any Willesden traffic that was on hand. The driver of Super-D 49277 of Willesden prepares to surrender the one-engine-in-steam token as Target 92 comes off the branch with the Hammersmith - Kew leg of the trip. (A E Bennet/transporttreasury.co.uk)

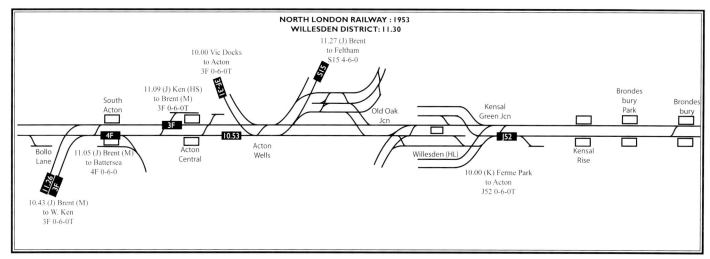

NORTH LONDON RAILWAY : 1953
WILLESDEN DISTRICT: 11.30

CONTROLLER'S LOG: Late morning is an unusual time of day for travelling post offices but the North London is no ordinary railway and adding to the general variety of traffic is a train of empty TPO's which are brought from Hornsey Carriage Sidings each morning to turn on the Dalston angle. This is a working of fairly recent date since the pre-war vehicles were equipped with traducers on both sides of each coach whilst those more recently

and Dalston East so if needs be, the method of working can be reversed. Propelling, however, is only permitted in clear weather and when fog descends as it often does in North London, the engine has to run round the train at both Dalston station and Dalston East.

Another form of unusual working happens when imports at Poplar exceed the booked train service - quite a regular occurrence - and a block trainload is made up for somewhere on the West

smaller than a 5XP 4-6-0 (a Devon Roads 4MT 2-6-0 can only take 39 vans at class C) which means commandeering a Jubilee from either Willesden or Camden loco and running it light to Poplar for the special. An experienced Controller will turn this to his advantage by insisting that the crew selected sign the road both to Poplar and to Rugby or Northampton so that they can work the train not only across the North London but down an appreciable

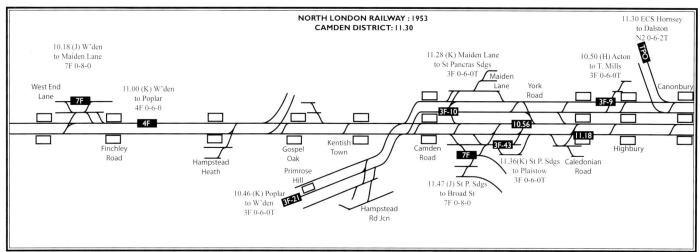

NORTH LONDON RAILWAY : 1953
CAMDEN DISTRICT: 11.30

introduced are one-sided and therefore have to be turned after each journey. Since dealing with the vehicles one by one on a turntable would be a cumbersome and time-consuming job, the TPO's are brought to Dalston station by a GNR 0-6-2T and propelled over the angle to Dalton East before returning to Hornsey Carriage sidings via Bounds Green. The concession to propel is granted only to the TPO service but applies in both directions between Dalston

Coast main line. How the train is dealt with depends on the volume and nature of traffic but if it is urgent traffic, fruit for example, and there are fifty wagons or less then the ideal is to load as many as possible into fitted vans so that the train can run as a class C express goods and enjoys a priority that is almost on a par with an express passenger.

The problem is finding a suitable engine since 50 wagons at class C requires nothing

section of the LNWR as well. When such an arrangement is made, it goes without saying that an exceptional effort is made to give both the light engine and the special train the highest possible priority. For more mundane traffic target 37 has to suffice, its 0-6-0T presently engaged in making up a train at Poplar for Willesden. The train will take only forty-seven wagons and will run at a considerably lower speed than a class C express!

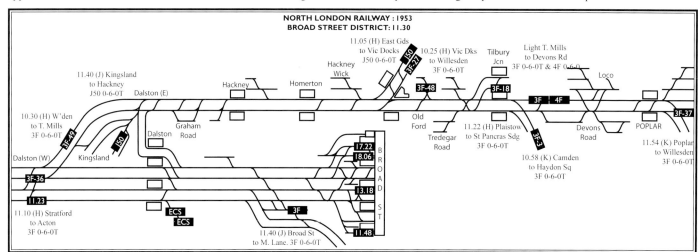

NORTH LONDON RAILWAY : 1953
BROAD STREET DISTRICT: 11.30

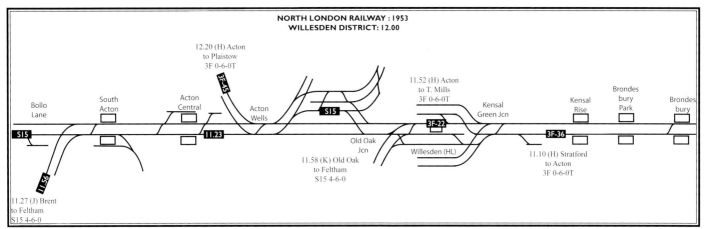

CONTROLLER'S LOG: There are still quite a number of trains at large although the threat of congestion has receded somewhat; a circumstance that is as well since, if the system is going to be graced by any special passenger trains, midday is about the time of day when they appear. It has to be stated, however, that the North London is not the first choice for the routing of trains - its own services leave precious little scope for additional trains - and

interesting to note that although the train passes through Stratford, it does not simply continue down the GE main line to Southend Victoria but takes, instead, the Forest Gate connection to the LTSR.

The return service leaves Southend at 18.45 to pass Victoria Park at 20.00, well after the evening peak has subsided. On the days that the train runs, close attention has to be paid to the state of the line between Dalston West

before the night trains. The trio of departures is made up of Target 12 at 12.40 with local traffic for St Pancras Sidings, a GN working at 13.27 for Ferme Park and. a Willesden turn at 13.57 which takes all LNW traffic apart that dealt with at Camden. Attention is drawn to the fact that the engine of the Willesden is a class 4 and will take 58 wagons of goods - the limit is 60 - against the 47 of a Standard 0-6-0 tank.

The Inspector is also reminded that the GN

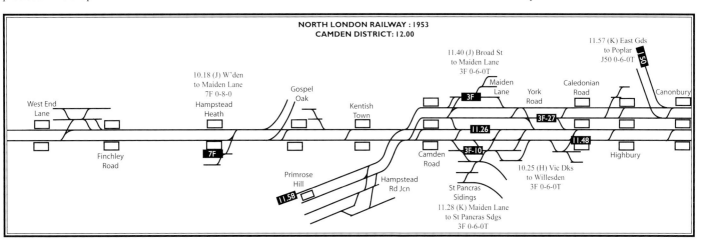

visiting trains, if not rare, are unusual. The usual visitor appears about once a week, usually on either a Wednesday or Thursday, during the summer holiday months and comes from either Tring or Watford Junction formed by an ordinary suburban set of non-corridors and a Watford 2-6-4 Tank. Running via Camden, the service passes Primrose Hill at about mid-day - the timings vary by a few minutes each time the train runs - and is allowed about thirteen minutes to reach Victoria Park, the train then running to Southend Central via Stratford, Forest Gate Junction, Barking and the LTSR line. It is

and Victoria Park, making sure that any goods trains for the Great Eastern are held back at Canonbury until the special has passed.

Such workings are irregular and special trains from further afield tend to be diverted away from the North London. Services, for example, from York to Dover are usually run up the Midland main line so that all the North London sees of them is over the short section between Acton Wells and Kew East.

Attention turns to Poplar for a quick chat with the Inspector. Three trains are booked to leave in close order after which there is very little

train runs direct to Ferme Park and does not take Clarence Yard traffic. Should it happen - and the PLA are quite adept at springing surprises on the LM Inspector - that there is a significant volume of Clarence Yard traffic then moving them is a simple matter of asking the Knebworth Controller if he will accept the 13.27 as a half and half: Clarence Yard's on the engine and Ferme Park's on the brake.

Making a change from the many Standard 3F 0-6-0 tanks in the area, one of the NLR 2F tanks appears from Poplar docks to run light to Devons Road for relief.

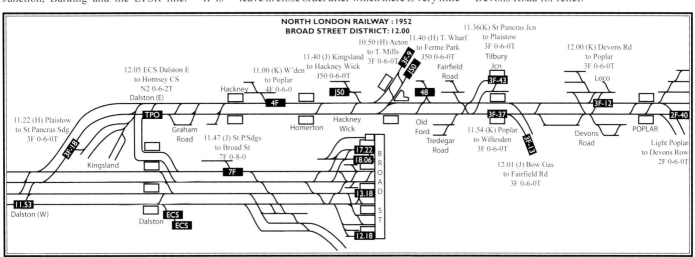

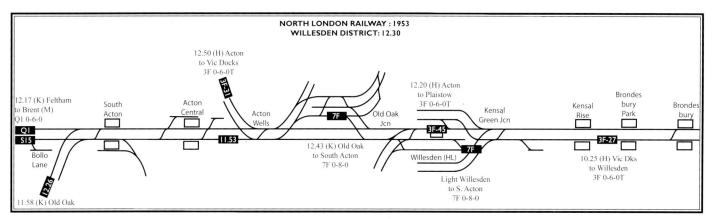

NORTH LONDON RAILWAY : 1953
WILLESDEN DISTRICT: 12.30

CONTROLLER'S LOG: It will have been noticed that one of the busiest locations on the North London is St Pancras Sidings so much so that the yard has a rightful claim to being the centre of the system. The reason for the level of activity - the yard has about forty arrivals and forty departures a day: a train every eighteen minutes - is the single-line branch from the Midland which hosts about a dozen trains in each direction, most being made up of wagons

thirty-seven but the latter has to have a vacuum braked brake van next to the engine and a 20-ton brake on the rear.

The yard is currently occupied with Target 18 which has just arrived from Plaistow and has forty minutes in which to shunt out any Midland traffic it may have brought before leaving for Camden.

There are some interesting developments taking place at the Western end of the section

(The service invites confusion of identity since the working to South Acton is Target 76, changing to Target 92 once the second 0-8-0 has taken over. The matter is generally resolved by simply referring to the train as the 'ammersmith!).

The use of a Super-D on the Hammersmith branch may seem an extravagance but it is a long diagram and water capacity has to be taken into account. 0-8-0's are in any case the

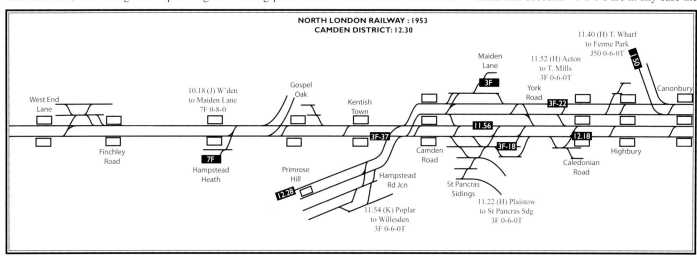

NORTH LONDON RAILWAY : 1953
CAMDEN DISTRICT: 12.30

that have arrived in main line goods workings from the North and either need to cross London without getting tied up in the coal traffic at Cricklewood or are destined for Poplar docks. The volume of traffic is impressive with the Kentish Town 3F 0-6-0T's bringing 28 wagons with each trip. There is also a single-line connection from St Pancras Sidings to the Great Northern at Kings Cross but this is less well used and normally has only one train; the 08.30 from Kings Cross, returning at 09.20. A J52 0-6-0T is allowed to bring twenty-three wagons of goods from Kings Cross and can return with

where a a 7F 0-8-0 is about to leave Old Oak Yard with daily trip for Acton Coal yard and Hammersmith. Since the train has to reverse at South Acton, the working is not allowed to leave Old Oak until another 0-8-0 is waiting at South Acton, ready to couple up to the rear of the train to take it over the Hammersmith branch.

The second Super-D, which has come light from Willesden Loco, can be seen crossing over at Kensal Green Junction and as soon as it has arrived at South Acton, the tip can be given to Old Oak to let the train leave.

standard LNW engine for trip working.

At the Eastern end of the line some old friends are on the point of leaving. Target 48 which has been shunting at Old Ford and knocking the 14.24 Camden into shape for some hours is on the point of leaving light for Devons Road where it will be relieved by a late turn crew before returning to Old Ford for another six hours of shunting. The J50 0-6-0T which has spent most of the morning shunting at Hackney Wick has finished its day's work and is on the point of leaving with a train for Ferme Park.

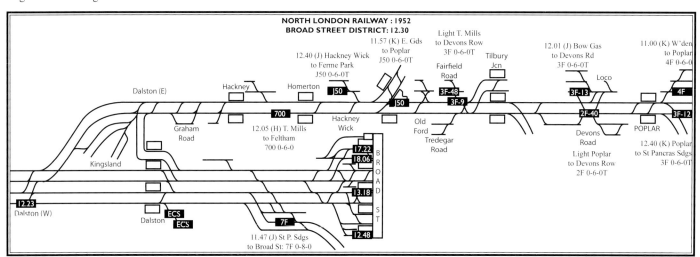

NORTH LONDON RAILWAY : 1952
BROAD STREET DISTRICT: 12.30

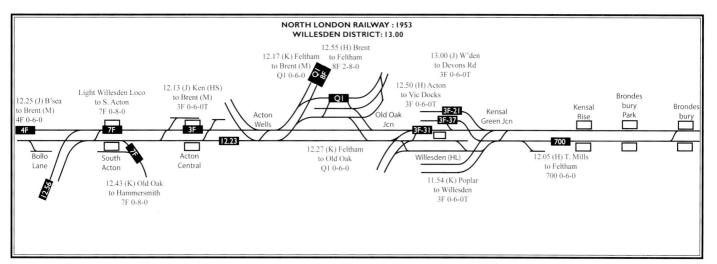

CONTROLLER'S LOG: One watches with some concern the activities at South Acton where the Hammersmith trip is in the process of reversing. It has been brought into South Acton by one LNWR 0-8-0 and will be taken forward by another which has come light from Willesden to back onto the rear of the train and work it up the branch. Ideally the manoeuvre will be accomplished without delay to the passenger service; the train departing for

press about the ex-LNER Scotch Goods, 15.00 Kings Cross Goods to Edinburgh (Niddrie), very little is heard of the LM equivalent which is rather sad since the latter is, in its early stages, a North London service. Leaving Broad Street at 13.10 the train is hauled as far as Camden by a parallel-boiler 2-6-0 which gives way to a 5XP 4-6-0 before repairing to Camden Loco to prepare for the 16.30 Euston - Bletchley passenger. The train is remarshalled

C - all wagons piped and at least half the train brake fitted - from Camden. The reason for the brakes not being connected at Broad Street is simply that most would have to be disconnected at Camden and this would cause unnecessary delay.

As the last checks are made to the 13.10, a pair of engines arrives coupled from Camden Loco. One is the Black 5 4-6-0 for the 13.43 Camden express goods - very often extended to

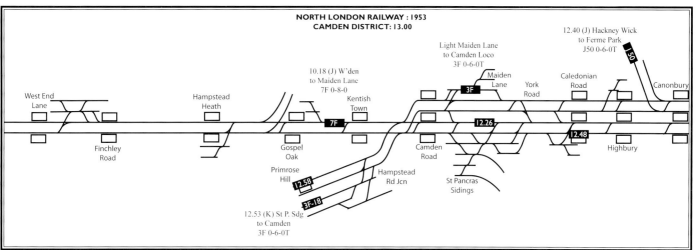

Hammersmith before the 12.23 Broad Street - Richmond comes into sight, and the inward engine getting away light to Willesden before any damage can be done to the 12.56 passenger from Richmond. The two-engine ritual is to minimise the time the train takes to reverse and is not attempted in the return direction; the train running through to Kew Bridge North and running round there.

Although one hears a great deal in the railway

during the engine change and on departure consists of forty-five wagons in three sections: Wigan (detached at Crewe), Carlisle exchange traffic and Glasgow (Buchanan Street). Not infrequently the train is oversubscribed and is run in two parts; the first being the booked service conveying only traffic for Scotland, the second taking the Wigan and Carlisle wagons.

Although the train leaves Broad Street as a class K unbraked service, it runs as a class

Crewe as a relief to the Glasgow train - whilst the other is Target 2, a Standard 3F tank which earlier worked the 10.30 Haydon Square to Camden and is on its way to take up the 14.35 trip to Devons Road. The North London gets its money's worth from the small 0-6-0T, its diagram keeping it in traffic for more than 24 hours. Later in the day it will work from Victoria Docks to Acton and is unlikely to return to Devons Road until the small hours.

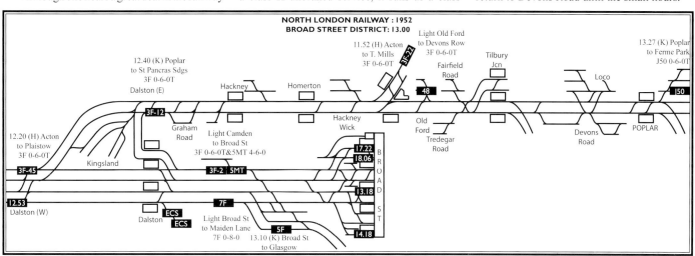

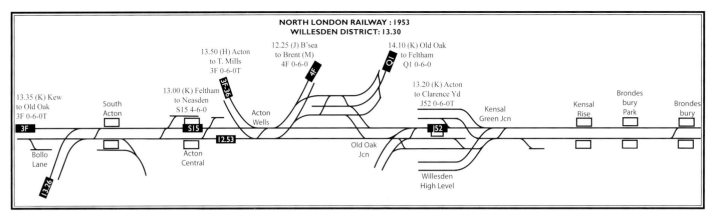

NORTH LONDON RAILWAY : 1953
WILLESDEN DISTRICT: 13.30

CONTROLLER'S LOG: One aspect of operations that might have escaped notice is the thoughtful way in which the off-peak passenger service is run from Broad Street, the Willesden electric leaving at eighteen minutes past the hour with the Richmond service following only five minutes later. This leaves an interval of twenty-five minutes between successive pairs of trains which allows the more important goods services to be run down the fast lines to Camden Road without fear of delaying the passenger service. The 13.10 and 13.32 departures from Broad Street Goods are beyond question, important services and it is wholly undesirable

variance of up to thirty minutes on either side of the schedule is not unusual - they are best regulated on the run.

One particular train that has be to carefully regulated between passenger trains and through services is the 10.18 Willesden to Maiden Lane which serves the intermediate yards on the Willesden - Kentish Town stretch and is now working Gospel Oak yard, the last port of call before terminating at Maiden Lane. With only two passenger trains an hour the prospects of a clash should be minimal but if it is given the road from somewhere like Finchley Road when a through goods is just getting to grips

mind. A J50 0-6-0 approaches Victoria Park for Clarence Yard with a goods from Victoria Docks whilst another passes Devons Road with a train from Poplar to Ferme Park. On the far side of the section a J52 0-6-0T passes Willesden with a 38-wagon Acton - Clarence Yard service which will run via Camden Road and reverse at Kingsland.

As ever, the area around Acton Wells - the crossroad of North London services in and out of Acton and North & South Western Junction workings between Brent Midland and Feltham - is a melting pot of trains; the continuum of through trains being varied with a little activity

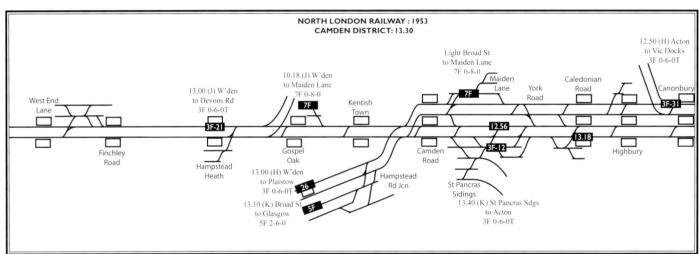

NORTH LONDON RAILWAY : 1953
CAMDEN DISTRICT: 13.30

that they should be relegated to the slow lines between Dalston West and Camden Road where they could quite easily find themselves at the rear of a queue of out of course trip workings. Were the passenger trains to be less imaginatively arranged, the results could be serious. The service into Broad Street is not so nicely arranged but since the arrival on the area of goods trains can be somewhat random - a

with the climb further back, the latter is likely to be brought to a stand and, if the engine is a 3F 0-6-0T hauling a full load, may have trouble restarting, a state of affairs that will very quickly react on the passenger service. Such matters are not usually allowed for in the time-table and in cases such as this intervention is justified.

Although it is only early afternoon, the goods service is shaping up with overnight traffic in

at Old Oak yard where the Q1 0-6-0 that arrived with the 12.27 from Feltham has turned and is preparing to leave with the 14.10 return service. On its way into Old Oak from the West is the local service from Kew Bridge North, train of mineral empties worked by a Willesden 3F 0-6-0T trip engine.

Old Oak, which operates in fits and jerks, will then remain quiet for the next three hours.

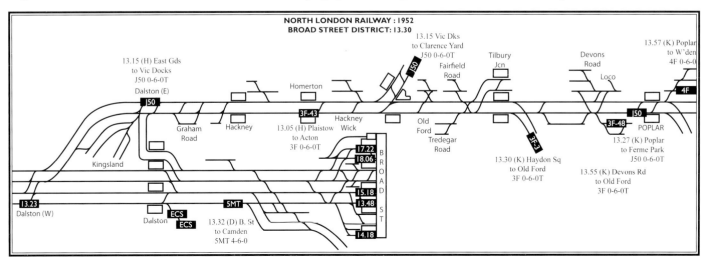

NORTH LONDON RAILWAY : 1952
BROAD STREET DISTRICT: 13.30

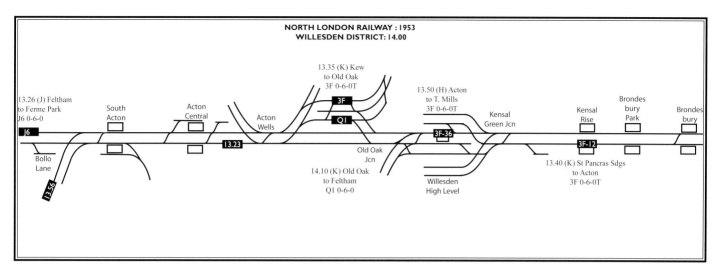

NORTH LONDON RAILWAY : 1953
WILLESDEN DISTRICT: 14.00

CONTROLLER'S LOG: A question that often arises is how the railway deals with large and exceptional consignments of perishable traffic that suddenly arrive by ship and cannot be dealt with by the ordinary service? The answer lies in the simple but effective methods of organisation the railways have evolved since 1830 which allow the network to operate in a highly flexible manner. The first point, however, is that exceptional traffics do not normally

the North East. The Broad Street traffic can be moved locally but the other traffic will have to be moved by special trains and the details will be passed over to the Timing & Diagramming Office who will issue a notice to all concerned showing the timings of the trains and where the engines and men are to come from.

A most important element is the provision of empty banana wagons and the 135 vehicles concerned will, unless they happen to be

to Poplar is a matter for the District Controller but if they come via Feltham, Willesden or Acton, he will probably arrange for a Devons Road engine and men to perform the requisite number of trips to get the wagons into Poplar. Those that come up the East Coast main line will be worked direct to Poplar by Kings Cross since their crews sign the road. When the ship berths, the PLA will keep the Poplar Inspectors advised who, in turn, will advise the Controller

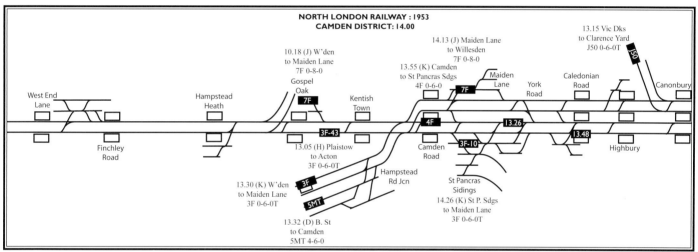

NORTH LONDON RAILWAY : 1953
CAMDEN DISTRICT: 14.00

appear out of the blue but are advised by the shipping company who give details of the ship, when and where it is due to dock, the volume of traffic - bananas, for example - and their destinations. This information will be received by the Regional Office who will convert the cargo tonnage into wagons and calculate that the shipment will mean 40 vans from Poplar to Broad Street, 50 from Poplar to Birmingham, 20 to Leeds and 25 for various destinations in

available locally (in which case they will be worked empty to Poplar to await the arrival of the ship), be passed over to the Central Wagon Office whose function it is to control and monitor the supply of empty wagons. They will locate the empty wagons and will instruct the appropriate Regional Offices to work them to the North London Railway, arriving about a week before the ship is due to dock. How the wagons find their way over the last few miles

of the time the loaded wagons are likely to be ready to depart.

Such matters are regarded as quite routine and so far as the District Controller is concerned, his main contribution is to make sure that the loco have allocated an engine and men to each of the workings. Once this is done the special trains become no different to any other except that they require much less attention than do the local trip services.

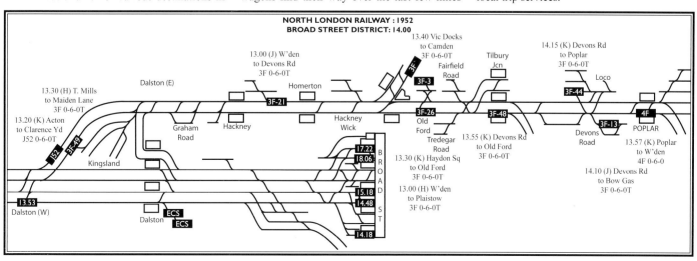

NORTH LONDON RAILWAY : 1952
BROAD STREET DISTRICT: 14.00

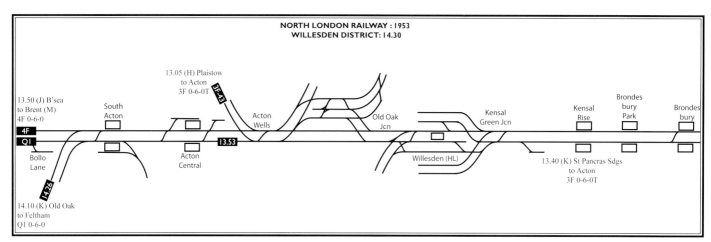

CONTROLLER'S LOG: With only an hour or so to go before the evening peak starts, an increased sense of urgency makes itself felt as one looks for workings that for one reason or another seem unlikely to finish their tasks before the rush-hour commences. Particular scrutiny is made of Targets 12 and 27 since they work the last trains from Acton and Willesden respectively and if either is delayed on the inward journey, then the 15.00 Willesden - Poplar and the 15.23 Acton - Temple Mills are likely to be lost. As it happens both trains have

at Victoria Park - to attach the Ilford tanks and then back onto the North London, passing Victoria Park at 15.25 to reach Shepherds Bush at 16.10 where the tanks will wait to be tripped to Kensington for attachment into a West of England Milk service. The 2-6-0 concerned works a long shift and will not return to Devons Road until almost ten tomorrow morning.

The area around St Pancras Sidings continues to swarm with activity; on one side Target 49 shunts the 13.30 from Temple Mills at Maiden Lane whilst on the other, a Willesden

very far away.

As ever, foreign engines add some colour to the proceedings and in addition to the J52 which is pounding its way up the bank to Clarence Yard with the 13.20 from Acton, a pair of J6 0-6-0's converge upon Hampstead Heath with Tottenham & Hampstead workings.

Although it is a little early to be thinking of traffic to connect with the overnight trains from Camden, there is still the interregnum of the peak hour to be considered and to ease any pressure that might arise later in the day, Target

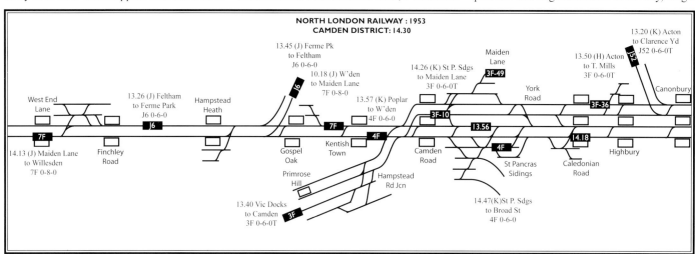

extended turn-round times, designed to absorb delays but nothing should be taken for granted.

Amongst all the coal and general goods traffic, milk is starting to make an appearance as a 4MT 2 6 0 rings off Devons Road Loco and runs light to Tredegar Road sidings to work the 14.40 Kensington milk empties; a service which takes a very circuitous path by running first of all to Channelsea, Stratford - with a reversal

4F 0-6-0 pulls onto the departure road with a train for Broad Street It will come out onto the up fast at York Road as soon as the 14.18 Broad Street to Willesden has passed on the down fast. In between target 10 navigates the four-road section with a transfer from St Pancras Sidings to Maiden Lane. It does no harm to remind the Maiden Lane Inspector to deal with Target 10 promptly since the 10.18 from Willesden is not

3 is arranged to serve both Haydon Square and Old Ford, clearing away the first tranche of any LNW overnight traffic that might be ready. Both depots have services to Camden later in the evening but Target 3 relieves some of the pressure. There will be inward traffic for Haydon Square until the morning but Old Ford will have an arrival from Camden in about an hour's time.

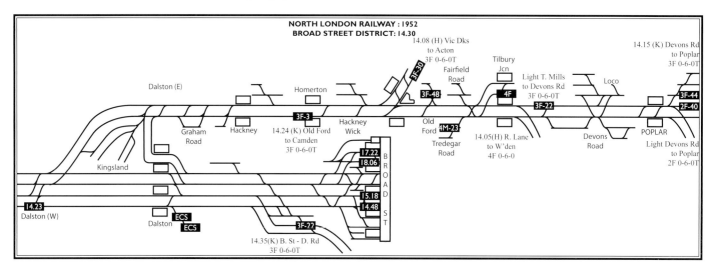

N2 0-6-2T 69589 rolls down the quarter-mile 1 in 60 bank immediately south of Dalston Junction and enters the station with an unidentified Great Northern train from Broad Street. Until their suspension during the war the Great Northern services were operated by the North London Railway using running powers that allowed a service of forty-four daily departures from Broad St to Gordon Hill (13 services), High Barnet (13), Alexandra Palace (10), New Barnet (5), East Finchley and Potters Bar (2 each) and one service to Cuffley. When the service resumed after the war it was operated by the Great Northern but ran only during the peak hours.

The N2's used on the Great Northern suburban services were far from being the only ex-LNER engines seen on the North London and much of the goods traffic from the East Goods, Finsbury Park, to Hackney and Poplar was handled by J50 0-6-0T's with J6 0-6-0's and J52 saddle tanks working between Ferme Park, Acton and Feltham. J50 (6)8968 of Ardsley (Wakefield) came to Hornsey in October 1952 and became a familiar sight on the East half of the North London. The class however had limited availability on the North London since it was barred between Canonbury Junction and Kew and between Gospel Oak and Ferme Park.

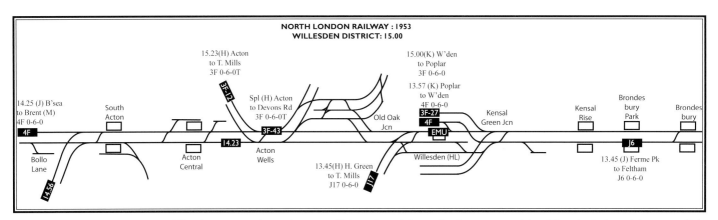

NORTH LONDON RAILWAY : 1953
WILLESDEN DISTRICT: 15.00

CONTROLLER'S LOG: Whilst the rate of change may have been imperceptible, there has nevertheless been a pronounced slackening of activity: the Kensal Green to Kentish Town section is very quiet with just one goods, a Great Northern service which entered the area at Gospel Oak, whilst the line east of Dalston is much quieter than it has been. The reason, of course, is to clear the way for the peak service and although there is an hour to go before Broad Street starts to hum with season tickets, a number of preparations are under way. The 3-car set that has been sitting in platform 5 since 10.50 this morning has been made up a

only sends one set light to Broad Street for the evening peak, all the others being fed into the system from Willesden High Level.

At various times in the early afternoon, discussions have been held with Mitre Bridge to ensure that the correct number of sets have been placed in diagram. In the unlikely event of their having to send out a three car set instead of a six car formation, it falls to us to manipulate the sets in traffic so that the shortfall can be made up with the minimum of harm. Usually, however, sufficient notice is given to allow the shortage to be made up from Croxley Green. It is with some satisfaction that we note the 15.00

approaching Victoria Park and has very little margin for delay since it has to get to Camden Road by 15.35 otherwise it will delay the Channelsea - Kensington Milk which in turn will delay the 15.37 Broad Street - Richmond. The margin is very tight but because of the state of play an extra six minutes is added to the train's schedule between Canonbury and Camden Road Junctions. If the train is not going to make the deadline then, as an alternative to letting it stand on the down goods at Camden road for two hours or more, consideration will have to be given to shunting the train in Maiden Lane and sending the engine light to Acton for

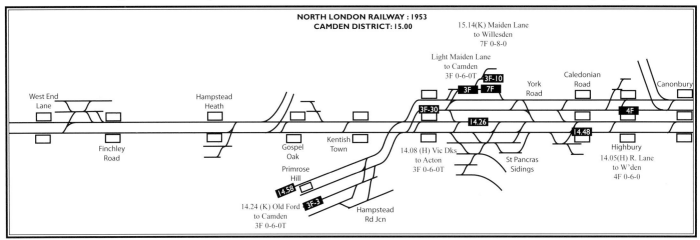

NORTH LONDON RAILWAY : 1953
CAMDEN DISTRICT: 15.00

6-coach set with the addition of the 13.58 ex Willesden Junction. The set will depart as the 15.18 to Watford Junction and later work the 17.47 Broad Street - Richmond. A set of empty DC coaches has come out of Mitre Bridge depot to reverse at Kensal Green Junction and form the 15.10 to Richmond and the 16.58 Broad Street to Watford. It is an interesting operational feature that although Mitre Bridge is the principal depot for the DC electrics, it

Willesden and the 15.23 Acton trains pulling out onto the main line in good time with, between them, a Hither Green to Temple Mills service which will take the Tottenham & Hampstead line from Gospel Oak and a Special from Acton to Devons Road. The latter is the final part of Target 43 which is available for Control Orders at Acton.

In the opposite direction, the 'whipper-in' is the 14.45 Temple Mills to Acton which is

its return working.

Another source of concern is Target 44, the 15.10 Poplar to St Pancras Sidings which has to run up the main line from Dalston West with no more than a three minute margin ahead of the Kensington Milk. The first step is to make sure that the signalman at Victoria Park understands that the normal laws of precedence must be reversed with the Class K - normally the lowest form of life - being given preference to a C!

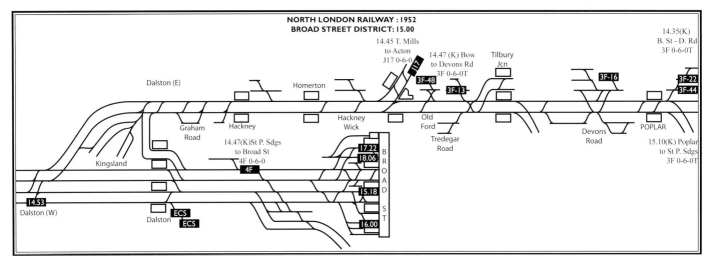

NORTH LONDON RAILWAY : 1952
BROAD STREET DISTRICT: 15.00

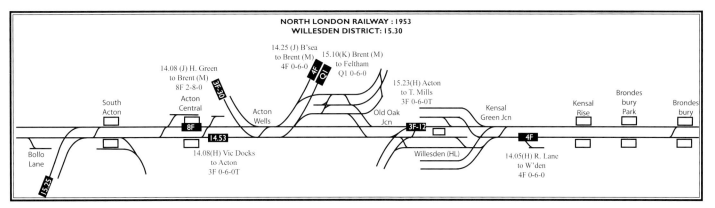

CONTROLLER'S LOG: *"Maiden Lane. Target 10: 47559 20 roughs."*

"You haven't pulled off for it yet?"

"It's ready to go. I'm just setting the road."

"Hold back. Have you had an Acton warned on Down 1?"

"Target 27 at thirty, Gospel Oak."

"No. Yes. Getting it from York Road now."

"Give the Acton the road then you can see about Target 10."

"Camden Road?"

"48219 and train for Brent, thirty Acton Wells."

wants a run down the Hampstead as soon as the down Watford passenger has cleared."

"What about the Milk?"

"The Milk is still back at Dalston. Anyway, I want the Acton goods first."

"Right you are."

"St Pancras Junction? Target 10 has 20 rough. Be with you in about fifteen minutes."

"What's it do next?"

"Your pilot for the next couple of hours and then light to Maiden Lane for the Parcels."

"Dalston West. Do you want this 3-2 down the slow and the Milk down No.2?"

"No. Both down No.2. In any case the

"Old Ford up at thirty-six and you can make the GN goods up at thirty-eight. Victoria Park."

"Target 27 up No.1 slow at thirty-six. Camden Road."

"Hello, Knebworth? Three-ten Vic Docks. 68982, Hornsey 12.30 men, 45 equal 45 Ferme Park includes two registered New Barnet."

"Nothing for you, yet. Wait. 69499 is the Broad Street turnover engine."

"Passenger up at thirty-seven. Acton Wells."

"Empty cars from Dalston for the four-fifteen Richmond at forty, behind the up

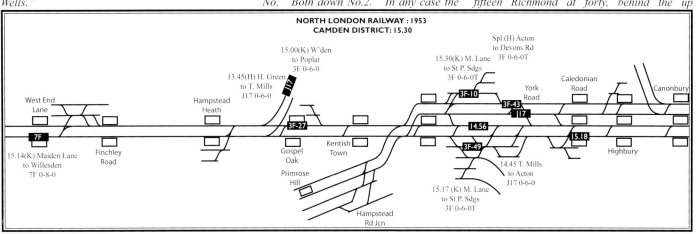

"Canonbury. What's this 3-2 on No.1 Down?"

"Special ex Acton. Right away Devons Road."

"Target 12 up by the High Level at thirty for Temple Mills."

"Channelsea Milk arrived at my home at thirty-one, Eastern. There's a 3-2 on the pound."

"Camden Road, hello."

"Next down No.1 is a 3-2 for Acton. It

3-2 is for St Pancras. I thought I'd told you once."

"OK. The 3-2'll be passed me at thirty-three and the milk at thirty-six."

"Junction? Next down No.1 after the passenger is Target 44 from Poplar. Take him straight in, it's got the Milk up its backside."

"Down Passenger time at Camden Road Acton down the Hampstead at thirty-five. Target 27 up No.1 at thirty five."

"Well done."

passenger."

"Canonbury Junction? You'll have engine 69499 off the GN in about twenty minutes. Light to Broad Street for the four-fifteen Hertford."

"69499. Special Acton up at forty."

"Sidings. Forty-four inside clear at forty. Where d'you want the engine?"

"Engine and Brake for the Kingsland pilot. Where's the Milk?"

"Just had it offered. It'll pass here at forty-two, down No.2. On time."

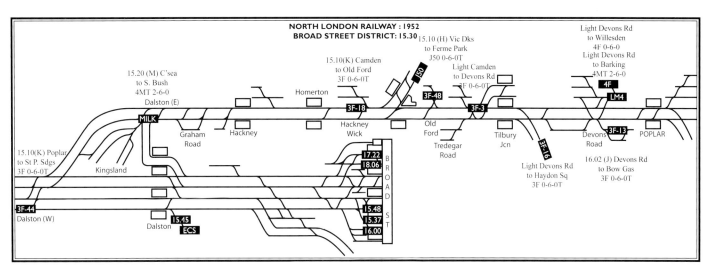

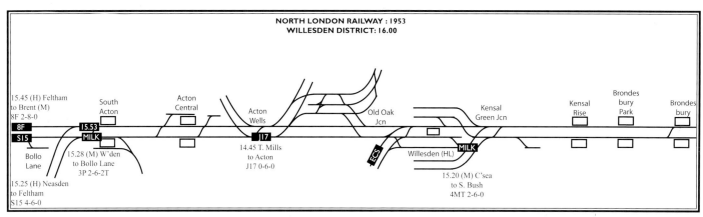

CONTROLLER'S LOG: Having successfully - one hopes - cleared the route of goods trains, the scene is set for the evening peak to start and whilst the service may be less than that of many other London termini, trains are due to leave Broad Street at an average of one every five minutes for the next hour; nine trains being North London electrics and three being Great Northern services. The method of working the latter is similar to that of the morning peak with a turnover engine arriving in Broad Street to work out the first train, the engine of which works the second and so on. All are worked by the Standard GNR N2 0-6-

for twenty-nine and thirty-three minutes respectively - and this allows a certain amount of operating flexibility. If things are running very badly on the up road, the booked diagrams will be abandoned and trains will be turned round as soon as they arrive. A spare set of men is kept at arms length to take over in the event of crewing problems

Goods traffic is not entirely eliminated and two services that are watched closely are the 15.30 Willesden to Devons Road which runs via Camden and the 16.06 Broad Street to Camden: both cut things very fine indeed. The latter may be run down the fast line in order

engines are also due at this time from Camden to Broad Street and, with luck, the order will be: Target 37 up the slow, the two light engines up the fast as far as Dalston Western, the Watford passenger up the fast, followed by Target 44 up the fast behind the passenger.

As can be seen from the line diagram, the eastern section is pretty quiet; mainly the result of having its supply of trains cut off. A Willesden - Poplar train is approaching Hackney whilst, behind it, an Acton to Temple Mills service takes the pound at Dalston Western Junction. One might have thought that with the Great Northern peak service tying up the

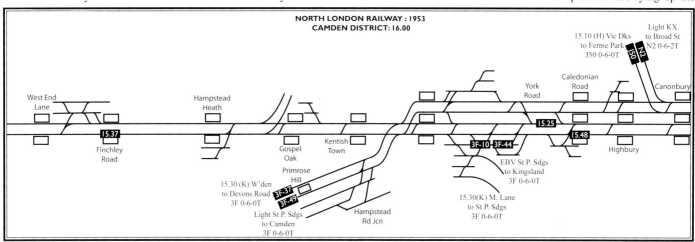

2T's except for the 16.43 departure which is worked by a B1 4-6-0.

Ensuring the punctuality of outward trains is of the first priority but so is that of the inward trains since any delay to them runs the risk of being passed onto the down service. As an insurance against trouble affecting the inward electrics, most are given extended turn-round times in Broad Street - the 16.04 and 16.13 arrivals, for example, remain in Broad Street

to get it out of the way at Hampstead Road as quickly as possible.

There is also Target 44 to be considered which runs engine and brake to Kingsland from St Pancras Sidings and has therefore to run along the up fast. Hopefully, Target 37 - the 15.30 from Willesden - will get to Camden Road in time to be crossed out of harms way on the up slow from whence it can get to Kingsland without doing too much damage. A pair of light

slow lines from Canonbury Junction to Dalston that these two goods trains would be the last for some time yet the GN - who carry considerable weight at timetable meetings - have managed to push through an East Goods - Victoria Park goods which passes Canonbury Junction at what would otherwise be the forbidden time of 16.18. Admittedly the train needs only two or three minutes to clear Dalston but it does illustrate how much muscle the GN has!

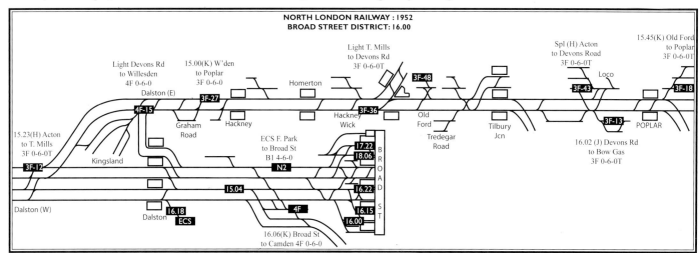

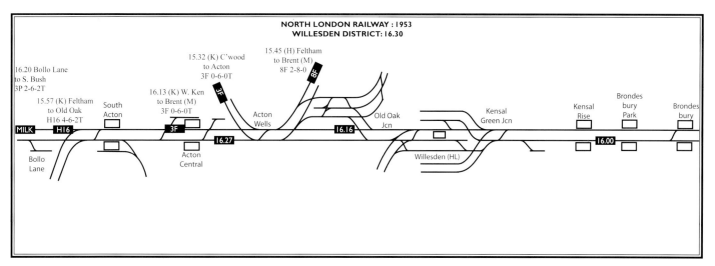

CONTROLLER'S LOG: Now we see the railway almost transformed and, apart from the St Pancras Sidings pilot, without a steam engine between South Acton and Dalston where Target 44 is crossing over to Kingsland and holding up the stock of the 16.56 Broad Street to Gordon Hill in the process. Not that the few minutes delay will do any harm since the stock cannot be admitted to its platform until the 16.35 Broad Street to Hertford has departed and its inward engine shunted out of the way.

Even the section east of Dalston is uncommonly quiet and the only main line service to be seen is the East Goods to Victoria Dock goods. Out of sight and adjacent to the Fenchurch Street - Shoeburyness line, Target 13 gets ready to haul a train of empties to Devons Road via Fairfield Road. This is the working's fourth departure from the Gas Works and the engine has one more trip to complete after this one.

Life is rather more interesting at the Kew end of the line where goods to and from Brent remains heavy. An 8F 2-8-0 has just taken the Midland line at Acton Wells with a Feltham - Brent service whilst behind it is a standard 3F 0-6-0T with a train for Brent from West Kensington. Following these is an H16 4-6-2T with a train of miscellaneous traffic for the

currently waiting for Target 44 to clear the road, to form the 16.43 to Royston.

ex-LNWR which will be remarshalled in Old Oak Yard, the Southern tank working back to Feltham with a train of coal in just over an hour's time. Finally, in a masterstroke of regulation, come the Bollo Lane milk empties which will run to Shepherds Bush via Old Oak Junction, West London Junction and Mitre Bridge. As a class C the train is theoretically entitled to a high degree of priority but somehow it has come to be placed fourth in a queue of slow moving minerals trains and will be calling at all signals

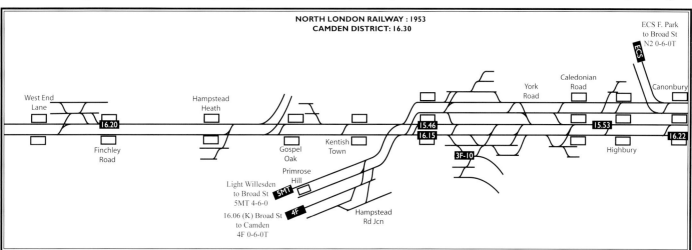

In any case Broad Street has its hands full with the two 2-6-4T's that have arrived coupled from Camden for the two steam-worked services to Tring and the N2 0-6-2T for the 17.06 Welwyn Garden City.

The first GN train to depart is the 16.35 for Hertford and is notable for the fact that its stock was worked, not by the usual 0-6-2T, but by a B1 4-6-0; the latter then backing onto the stock

to Old Oak. A cynic might say that given the class of engine booked to the train, an LMS 3P 2-6-2T, it would do no better with a clear run!

Kingsland Yard is about to have the attentions of two trains at once. Target 37 en route from Willesden to Devons Road is putting off wagons of coal for the adjacent LNW yard; vehicles that Target 44 will shunt and position as soon as 37 has left.

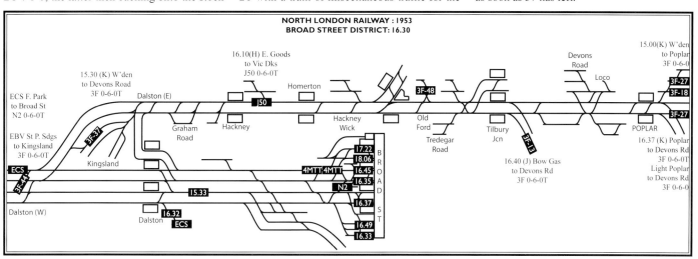

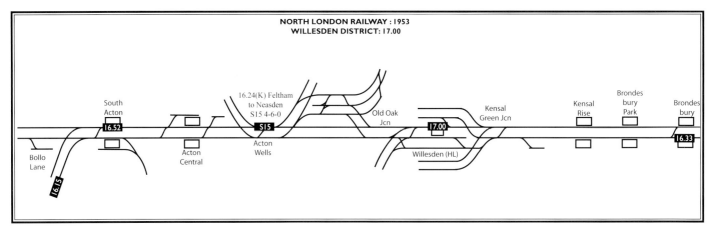

NORTH LONDON RAILWAY : 1953
WILLESDEN DISTRICT: 17.00

CONTROLLER'S LOG: The embargo has now fallen on the western end of the section which, apart from a solitary Feltham to Neasden train, is free from steam workings. In fact the only steam train at work on the main line is Target 37 which is passing Victoria Junction en route to Devons Road after putting off part of its load at Kingsland. A very different railway to that which was evident an hour or two ago - how useful an extra pair of rails would be between Camden Road and Kensal Green! Not the least of the problems caused by the peak service is the fact that the three hour closure to

wagons; each train being limited to thirty-five wagons as far as Camden where another twenty are added whilst the engines are relieved by sets of main line crews and worked through to various points on the West Coast. The odd-man out is the 22.02 from Broad Street which does not call at Camden (other than a two-minute pause to change crews) but runs through to Stockport. The activity at Camden goods during this period has to be seen to be believed and life would be a great deal easier if the movement of goods from Broad Street did not have to wait until the peak had finished before

17.22 and 18.02, the only concession made to passengers in the Harrow and Watford areas is to run the 16.49 and 17.17 electrics non-stop to Willesden Junction. The effect is more psychological than real since the overall saving in time is no more than five minutes and one wonders whether the timetable could not be redrafted to incorporate a number of limited stop trains that would emulate the steam timing of thirty-nine minutes to Watford Junction. The all-stations electric takes sixty-three minutes for the 22-mile journey and can scarcely be described as an advertisement for

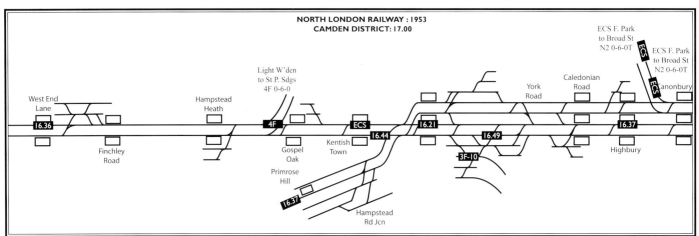

NORTH LONDON RAILWAY : 1953
CAMDEN DISTRICT: 17.00

goods traffic means that when the embargo is lifted, freight operations start like a cork from a shaken bottle. Whilst the line is given over to season-ticket holders, goods traffic is being loaded and has to connect with services from Camden, Willesden and Clarence Yard. The most urgent traffic comes from Broad Street goods which between six o'clock and ten, despatches no less than ten main line goods trains for a total of three hundred and fifty

sending the first of the trains out.

The engine for these trains drift over light in one's and two's, the first - a Black Five 4-6-0 from Willesden Loco for the 18.11 goods - waiting outside Broad Street for the road into the goods yard.

For the rest, the service is a monotony of electric trains with very little to distinguish one from another. Almost all are stopping trains and, apart from the two steam departures at

modern traction.

Line occupation is a problem when it comes to mixing trains of widely differing speeds but as things are at the moment, the Harrow, Bushey and Watford passengers tend to ignore the electric services and instead overcrowd the two Tring steam services. Why, one wonders, is it not possible to divide trains at Willesden Junction; the leading three coaches making limited stops between there and Watford.

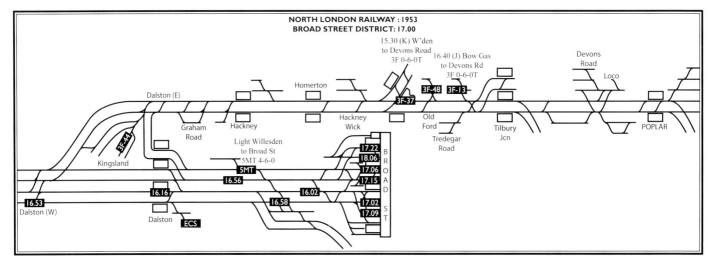

NORTH LONDON RAILWAY : 1953
BROAD STREET DISTRICT: 17.00

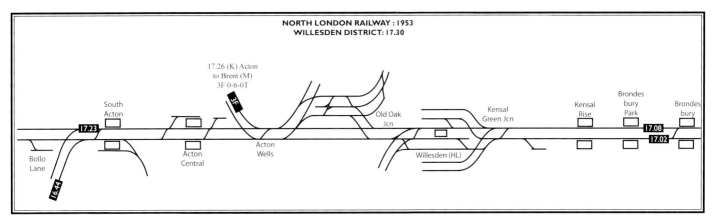

NORTH LONDON RAILWAY : 1953
WILLESDEN DISTRICT: 17.30

CONTROLLER'S LOG: To the spectator standing on Caledonian Road station, the sight of electric trains arriving and departing every few minutes must be fairly impressive (although he will get more for his money south of the Thames) yet to the operator the peak period is rather a dull time since it is made up of passenger trains which require very little in the way of intervention and most rush hours call for little more effort than that needed to record the progress of trains. One's mind is kept alert by imagining problems such as the trailing set of the 17.12 becoming derailed - no injuries - at

jacking the bogies up and swinging them onto the rails. Just the sort of scenario that provides the opportunity for advancement!

The focus is still on the electric service but there are a few more steam workings in evidence than there were half an hour ago. One is an Acton to Brent(M) trip - not a route upon which an embargo is placed - and another is a Poplar to Finsbury Park goods which should not reach the Great Northern until the worst of their peak service is over. The tricky part will be filtering the train from Canonbury Junction to Finsbury Park since the GN service from Broad Street is

a Watford Junction 2-6-4T.

The sixty minutes between five and six is the busiest part of the peak service with twelve LMS and six GN trains leaving Broad Street where the level of activity is quite interesting. On the GN (or steam) side of the station, the 17.26 to Cuffley has just pulled out of platform 3; the engine that brought the stock in following the train to the end of the platform where it is held until the empty stock for the 17.45 to Hatfield arrives in platform 1 at 17.29. The engine is then shunted across to platform 1 to work the train to Hatfield. When the train

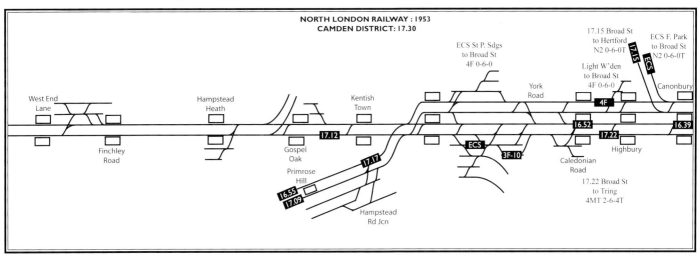

NORTH LONDON RAILWAY : 1953
CAMDEN DISTRICT: 17.30

Gospel Oak. The solution: call out the SM's at Gospel Oak and Kentish Town and get them to put in single line working over the up line whilst arranging for the passengers in the 17.12 to be transferred to the front unit which can be uncoupled and run forward without too much delay. How long the single-line working has to go on for depends upon how quickly the unit can be rerailed but it should be possible to drop the tool vans behind it and get the job done by

quite heavy at the time the Poplar train gets to Dalston and the margins in the timetable are, to say the least, optimistic.

Pulling out of St Pancras Sidings is the empty stock for the 18.02 Broad Street to Tring, the engine working it being a Willesden 4F 0-6-0 which will later work the 20.10 Broad Street to Camden goods. As the stock draws out of the siding, it is passed by its partner, the 17.22 Broad Street to Tring which is worked by

leaves at 17.45, the engine that brought that stock in will work the 17.53 to New Barnet and so the routine goes on. The odd man out is the 18.06 to Hertford North, the stock of which has been berthed in Broad Street since arriving with the 09.04 from Gordon Hill during the morning peak. This reduces the inward engines by one and to compensate for the loss the engine for the 17.06 to Welwyn Garden City comes in light from Kings Cross.

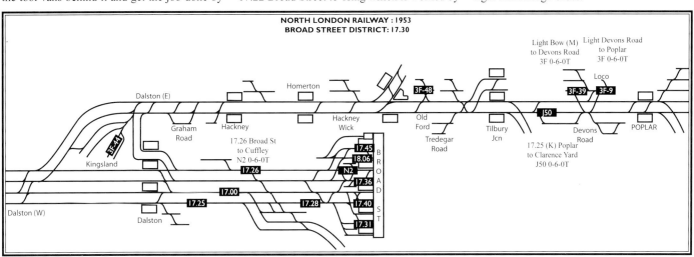

NORTH LONDON RAILWAY : 1953
BROAD STREET DISTRICT: 17.30

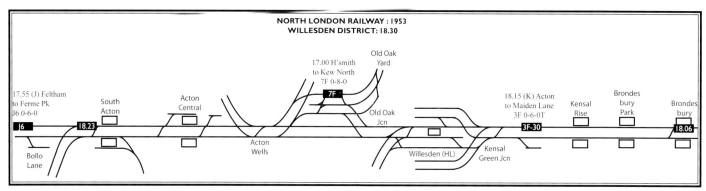

NORTH LONDON RAILWAY : 1953
WILLESDEN DISTRICT: 18.30

CONTROLLER'S LOG: The peak service is in its final moments, the remnant being the 18.32 Broad Street to Cuffley which will be followed as far as Finsbury Park by the engine which brought the empty stock in. The electric side of the station is similarly quiet with only three trains departing in the thirty minutes to seven o'clock.

Goods trains start to crawl out of the woodwork and life becomes altogether more interesting. There is not much more you can do with passenger trains other than watch them make their way up and down the line but goods

at the eastern end of the line, one being the 18.28 from Haydon Square and the other being the 19.00 from Old Ford: both former LNW goods depots. The Haydon Square service is of note since it is a class E express goods which, whilst unremarkable anywhere else, has a considerably higher priority than the rank and file class H, J and K's that make up the normal North London fare. Class E trains are only permitted to convey oil-axlebox vehicles and are the highest classification of goods train that a standard 3F 0-6-0T may work. Interspersed in this trains are a pair of light engines; the first

and 20.10 departures from Broad Street Goods can be seen passing Hampstead Heath on their way from Willesden Loco.

With the return of goods activity comes the appearance of foreign engines: two GNR J6 0-6-0's enter the district with Feltham - Ferme Park services, one at Kew with an up train and the other approaching Gospel Oak with a down service. Both are routed via the Tottenham & Hampstead. A third foreigner takes the angle at Dalston Western with the 17.50 Acton to Temple Mills.

The daily Hammersmith trip approaches

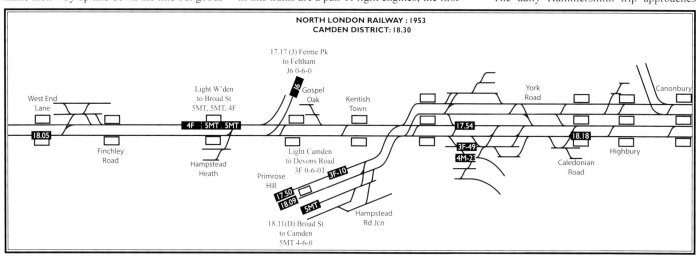

NORTH LONDON RAILWAY : 1953
CAMDEN DISTRICT: 18.30

trains require a considerable amount of work. You have to ensure that you have a load for each train, agree both the outward and the return load with the receiving district, divert the train if no traffic is available at the booked starting point, haggle with the receiving Controller as to whether the engine and crew should be sent for the back working and a hundred other matters associated with goods train work.

Two highly important services which have to make connections at Camden can be seen

being the relieving Broad Street pilot and the second being the engine for the 20.00 Victoria Docks - Acton.

The first of the evening express goods services from Broad Street, the 18.11 to Camden, has barely waited for the peak service to finish and has followed the 18.09 Broad Street to Watford as far as Hampstead Road Junction where it has been turned onto one of the arrival roads prior to making up its load before leaving for the North. The engines for the 19.35, 19.52

Old Oak at the end of its journey. It is an interesting working that takes an LNW 0-8-0 into an unlikely area of London and makes an interesting sight on the outward trip where one 0-8-0 has to haul the train to South Acton and another has to come on to the rear of the train for the reversal. On the return journey, the train does not reverse at South Acton but runs to Kew East Yard where the 0-8-0 runs round its train and collects any traffic that is on hand for Willesden and the North.

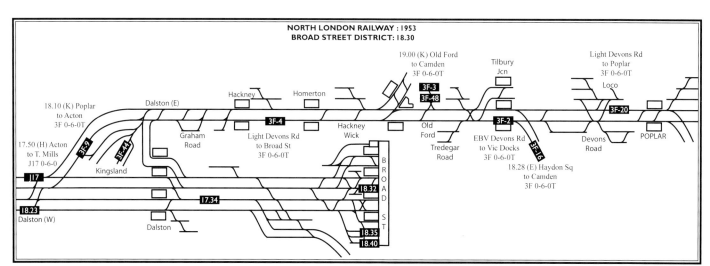

NORTH LONDON RAILWAY : 1953
BROAD STREET DISTRICT: 18.30

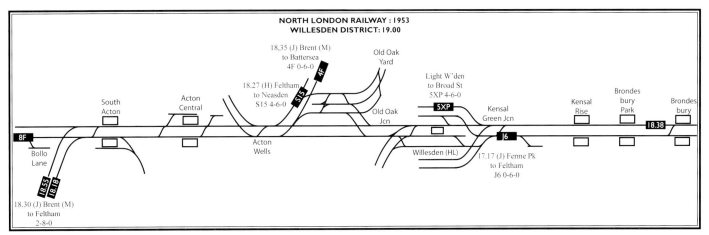

NORTH LONDON RAILWAY : 1953
WILLESDEN DISTRICT: 19.00

CONTROLLER'S LOG: The rush to get traffic to Camden in a hurry has produced an interesting regulating problem on the Dalston/Camden Road section. The gap between the 18.40 Broad Street to Watford and the 18.52 Broad Street to Richmond is just broad enough to accommodate an express goods as far as Camden Road yet into this space we have to fit two - the 18.45 Broad Street - Camden and the 18.28 Haydon Square - Camden - and hope that the 18.52 passenger remains unscathed. The slow, or No.1 line, cannot be used since it is occupied by the Target 9, the 18.10 Poplar -

will flog the engine a little and keep ahead of the passenger which, of course, has to call at all stations. Of all the trains from Broad Street, the 18.52 will probably be the one that the District Superintendent chooses to travel on and tomorrow there will be questions asking why it was checked all the way to Camden Road. Other trains that are on the run for Camden include services from Old Ford and Poplar.

Not all roads lead to Camden since a proportion of the traffic arriving in the docks is destined for the West of England and now the peak has finished, there will a steady flow of

steeply graded connection are on the generous side and the 3F 0-6-0T's that usually work the trips are allowed to take twenty-eight wagons of goods from the Midland and forty-five downhill - with wagon brakes applied - from the North London.

Its ports being largely industrial, fish traffic does not play a great part in the life of the North London but in the evenings it does act as a link between the Great Eastern and the Great Western by sending an engine to Stratford Market to take over the 15.50 from Beccles which brings in fish from both Yarmouth and Lowestoft. The train

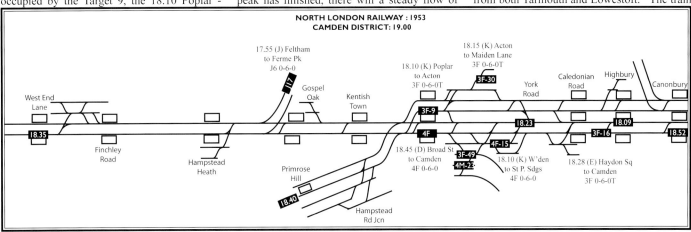

NORTH LONDON RAILWAY : 1953
CAMDEN DISTRICT: 19.00

Acton which is waiting for a road from Camden Road and will be there until the 18.52 Broad Street - Richmond has cleared. Target 9 could have been held at Western Junction to let the two Camden trains go down the slow line but this would have reacted on the string of trains coming down via Hackney.

Normally a class E worked by a class 3 engine would be loaded to forty-eight wagons but since the Haydon Square train is limited to thirty, there is a fighting chance that the driver

services to Acton from Poplar, Victoria Docks and Tilbury via Plaistow. Unlike Camden where the main line departures tend to be grouped between eight and midnight, services from Acton are more evenly spread; a factor that lessens the pressure a little on the North London. Another terminus that sees a steady flow of traffic is St Pancras Goods and the pilot that shuttles between St Pancras Sidings and Church Yard Sidings has been kept busy for some time. The loadings permitted on this

can load to thirty-five wagons or more and runs in two sections; the train being divided at Old Oak into an Acton section and a smaller LSWR section for Feltham. The engine concerned, a 4MT 2-6-0 is ringing off Devons Road loco and will run to Stratford Market via a reversal at Victoria Park. The LSWR section is worked from Old Oak by a Feltham S15 4-6-0.

A Crewe North Jubilee 5XP 4-6-0 backs down from Willesden Loco and makes its way to Broad Street for the 20.23 to Camden.

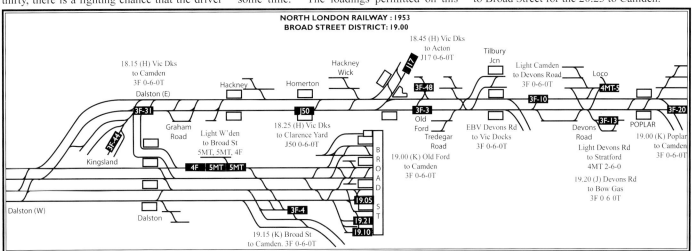

NORTH LONDON RAILWAY : 1953
BROAD STREET DISTRICT: 19.00

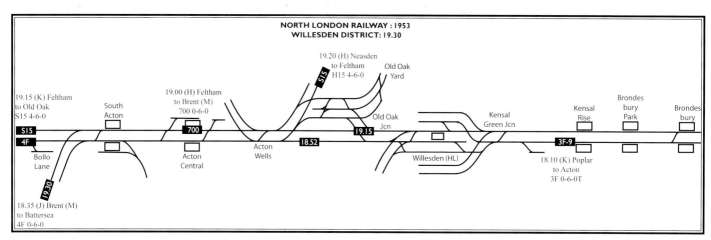

NORTH LONDON RAILWAY : 1953
WILLESDEN DISTRICT: 19.30

CONTROLLER'S LOG: In addition to the Stratford - Acton fish, the North London is responsible for another East-West connection in the form of the 19.15 Barking to Willesden Parcels which can be seen approaching Tilbury Junction after calling at all the LTSR stations on its route. Terminating in Willesden Junction the train will be routed via Primrose and Camden and will follow the 19.42 Broad Street to Watford from Dalston.

On most railways any half-decent passenger train should leave a goods train standing but not on the North London! Target 9, the 18.10 Poplar to Acton, was held at Camden Road to follow the 18.52 Broad Street to Richmond yet, allowing for a couple of minutes for the goods to get on the move once it had been given the road, the two trains have pretty well kept pace with each other for the last twenty minutes. The reason, of course, is because the passenger calls at all stations and it is only the stopping nature of the electrics that allows such a heavy programme of goods trains to be run. However, it is unwise to reverse the process by giving a goods train the road immediately ahead of a passenger!

Broad Street is considerably quieter than is was an hour ago, the steam workings have finished completely and the service is about to decline to the level of one Richmond service every half an hour, the last through service to Watford being the 19.42 departure. It needs hardly to be said that the complete absence of passenger trains on the Camden Road - Camden section makes the working of goods trains a great deal easier.

The four track section is the usual tangle of trains with Target 4 running the gauntlet of the 19.21 Broad Street - Watford: one gazes at its position on the peg-board, willing it to get to York Road and inside clear on the arrival line in the time it takes the electric to call at Highbury and Caledonian Road. Running parallel to Target 4 is a J17 0-6-0 with the 18.45 Victoria Docks to Acton which will be given a run from Camden Road ahead of the 19.28 Broad Street to Richmond. The thirteen minute margin should just about see the J17 clear of the main line at Acton Wells without harming the electric.

A second J17 can be seen at Hackney with a Victoria Docks to Old Oak train of LSWR exchanges and a third will soon enter the system at Gospel Oak with a Tottenham & Hampstead service from Temple Mills.

A number of light engines are making their way from Willesden Loco to Broad Street for the goods workings: one is passing Canonbury and another is at West End Lane. Both are 4-6-0's from distant parts of the LMS, one being a Jubilee or Patriot 5XP 4-6-0 from Crewe North Loco and the other, a Black Five from Warrington.

Foreign engines are also - as they often are - in evidence West of Acton Wells where a 700 0-6-0 and an S15 4-6-0 make their way to Brent and Old Oak respectively.

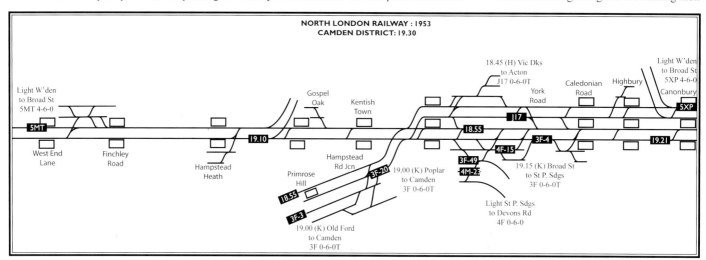

NORTH LONDON RAILWAY : 1953
CAMDEN DISTRICT: 19.30

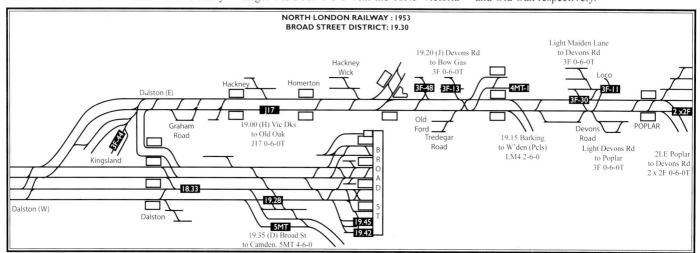

NORTH LONDON RAILWAY : 1953
BROAD STREET DISTRICT: 19.30

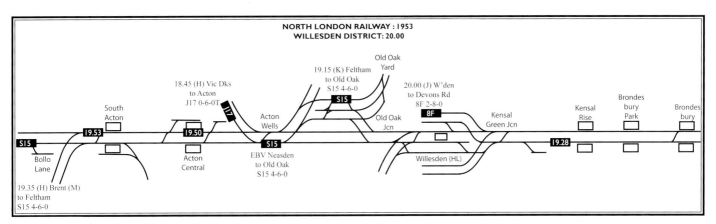

CONTROLLER'S LOG: East of Acton Wells, large engines are the exception to the rule and the most a casual observer is likely to see is the odd G2a that operates between Camden or Willesden and Broad Street. 8F 2-8-0's are quite uncommon and the only train to be diagrammed to one is pulling away from the High Level sidings at Willesden with fifty wagons of coal for Devons Road: some of tomorrow's supply for Bow Gas. Since the limit for the train is fifty wagons whilst an 8F

Old Oak. A third train, the 19.00 from Victoria Docks, is about half an hour away at Finchley Road whilst a fourth - the Stratford Fish - is approaching Victoria Park.

On paper the S15 arriving with the 19.15 from Feltham returns with the 20.52 Old Oak to Feltham and since this is the last service to Feltham for some time, one has to look very carefully at the traffic already in Old Oak yard and that being brought down by the 19.00 from Victoria Docks. The latter will be mainly goods

one for the Great Western and the other for the London South Western. The former is taken forward by the train engine at 21.15 whilst the remainder is worked to Feltham by the S15 4-6-0 that came in from Neasden.

Traffic is moving nicely between Broad Street and Camden with one train running down the goods arrival towards Camden, another passing Dalston Junction whilst a third waits for the right away from Broad Street. Waiting to enter the yard is a 5XP 4-6-0 that has just

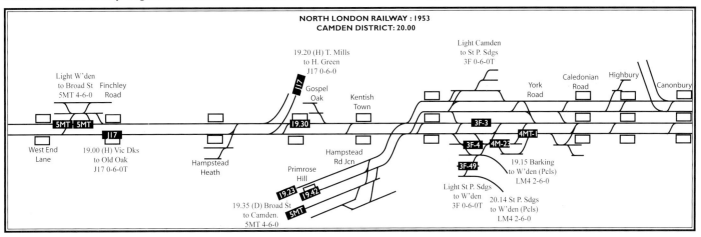

is able to handle sixty-three, the use of such a large engine is not, strictly speaking, necessary but since the return working runs through from Devons Road to Overseal, near Burton on Trent, the use of a Standard 2-8-0 is considered desirable.

Old Oak sidings is getting ready for one of its periodic bouts of activity with a number of trains closing in. An S15 4-6-0 is arriving with a train of empties from Feltham whilst another S15, conveying nothing more than a brakevan, that has come in from Neasden, reverses and crosses over at Acton Wells before backing into

traffic as opposed to coal and it may be a good idea to run the Victoria Docks train onto the goods line at Old Oak Junction, change engines and run it forward as the 20.52. The Southern will moan about the loss of one of their bogie brake vans but it is a small price to pay! The J17 will have to go into the yard to be given a brakevan - not the Southern one! - to take to Acton for its back working, the 21.23 Acton - Temple Mills.

By the time all this has been sorted out, the Stratford Fish will be at Acton Wells, reversing into Old Oak Yard where it divides into two:

arrived from Camden whilst another pair of 4-6-0's approaches Finchley Road.

The urgency with which these trains are worked cannot be understated and almost all run as class D express goods which require at least one-third of the wagons to be vacuum braked. There is a higher classification available - Class C (50% of the train vacuum fitted) - but this is not greatly used on the London Midland who prefer the class D which can convey a greater load for the sacrifice of a little speed. The urgency of these trains is emphasised by the fact they run over the fast line to Camden Road.

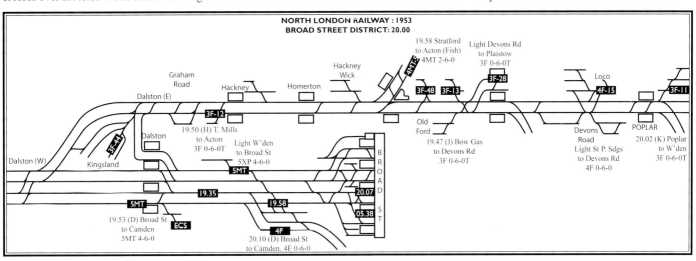

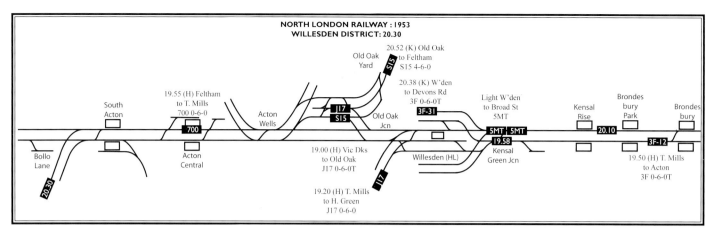

NORTH LONDON RAILWAY : 1953
WILLESDEN DISTRICT: 20.30

CONTROLLER'S LOG: Willesden High Level platform is an interesting place to be at this moment. A pair of 4-6-0's for Broad Street, coupled, have just passed on the connecting line from the LNW to the North London and are following the 20.10 Richmond Broad Street. Such a movement may seen straightforward but running tender-first for eleven miles is no joke and on wet nights the engines may run tender-first only to reach Broad Street the wrong way round because no-one has passed the message main line just ahead of the 19.58 Broad Street - Richmond.

A short distance away another J17 has arrived on the reception line at Old Oak Junction with the 19.00 ex Victoria Docks and is about to back up to the yard. Once its train has been disposed of, the engine will be given a brakevan to take to Acton for the back working, the 21.33 Acton to Temple Mills. A pair of Southern S15 4-6-0's wait at Old Oak, one preparing to leave with the 20.52 goods to Feltham and the other for Devons Road.

The Ferme Park train conveys thirty-eight wagons of London & South Western traffic with a brake each end so that its reversal will not be delayed for want of a brakevan. The J50 0-6-0T will return light to East Goods and a Devons Road 4MT 2-6-0 will turn up in a couple of hours time to take the train forward to Old Oak where it will be worked forward to Feltham by a Southern engine in the early hours of the morning.

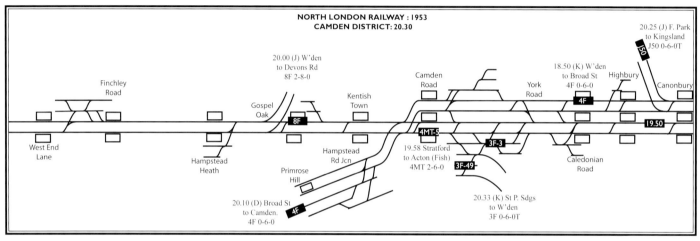

NORTH LONDON RAILWAY : 1953
CAMDEN DISTRICT: 20.30

on! We try and remember to get one of the signalmen on the route to call out whether they are chimney or tender-first and if the former run them up to Dalston Eastern to turn then on the angle. (Even this precaution falls down when some joker sends a pair of engines coupled chimney to chimney...........)

Following the two engines from Brent Yard is Target 31 with a train - Bow Gas and Loco coal - for Devons Road whilst in the opposite direction a Great Eastern J17 0-6-0 takes the West London line to Hither Green, clearing the waiting for the Southern's share of the Great Eastern Fish which is passing Camden Road.

As though the section was not already sufficiently cosmopolitan, an LSWR '700' 0-6-0 pulls through Acton Central with a train for Temple Mills via Camden Road. This part of the world really is a trainspotter's dream!

In the west, the Great Northern pays its last respects for the day with a Ferme Park - Kingsland train. To clear the way for it, target 44 which has been shunting Kingsland for some time, will leave at 20.45 with a train of empties Broad Street passenger station is at its most depressing with the passenger service reduced to a half-hourly service to Richmond. The Watford service which in the period between the two peaks ran only to Willesden Junction, has now ceased altogether; the last Watford departure from Broad Street being the 19.42.

The station is now preparing for the morning peak by making sure the 'terminators' contain the correct number of sets and are in proper condition for the morning service. The stock for the 05.38 Richmond is already in place.

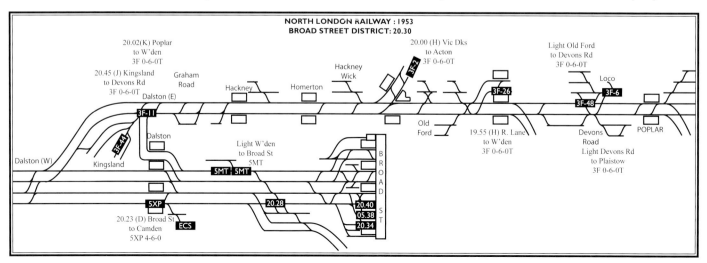

NORTH LONDON RAILWAY : 1953
BROAD STREET DISTRICT: 20.30

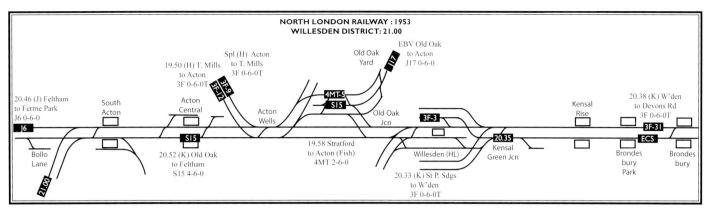

NORTH LONDON RAILWAY : 1953
WILLESDEN DISTRICT: 21.00

CONTROLLER'S LOG: Activity is at its greatest at Old Oak where the Stratford Fish is about to reverse into the Yard; an S15 4-6-0 waiting to back onto the Feltham section as soon as the train has divided. Another S15 has just left the yard with the 20.52 to Feltham whilst the J17 0-6-0 that arrived with the 19.00 from Temple Mills is about to leave with its brakevan for Acton and the 21.23 back to Temple Mills. If Willesden loco have been able to send a pilotman over, the J17 will have turned on Mitre Bridge Angle, if not the engine

be able to clear some of the back log. "What," he asks, "is the engine number? "47483." he is told and after a few minutes he comes back, complaining that the engine is no good since it will only take 24 wagons of coal which will scarcely make a dent in the pile. When he stops to take a breath, it is suggested to him that he uses 47483 on a special of goods for Temple Mills since goods is lighter than coal and if he runs the train as a class H, the engine will take 45 wagons. "But what about the coal?" Reading asks and is told that Target 5, which is

and the temptation exists to tell them that if they have a glut of traffic, to dig out some of their Hall 4-6-0's and move some of it themselves. The wish dies unspoken since GWR engines have never been cleared over the North London: everything but a King can run the few yards from Acton to Acton Wells but no authority for GWR engines to travel further exists and that is the same thing as a ban.

The area around York Road has quietened down a lot. Target 49 is busy shunting out Midland traffic at St Pancras Sidings but the

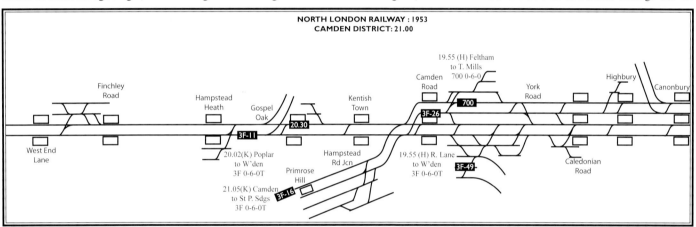

NORTH LONDON RAILWAY : 1953
CAMDEN DISTRICT: 21.00

will have to work back tender first to Temple Mills: a grim prospect on a wet night although the J17's are particularly well equipped with weather-proof tarpaulins. In the meantime a Standard 3F 0-6-0T arrives at Acton with Target 12 from Temple Mills and will return with the 21.45 Acton - Temple Mills.

The Reading Controller has been on the line from time to time commenting on the build-up of North London traffic at Acton and it has been pointed out to him several times - not that it is a secret - that Target 9 which arrived in Acton an hour ago has no back working and should

also unbalanced at Acton in a couple of hours time, has 43021 in the working which will take twenty-nine of coal. He is also reminded that Target 2 in an hour's time will also shift 24 wagons of coal. Shortly before nine o'clock he comes back and announces - as though it was his private scheme - that 47483 will be working a 21.00 special Acton to Temple Mills with a train of Whitemoor traffic and that there will be two other specials at 22.30 and 23.30 with Temple Mills coal.

The Western tend to regard you in much the same way as a belted Earl might view an Aztec

main object of interest is the LSWR '700' 0-6-0 which, far from home, is passing on the up slow with a Feltham - Temple Mills goods. A trio of Standard 0-6-0T's pass in close order, two heading for Willesden with trains from Poplar and Ripple Lane whilst the third is bound for Acton with a train from Victoria Docks.: A fourth - Target 16 - is on its way to St Pancras Sidings from Camden and will head light for Devons Road Loco as soon as it has placed its train. Traffic from Broad Street remains brisk with one Black 5 pulling away for Camden whilst two others approach from Willesden.

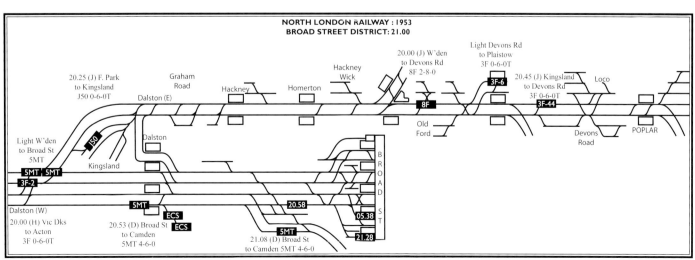

NORTH LONDON RAILWAY : 1953
BROAD STREET DISTRICT: 21.00

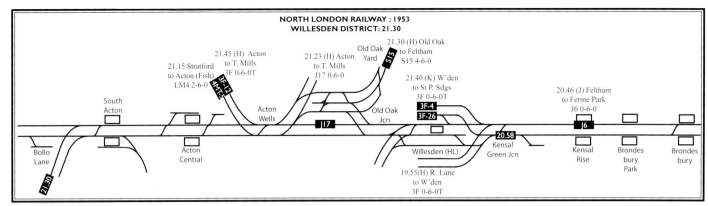

NORTH LONDON RAILWAY : 1953
WILLESDEN DISTRICT: 21.30

CONTROLLER'S LOG: The special Acton to Temple Mills - Target 9 - makes its way towards Western Junction which suggests that it is about time to tell the Great Eastern about it. "*Stratford? Special class H Acton, Temple Mills. 47483, Devons Road five-forty, forty-five equal forty-five. Two Lincoln fitted, one Cambridge Green Arrow, one Boston registered on the engine and forty-one Temple Mills. Nine-fifteen at Victoria Park.*" After a pause he responds by saying that he will give

that by the time the matter has been attended to, there will barely be time to run light to Devons Road without incurring overtime. On the other hand, if the crew do take the train, they will probably come to a stand at Victoria Park and demand instant relief. One can respond with threats of eventual disciplinary action but the reality is that a train is blocking the running line and there is precious little that can be done about it.

Before the train leaves Temple Mills, it

Target 9 - is he an overtime merchant?" When the answer comes back that he is a young passed man who works more Sundays than the Bishop of Stepney and is fighting tooth and nail for a ninety hour week you know your troubles are over. "*Special ten-thirty Temple Mills to Acton with Target 9 engine and men: will you take it?*" comes the question a few minutes later. The answer: "*Wheel it in!*"

Matters are still pretty brisk in the Willesden area. The Channelsea Fish has left Old Oak

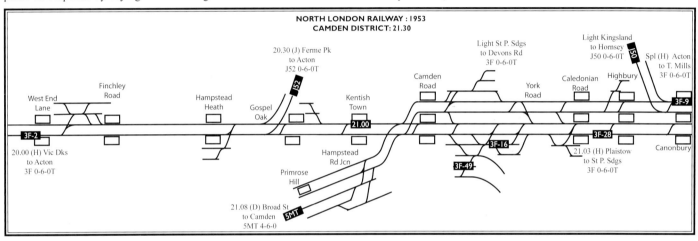

NORTH LONDON RAILWAY : 1953
CAMDEN DISTRICT: 21.30

47483 a train of empties for Acton to bring back. This puts us in an awkward position because the crew's day finishes at half past one and they are hardly going to agree to leave Temple Mills for Acton at half-past ten with only three hours of their shift left. Theoretically they might be able to do it but given the probability of delays en route and the fact that Acton will find a train of Poplar traffic for them to work back to Devons Road, nine drivers out of ten will find some excuse not to cooperate. The usual ploy is to find some minor defect with the engine - which is not difficult - and demand a fitter knowing

has to be formally offered and although this is merely a telephone formality, it could in theory be refused but in practice refusals are hard to justify and one has to make the best of things. A list of spare Devons Road crews - approximately one in twelve turns has no diagrammed work - is consulted to see whether the facilities exist to relieve 47483 at Victoria Park on its way back from Temple Mills: a fresh crew might manage two unscheduled return trips between Temple Mills and Acton but there is one course of action that has to be taken before anything else is done: "*Devons Road Loco? Who's on

for Acton and an S15 4-6-0 is about to pull out of Old Oak with a train for Feltham. On the adjacent main line a Great Eastern J17 0-6-0 passes with an Acton - Temple Mills (via Kingsland) service. Behind it, Target 12 gets ready to leave Acton with another train for Temple Mills.

Devons Road Loco rings up to ask if target 25 is running as booked. This is an engine that goes out for the 22.58 Plaistow - Acton and the 01.25 return but calls at Tredegar Road to pick up any LTSR traffic that might have been placed there by Target 48 during the day.

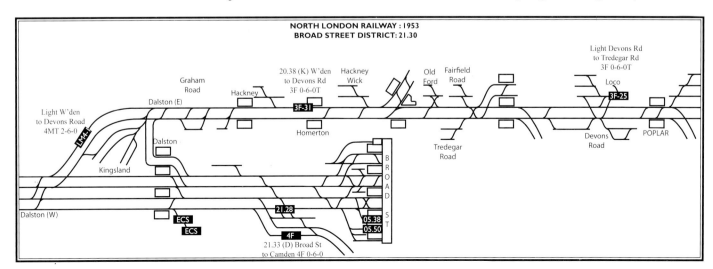

NORTH LONDON RAILWAY : 1953
BROAD STREET DISTRICT: 21.30

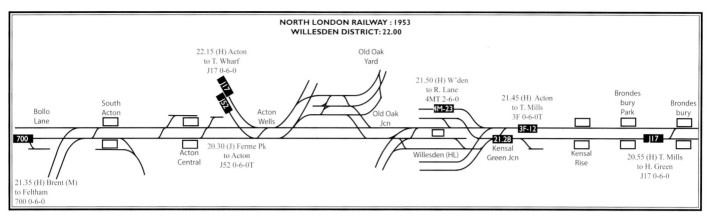

NORTH LONDON RAILWAY : 1953
WILLESDEN DISTRICT: 22.00

CONTROLLER'S LOG: Witness now one of the strange sights of the North London: an electric passenger train on the slow line at Camden Road. The slow lines are generally reserved for goods trains in order to leave the fast lines clear for passenger traffic and because of this they were never electrified except for a short stretch of third rail which was laid between Camden Road and York Road Junction. The reason for this was to allow electric trains to terminate in the up slow platform at Camden Road; the short electrified stretch permitting them to run empty to York Road where they

could reverse, crossover and return to Camden Road. It is not a facility that is used very much and is usually limited to the 21.05 Watford - Camden Road staff train which runs down the goods line to York Road before returning to form the 22.11 Camden Road - Harrow. Were the working to use the fast lines, then it would delay the 21.30 Richmond - Broad Street which calls at Camden Road at 22.02.

The fact the 22.11 Camden Road - Harrow - Watford is the first down electric to run via

Primrose Hill for two hours confirms the rundown of the passenger service and is a signal that the fast lines can be used by class H and J goods trains without much fear of delaying passenger trains.

For some time there has been a steady stream of express goods trains from Broad Street to Camden, worked by main line engines which attach and detach traffic at Camden before continuing forward down the LNWR main line. The train waiting to follow the 21.58 Broad Street - Richmond passenger is the odd-man out since it conveys a full train -

forty five wagons - of conflats and containers for Stockport Edgeley. This is very much a showcase train - heaven help the man who delays it - which runs non-stop from Willesden, where two minutes are allowed for a change of crews, to Stockport except for a pause at Bramhall to allow a Crewe - Manchester news train to proceed from Cheadle Hulme. Water is taken from troughs and arrival in Edgeley Yard is at 03.23. It is as well to remind Hampstead Road Junction that the train must be run main

line to Camden and not, like the other trains, down one of the goods reception roads.

Target 2 has just arrived in Acton from Victoria Docks, an event that prompts Reading to offer a special of general PLA traffic to Poplar, leaving in about half an hour with Target 2's engine and men. Poplar does not work a night shift so the special is accepted to Devons Road Yard; the traffic to be tripped to Polar in the morning. Reading also adds that he proposes to use the 2-6-0 on Target 5 - the engine and men that arrived with the Channelsea Fish - for a special to Temple Mills, leaving at about

eleven. He has cleared the train with Stratford but is letting us know as a polite formality.

As it happens Target 5's crew do not sign off until after two o'clock so there should be no difficulty in their getting to Temple Mills and light to Devons Road before that time. If Stratford decides to load the engine back to Acton, so long as he gives an hour or so of warning, we can send a set of spare men to Victoria Park to relieve the engine and, if needed, do a couple of extra Acton trips.

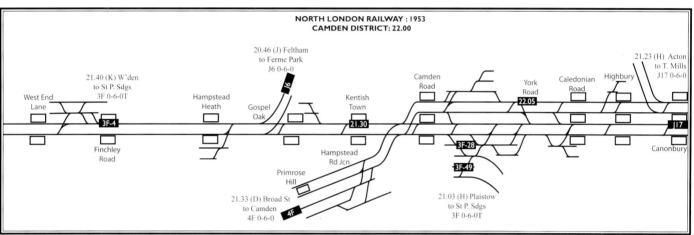

NORTH LONDON RAILWAY : 1953
CAMDEN DISTRICT: 22.00

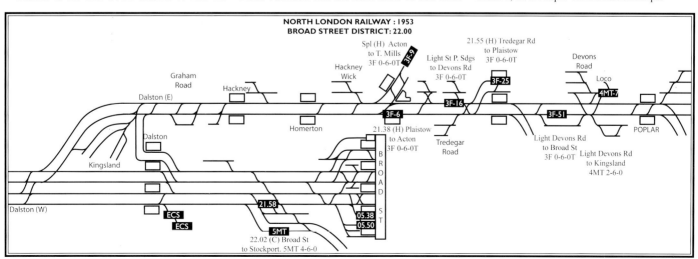

NORTH LONDON RAILWAY : 1953
BROAD STREET DISTRICT: 22.00

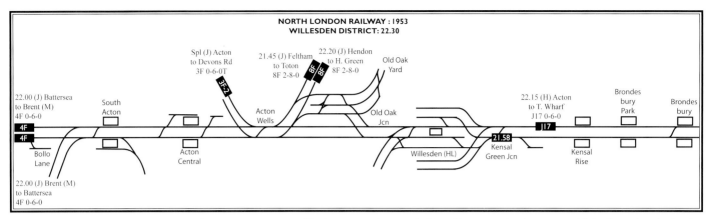

CONTROLLER'S LOG: As though demonstrating that not all goods traffic goes from South to North, an express goods - a class C, no less - joins the system at Kensal Green Junction, the service being the 14.50 Fleetwood to Broad Street which conveys fish and other high-grade traffic from the North. The engine is a Willesden 5XP 4-6-0 which works through from Crewe and, since Willesden has two of each type, has a fifty-fifty chance of being one of the parallel-boilered 'Patriot' type. Enthusiasts who sit up late to see the train should be warned

Devons Road is the stale engine - probably with an ash pan whose contents are uncomfortably close to the bars.

One of the unpopular 4MT 2-6-0's has run light from Devons Road to Kingsland to work the 22.40 to Old Oak, a train of LSWR traffic that was brought in from Ferme Park two hours ago by a J52 0-6-0T. Noting that there is a little LSWR traffic on hand at Kingsland, the shunter is told to liaise with the guard of the 22.40 and use the engine to attach them to the thirty-eight wagons that have come from the

empties for Toton which allows it to be loaded to seventy wagons instead of the normal forty-four. The engine, however, will not go through (at least, not unless the Midland is on the floor for engines) but will be replaced at Brent by another 8F 2-8-0 whilst another thirty wagons are added to the train. The train in the opposite direction is a Hendon - Hither Green coal service which follows a rather interesting route via Kew, Barnes, Clapham Junction, Factory Junction, Brixton, Nunhead and Lewisham. North London trains to Hither Green follow a

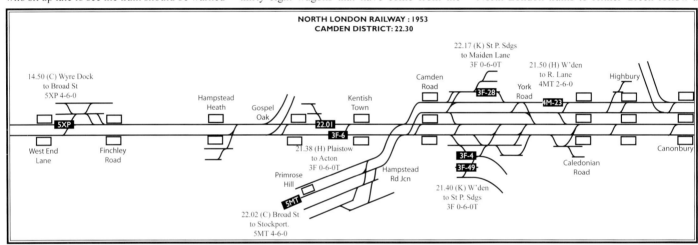

that disappointment can reign since the train is occasionally worked from Crewe by one of the LMS diesels which are (except for 10800) barred from the North London system, resulting in an everyday 4-6-0 or 2-6-0 taking over from Willesden.

One might wonder why there are two Target 50's on the board one passing Graham Road on the up road and the other disappearing into Broad Street Goods. The reason is that one has just relieved the other: the Broad Street pilot is a 24-hour duty and the engine heading towards

Great Northern. The limit from Kingsland to Old Oak is forty-eight wagons; ten greater than that allowed between Finsbury Park and Kingsland. On reaching Old Oak, the train will be worked forward by a Southern S15 4-6-0 whilst the 4MT 2-6-0 will be given a train of milk empties to take to Kensington.

Midland traffic is quite strong at the western end of the line with a pair of 4F 0-6-0's passing each other at Kew with Battersea trains whilst a pair of 8F 2-8-0 meet the other side of Acton Wells. The northbound train is made up with

different route by taking the West London line at Willesden High Level Junction and travelling to Clapham Junction via Kensington Olympia.

Cutting across its path is Target 2 and its 0-6-0T with forty-five wagons of goods on a special from Acton to Devons Road. Since it stays within North London boundaries, the only formality required is to let the Devons Road Inspector know what it is bringing and the time it is likely to arrive. This special will be followed by Target 5 whose 4MT 2-6-0 will work a special Acton to Temple Mills.

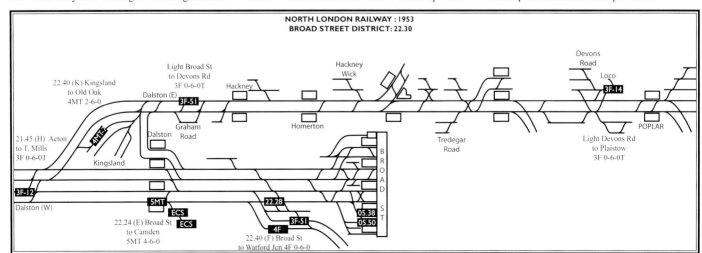

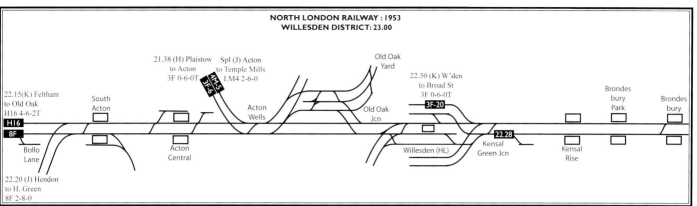

CONTROLLER'S LOG: *"Southend? Target 23 on its way to you. 43001, Devons Road ten-forty men, 31 equal 35 for Ripple Lane."*

"Kew. Hither Green goods down at fifty-seven. What's this that's coming on the up?"

"Old Oak."

"Passenger from Broad Street at fifty-eight."

"Gospel Oak. Old Oak goods down at fifty-eight."

"Victoria Park. I've got a set of men here to relieve Target 23."

"Devons Road Loco? Who's on Target 5. He wants to finish a couple of hours before his time."

"Half a minute .... We had to put a three o'clock spare man in there, the booked chap went sick. My mate should have told you."

"Well, he didn't. Anyway Target 5 wants relief at Victoria Park for Temple Mills in about forty-five minutes."

"Passenger down at oh-one, Kensal Green."

"I've got an eleven-thirty set."

looks as though it's going to be running between Temple Mills and Acton all night. It's just left Acton for Temple Mills and may want relief on the way back. Have your bloke standing by and I'll let you know."

"Stratford? Special Target 5 just leaving Acton. 43021 twenty-nine including fifteen Brimsdown."

"What's his next working?"

"As required. Fresh crew. Can load back if required."

"That's most obliging of you. He can have an Acton load to return with. I'll give you the

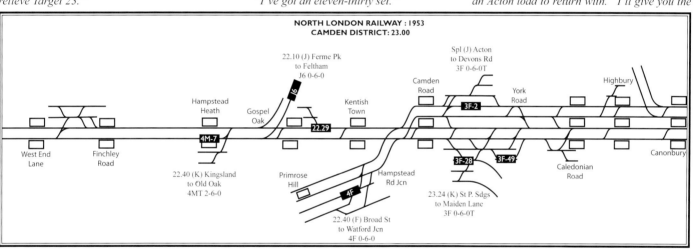

"Next up to you. engine 43001."

"Southend. 22.58 ex Plaistow. Target 25 engine and men. 47499, forty five empties Acton."

"Reading. Special Acton - Temple Mills. Away at fifty-nine. 43021, Target 5 engine and men, twenty-nine Temple Mills including fifteen Brimsdown CEA. Loco relief at Victoria Park."

"His day's not up until two twenty-four. What's he playing at?"

"I'm just passing the message on."

"Right send them to Victoria Park. They'll be as required at Temple Mills."

"York Road. What's this 3-2 coming up the goods to me?"

"Right away Devons Road."

"Thames Wharf goods up at oh-two. Eastern Junction."

"Feltham up at oh-two, Western."

"Hampstead Road. Target 85 down main to goods arrival 1 at two."

"Guards inspector? I may want a guard about midnight at Victoria Park. Target 5

details nearer the time."

"Target 20 up the main, oh-five at Kensal Green."

"Devons Road. I've got engine 47564 here from Broad Street. What's it for?"

"Loco."

"Target 23. Oh-five to eight, getting relief. Where d'you want the relieved set that's been relieved?"

"Tell 'em to sign off at the Loco."

"Where shall I send the engine off the Wyre Dock?..............."

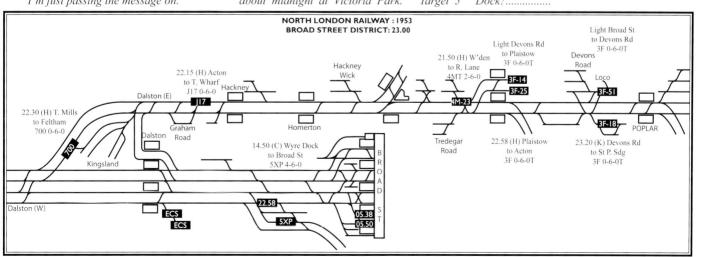

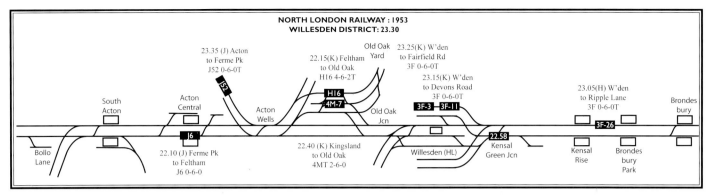

NORTH LONDON RAILWAY : 1953
WILLESDEN DISTRICT: 23.30

CONTROLLER'S LOG: The passenger service which has been wilting for some hours is finally about to expire altogether. The 22.58 from Broad Street is approaching Willesden on its way to Richmond after which it will run empty to Mitre Bridge. Its opposite number, the 23.05 ex-Richmond is at Finchley Road and will stable at Broad Street to form the 05.09 to Camden Road in the morning. The system will then be totally free for the operation of goods traffic; the North London's raison d'etre.

And what a variety of goods traffic there is, especially at the Acton end of the District.

Northern engine, a J6 0-6-0, strives to reach Acton South before the 22.58 Broad Street electric catches up with it.

Traffic in the Camden area is almost as varied: an LSWR 700 0-6-0 running down Hampstead bank with a Temple Mills - Feltham service and a Great Eastern J17 0-6-0 approaching Gospel Oak from the Tottenham & Hampstead direction with a Temple Mills to Hither Green train. At York Road a transfer from St Pancras Sidings to Maiden Lane waits for a special Acton to Temple Mills to pass whilst a J52 0-6-0T with an East Goods to Acton

it has been possible to sit back and see the entire timetable unfold before you. Today, everything has run to time and the trains have behaved themselves. Tomorrow half - perhaps all - the system will be shrouded in a London Particular - a fog so dense that even walking through Leicester Square itself is difficult - with trains standing at every signal and barely moving. Not infrequently under these conditions a set of men will relieve a train and then, eight hours later, be themselves relieved without the train having moved an inch. This was railway work at its worst: Frustration for

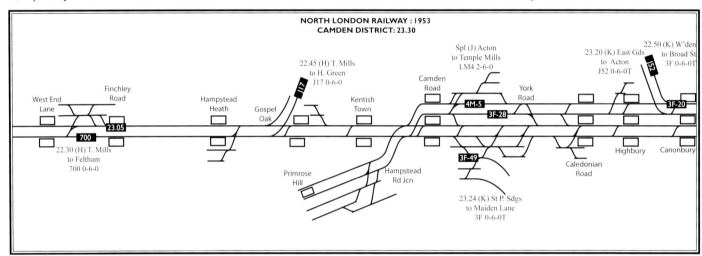

NORTH LONDON RAILWAY : 1953
CAMDEN DISTRICT: 23.30

Three goods trains form a procession from Willesden High Level Sidings, running to Ripple Lane, Devons Road and Fairfield Road respectively. All are worked by Devons Road Standard 3F 0-6-0T's. At Old Oak, the 22.40 from Kingsland waits to back into the yard as an H16 4-6-2T passes with a service from Feltham whilst a Great Northern J52 0-6-0T adds to the jollity by pulling away from Acton with a Tottenham, & Hampstead service to Ferme Park. On the down main line another Great

train receives a check from Target 20 as it get preference through Canonbury Junction with a Willesden to Broad Street service. The last mentioned could be run on the fast line from Camden Road but just in case Broad Street Goods are unable to take it straight in, it is safer to run it up the slow line just in case it has to be held back until the 23.05 Richmond passenger has passed.

And so a twenty-four hour stretch on the North London draws to an end; a day when

the Controller at being unable to move more than a small fraction of traffic, irritation on the part of signalmen who were having to signal trains under the most trying of conditions and unspeakable for train crews who had to spend hours on freezing cold engines, scarcely able to see each other yet having to remain on the alert in case their signal should come off.

The day after might be as clear as a bell and then a light engine derails itself right across the junction at Camden Road.............!

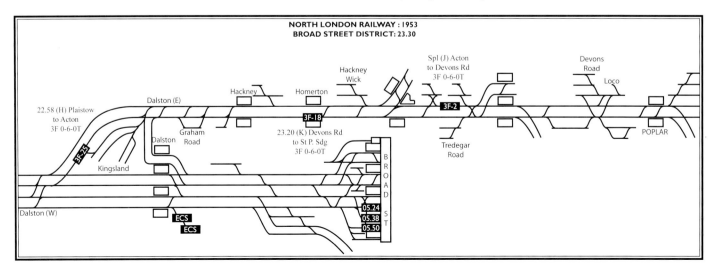

NORTH LONDON RAILWAY : 1953
BROAD STREET DISTRICT: 23.30

NORTH LONDON EMU CARRIAGE WORKINGS (1953)

C/Working 1

Arr	Station	Dep
	Watford Jcn	04.50
	Euston	05.47
06.32	Watford Jcn	06.44
07.47	Broad St	08.06
09.08	Watford Jcn	09.18
09.30	Croxley Gn CS	
	Berth	
	Croxley Gn CS	16.28
16.45	Bushey	16.46
17.26	Euston	17.40
18.22	Watford Jcn	18.38
19.23	Euston	19.32
20.18	Watford Jcn	20.34
21.19	Euston	21.34
22.19	Watford Jcn	22.30
23.15	Euston	23.30
00.15	Watford Jcn	

C/Working 2

Arr	Station	Dep
	Croxley Gn CS	05.57
06.07	Watford Jcn	06.18
07.03	Euston	07.16
08.04	Watford Jcn	08.23
09.13	Broad St	09.30
10.32	Watford Jcn	11.00
11.44	Euston	11.52
12.37	Watford Jcn	12.45
13.29	Euston	13.37
14.22	Watford Jcn	14.30
15.14	Euston	15.22
16.07	Watford Jcn	16.32
17.19	Euston	17.30
18.17	Watford Jcn	18.33
19.34	Broad St	

C/Working 3

Arr	Station	Dep
	Croxley Gn CS	05.40
05.50	Watford Jcn	06.02
06.47	Euston	07.00
07.45	Watford Jcn	08.09
09.08	Broad St	09.14
09.58	Mitre Bridge CS	
	Berth	
	Mitre Bridge CS	16.05
16.18	Willesden HL	16.20
16.54	Broad St	17.09
18.07	Watford Jcn	18.15
18.25	Croxley Gn CS	

C/Working 4

Arr	Station	Dep
	Watford Jcn	05.18
06.18	Broad St	06.25
07.27	Watford Jcn	07.46
08.38	Broad St	08.53
09.01	Dalston Jcn	
	Berth	
	Dalston Jcn	16.32
16.39	Broad St	16.53
17.54	Watford Jcn	18.06
18.17	Croxley Gn CS	

C/Working 5

Arr	Station	Dep
	Croxley Gn CS	06.11
06.22	Watford Jcn	06.38
07.22	Euston	07.29
08.15	Watford Jcn	08.27
09.12	Euston	09.18
10.04	Watford Jcn	10.10
10.20	Croxley Gn CS	
	Berth	
	Croxley Gn CS	15.54
16.09	Bushey	16.10
16.52	Euston	17.02
17.48	Watford Jcn	17.58
18.08	Croxley Gn CS	

C/Working 6

Arr	Station	Dep
	Croxley Gn CS	06.45
06.56	Watford Jcn	07.03
07.11	Croxley Grn	07.15
07.28	Watford Jcn	07.48
07.55	Croxley Grn	08.01
08.48	Euston	08.56
09.41	Watford Jcn	09.48
09.58	Croxley Gn CS	
	Berth	
	Croxley Gn CS	14.25
14.35	Watford Jcn	15.00
15.45	Euston	15.52
16.38	Watford Jcn	16.46
17.33	Euston	17.52
18.36	Watford Jcn	18.55
19.54	Broad St	20.07
20.14	Dalston Jcn	

C/Working 7

Arr	Station	Dep
	Watford Jcn	06.05
06.12	Croxley Green	06.21
06.29	Watford Jcn	06.57
07.42	Euston	07.52
08.36	Watford Jcn	08.52
09.00	Croxley Green	09.04
09.11	Watford Jcn	09.42
10.26	Euston	10.37
11.22	Watford Jcn	11.30
12.14	Euston	12.22
13.07	Watford Jcn	13.15
13.59	Euston	14.07
14.52	Watford Jcn	15.33
16.34	Broad St	16.44
17.36	Richmond	17.54
18.44	Broad St	19.05
20.07	Watford Jcn	20.19
21.04	Euston	21.21
22.06	Watford Jcn	22.24
23.08	Euston	23.19
00.04	Watford Jcn	

C/Working 8

Arr	Station	Dep
	Dalston Jcn	06.21
06.31	Broad St	06.47
07.51	Watford Jcn	08.15
09.00	Euston	09.08
09.54	Watford Jcn	10.12
11.10	Broad St	11.18
11.47	Willesden New	11.58
12.26	Broad St	12.48
13.17	Willesden New	13.28
13.56	Broad St	14.48
15.48	Watford Jcn	16.13
16.22	Rickmansworth	16.25
16.34	Watford Jcn	17.18
18.05	Euston	18.16
19.01	Watford Jcn	19.14
19.58	Euston	20.07
20.52	Watford Jcn	21.15
21.59	Euston	22.07
22.52	Watford Jcn	22.57
23.07	Croxley Gn CS	

C/Working 9

Arr	Station	Dep
	Broad St	05.50
06.51	Watford Jcn	07.05
08.08	Broad St	08.23
09.15	Richmond	09.28
10.16	Broad St	10.30
10.40	Dalston Jcn	
	Berth	
	Dalston Jcn	15.17
15.27	Broad St	15.37
16.27	Richmond	16.36
17.26	Broad St	17.40
18.32	Watford Jcn	18.50
19.34	Euston	19.49
20.34	Watford Jcn	20.56
21.41	Euston	21.54
22.39	Watford Jcn	23.05
23.51	Euston	00.00
00.47	Watford Jcn	

C/Working 10

Arr	Station	Dep
	Euston CS	06.35
06.40	Euston	06.53
07.40	Watford Jcn	07.57
08.56	Broad St	09.09
10.10	Watford Jcn	10.30
11.14	Euston	11.22
12.07	Watford Jcn	12.15
12.59	Euston	13.07
13.52	Watford Jcn	14.00
14.44	Euston	14.52
15.37	Watford Jcn	16.11
16.57	Euston	17.16
18.01	Watford Jcn	18.33
19.34	Broad St	
	Stable	

C/Working 11

Arr	Station	Dep
	Croxley Gn CS	08.20
08.32	Watford Jcn	08.48
09.39	Broad St	09.55
10.43	Mitre Bridge CS	
	Berth	
	Mitre Bridge CS	16.40
16.55	Willesden HL	17.00
17.33	Broad St	17.43
18.46	Watford Jcn	18.59
19.43	Euston	19.52
19.57	Euston CS	

C/Working 12

Arr	Station	Dep
	Euston CS	05.55
06.00	Euston	06.15
07.02	Watford Jcn	07.19
08.20	Broad St	08.40
09.29	Richmond	09.45
10.33	Broad St	10.53
11.43	Richmond	11.56
12.44	Broad St	12.53
13.43	Richmond	13.56
14.44	Broad St	14.53
15.43	Richmond	16.16
17.05	Broad St	17.17
18.11	Watford Jcn	18.20
18.30	Croxley Green CS	

C/Working 13

Arr	Station	Dep
	Broad St	05.09
05.24	Camden Road	05.33
05.48	Broad St	06.05
06.56	Richmond	07.10
08.00	Broad St	08.10
09.00	Richmond	09.15
10.03	Broad St	10.12
10.57	Mitre Bridge CS	
	Berth	
	Mitre Bridge CS	16.20
16.34	Willesden HL	16.37
17.12	Broad St	17.25
18.21	Croxley Green	18.25
18.40	Croxley Green CS	

C/Working 14

Arr	Station	Dep
	Watford Jcn	05.32
06.17	Euston	06.33
07.18	Watford Jcn	07.38
08.23	Euston	08.32
09.17	Watford Jcn	09.32
10.27	Broad St	10.45
11.35	Mitre Bridge CS	
	Berth	
	Mitre Bridge CS	16.30
17.20	Broad St	17.31
18.22	Richmond	18.38
19.29	Broad St	19.45
19.50	Dalston Jcn	

C/Working 15

Arr	Station	Dep
	Mitre Bridge CS	05.05
05.20	Kensal Green Sdg	05.30
05.32	Willesden HL	05.33
05.50	Richmond	06.03
06.53	Broad St	07.07
07.59	Richmond	08.15
09.04	Broad St	09.23
10.13	Richmond	10.26
11.14	Broad St	11.23
12.13	Richmond	12.26
13.14	Broad St	13.23
14.13	Richmond	14.26
15.14	Broad St	15.40
16.49	Watford Jcn	17.00
17.46	Euston	18.03
18.43	Bushey	18.44
18.54	Croxley Green CS	

C/Working 16

Arr	Station	Dep
	Mitre Bridge CS	04.15
04.29	Kensal Green Jn	04.33
04.36	Willesden New	04.48
05.02	Euston	05.10
05.57	Watford Jcn	06.14
07.16	Broad Street	07.28
08.30	Watford Jcn	08.40
09.24	Euston	09.34
10.19	Watford Jcn	10.26
10.36	Croxley Green CS	
	Berth	
	Croxley Green CS	15.22
15.32	Watford Jcn	15.55
16.41	Euston	16.50
17.35	Watford Jcn	17.45
17.55	Croxley Green CS	

C/Working 17

Arr	Station	Dep
	Broad Street	05.24
06.13	Richmond	06.23
07.12	Broad Street	07.22
08.14	Richmond	08.29
09.19	Broad Street	09.34
10.20	Mitre Bridge CS	

C/Working 18

Arr	Station	Dep
	Broad St	05.38
06.31	Richmond	06.54
07.43	Broad St	07.53
08.44	Richmond	08.56
09.45	Broad St	09.53
10.43	Richmond	10.56
11.44	Broad St	11.53
12.43	Richmond	12.56
13.44	Broad St	13.53
14.43	Richmond	14.56
15.44	Broad St	16.22
17.21	Watford Jcn	17.38
18.24	Euston	18.44
19.30	Watford Jcn	19.44
20.00	Stonebridge Park CS	

C/Working 19

Arr	Station	Dep
	Mitre Bridge CS	04.25
04.50	Willesden HL	04.52
05.07	Richmond	05.20
06.07	Broad St	06.35
07.26	Richmond	07.40
08.30	Broad St	08.47
09.48	Watford Jcn	09.55
10.05	Croxley Green CS	
	Stable	
	Croxley Green CS	16.33
16.43	Watford Jcn	16.55
17.54	Broad St	18.05
18.56	Richmond	19.15
20.06	Broad St	20.28
21.18	Richmond	21.30
22.17	Broad St	22.28
23.18	Richmond	23.43
23.57	Willesden HL	00.04
00.17	Mitre Bridge CS	

C/Working 20

Arr	Station	Dep
	Croxley Green CS	14.45
14.55	Watford Jcn	15.10
15.56	Euston	16.10
16.56	Watford Jcn	17.06
18.09	Broad St	18.18
19.07	Richmond	19.30
20.20	Broad St	20.40
20.45	Dalston Jcn	

C/Working 21

Arr	Station	Dep
	Watford Jcn	05.45
06.45	Broad St	07.03
07.50	Harrow	08.07
08.51	Broad St	09.06
09.50	Mitre Bridge CS	
	Stable	
	Mitre Bridge CS	15.50
16.05	Kensal Green Sdg	16.23
16.25	Willesden HL	16.27
16.43	Richmond	16.52
17.42	Broad St	17.56
18.55	Watford Jcn	19.20
19.28	Croxley Green	19.43
19.51	Watford Jcn	19.59
20.16	Harrow	

C/Working 22

Arr	Station	Dep
	Harrow	06.58
07.13	Watford Jcn	07.25
08.10	Euston	08.18
09.03	Watford Jcn	09.15
09.58	Euston	10.10
10.55	Watford Jcn	
	Berth	
	Watford Jcn	15.04
16.04	Broad Street	16.33
17.24	Richmond	17.38
18.28	Broad Street	18.40
19.41	Watford Jcn	19.48
20.32	Euston	20.38
21.23	Watford Jcn	21.34
22.18	Euston	22.34
23.19	Watford Jcn	23.35
00.20	Euston	00.45
01.29	Watford Jcn	

C/Working 23

Arr	Station	Dep
	Mitre Bridge CS	05.55
06.08	Willesden HL	06.10
06.41	Broad St	06.54
07.57	Watford Jcn	08.58
09.53	Broad St	10.18
10.47	Willesden New	10.58
11.26	Broad St	11.48
12.17	Willesden New	12.28
12.56	Broad St	14.18
14.47	Willesden New	14.58
15.26	Broad St	16.00
16.51	Richmond	17.08
17.58	Broad St	18.09
19.10	Watford Jcn	19.23
20.24	Broad St	20.34
21.19	Mitre Bridge CS	

C/Working 24

Arr	Station	Dep
	Harrow	06.28
06.45	Watford Jcn	07.09
07.55	Euston	08.04
08.50	Watford Jcn	09.09
10.08	Broad St	10.23
11.13	Richmond	11.26
12.14	Broad St	12.23
13.13	Richmond	13.26
14.14	Broad St	14.23
15.13	Richmond	15.25
16.13	Broad St	16.49
17.44	Watford Jcn	18.00
18.45	Euston	19.00
19.45	Watford Jcn	19.57
20.43	Euston	20.54
21.39	Watford Jcn	21.54
22.38	Euston	22.48
23.32	Watford Jcn	

C/Working 25

Arr	Station	Dep
	Dalston Jcn	06.16
06.23	Broad Street	06.50
07.42	Richmond	07.56
08.45	Broad Street	08.58
09.49	Richmond	10.02
10.50	Broad Street	
	Berth	
	Broad Street	13.18
13.47	Willesden New	13.58
14.26	Broad Street	15.18
16.21	Watford Jcn	16.39
17.38	Broad Street	17.47
18.39	Richmond	18.55
19.45	Broad Street	19.58
20.48	Richmond	21.00
21.47	Broad Street	21.58
22.50	Richmond	23.05
23.52	Broad Street	

C/Working 26

Arr	Station	Dep
	Croxley Green CS	07.35
07.53	Bushey	07.54
08.30	Euston	08.37
09.16	Bushey	09.17
09.24	Croxley Green CS	
	Berth	
	Croxley Green CS	16.02
16.12	Watford Jcn	16.34
16.44	Rickmansworth	16.50
17.01	Watford Jcn	17.28
18.13	Euston	18.33
19.19	Watford Jcn	19.30
20.15	Euston	20.23
21.08	Watford Jcn	21.24
22.09	Euston	22.21
23.06	Watford Jcn	23.20
00.05	Euston	00.22
01.05	Watford Jcn	

C/Working 27

Arr	Station	Dep
	Stonebridge Park C	06.10
06.27	Willesden New	06.29
07.00	Broad Street	07.18
08.20	Watford Jcn	08.37
09.36	Broad Street	09.45
10.48	Watford Jcn	11.26
11.36	Croxley Green CS	
	Berth	
	Croxley Green CS	15.40
15.50	Watford Jcn	16.02
17.01	Broad Street	17.12
18.02	Richmond	18.23
19.14	Broad Street	19.42
20.43	Watford Jcn	21.05
21.49	Camden Road	21.50
21.54	Maiden Lane Jcn	22.05
22.07	Camden Road	22.05
22.38	Harrow	

C/Working 28

Arr	Station	Dep
	Watford Jcn	06.25
07.25	Broad Street	07.35
08.26	Richmond	08.44
09.33	Broad Street	09.47
10.35	Mitre Bridge CS	
	Stable	
	Mitre Bridge CS	14.50
15.04	Kensal Green Sdg	15.10
15.11	Willesden HL	15.12
15.28	Richmond	15.53
16.42	Broad Street	16.58
17.59	Watford Jcn	18.09
19.09	Broad Street	19.28
20.18	Richmond	20.30
21.19	Broad Street	

C/Working 29

Arr	Station	Dep
	Croxley Green CS	15.27
15.44	Bushey	15.45
16.28	Euston	16.38
17.25	Watford Jcn	17.34
18.34	Broad Street	18.52
19.43	Richmond	19.53
20.03	Acton Central	20.11
20.17	Willesden HL	20.23
20.50	Mitre Bridge CS	

C/Working 30

Arr	Station	Dep
	Mitre Bridge CS	05.20
05.41	Kensal Green Sdg	06.00
06.02	Willesden HL	06.05
06.19	Richmond	06.40
07.29	Broad Street	07.38
08.39	Watford Jcn	08.55
09.38	Euston	09.54
10.41	Watford Jcn	10.55
11.05	Croxley Green CS	
	Berth	
	Croxley Green CS	15.07
15.18	Watford Jcn	15.46
16.47	Broad Street	17.02
17.54	Richmond	18.06
18.58	Broad Street	19.21
20.22	Watford Jcn	20.45
21.30	Euston	21.38
21.43	Euston CS	

C/Working 31

Arr	Station	Dep
	Dalston	05.57
06.03	Broad Street	06.20
07.12	Richmond	07.25
08.15	Broad Street	08.26
09.26	Watford Jcn	09.39
09.50	Croxley Green CS	
	Berth	
	Croxley Green CS	14.50
15.05	Watford Jcn	15.24
16.11	Euston	16.25
17.11	Watford Jcn	17.21
18.21	Broad Street	18.35
19.25	Richmond	19.50
20.40	Broad Street	20.58
21.49	Richmond	22.01
22.47	Broad Street	22.58
23.49	Richmond	00.04
00.35	Mitre Bridge CS	

C/Working 32

Arr	Station	Dep
	Croxley Green CS	06.35
06.47	Croxley Green	06.56
07.04	Watford Jcn	07.16
07.24	Croxley Green	07.28
08.33	Broad Street	08.43
08.48	Dalston Jcn	
	Berth	
	Dalston Jcn	16.18
16.25	Broad Street	16.37
17.40	Watford Jcn	17.50
18.50	Broad Street	19.10
20.00	Richmond	20.10
21.00	Broad Street	21.28
22.18	Richmond	22.29
23.17	Broad Street	

C/Working 33

Arr	Station	Dep
	Croxley Green CS	08.10
08.25	Croxley Green	08.28
09.26	Broad Street	09.40
09.45	Dalston Jcn	
	Berth	
	Dalston Jcn	15.45
15.53	Broad Street	16.15
17.06	Richmond	17.23
18.12	Broad Street	18.23
19.20	Bushey	19.21
19.33	Croxley Green CS	

NORTH LONDON EMU CARRIAGE WORKINGS (1953)

C/Working 34

Arr	Station	Dep
	Croxley Green CS	16.08
16.20	Bushey	16.21
17.16	Broad Street	17.28
18.30	Watford Jcn	18.45
18.52	Croxley Green	18.56
19.15	Croxley Green CS	

C/Working 35

Arr	Station	Dep
	Croxley Green CS	05.13
05.24	Watford Jcn	05.48
05.58	Croxley Green	06.03
06.13	Watford Jcn	06.23
06.30	Croxley Green	06.34
06.42	Watford Jcn	06.51
07.01	Rickmansworth	07.06
07.17	Watford Jcn	07.29
07.37	Croxley Green	07.41
07.49	Watford Jcn	08.03
08.11	Croxley Green	08.15
08.22	Watford Jcn	08.31
08.38	Croxley Green	08.41
08.48	Watford Jcn	09.00
09.10	Rickmansworth	09.14
09.24	Watford Jcn	09.34
09.41	Croxley Green	09.44
09.51	Watford Jcn	09.59
10.08	Croxley Green CS	
	Berth	
	Croxley Green CS	15.15
15.26	Watford Jcn	15.49
15.56	Croxley Green	16.01
16.09	Watford Jcn	16.19
16.26	Croxley Green	16.32
16.40	Watford Jcn	16.53
17.00	Croxley Green	17.06
17.14	Watford Jcn	17.23
17.30	Croxley Green	17.39
17.46	Watford Jcn	17.52
18.00	Croxley Green	18.07
18.14	Watford Jcn	18.25
18.33	Croxley Green	18.41
18.48	Watford Jcn	19.02
19.11	Croxley Green	19.17
19.26	Watford Jcn	19.33
19.43	Croxley Green	19.52
20.02	Watford Jcn	20.29
20.39	Croxley Green CS	

C/Working 36

Arr	Station	Dep
	Croxley Green CS	05.30
05.35	Croxley Green Jcn	05.38
05.45	Croxley Green	05.57
06.05	Watford Jcn	06.29
06.39	Rickmansworth	06.47
06.58	Watford Jcn	07.11
07.20	Rickmansworth	07.25
07.35	Watford Jcn	07.43
07.52	Rickmansworth	07.56
08.06	Watford Jcn	08.12
08.22	Rickmansworth	08.31
08.41	Watford Jcn	08.44
08.54	Rickmansworth	08.57
09.06	Watford Jcn	09.13
09.20	Croxley Green	09.26
09.34	Watford Jcn	09.44
09.54	Rickmansworth	09.58
10.08	Watford Jcn	10.16
10.26	Croxley Green CS	
	Berth	
	Croxley Green CS	16.24
16.36	Watford Jcn	16.57
17.06	Rickmansworth	17.13
17.23	Watford Jcn	17.32
17.41	Rickmansworth	17.47
17.57	Watford Jcn	18.02
18.13	Rickmansworth	18.17
18.27	Watford Jcn	18.35
18.44	Rickmansworth	18.52
19.03	Watford Jcn	19.08
19.17	Rickmansworth	19.28
19.39	Watford Jcn	19.46
19.54	Croxley Green	20.09
20.16	Watford Jcn	20.29
20.39	Croxley Green CS	

C/Working 37

Arr	Station	Dep
	Croxley Green CS	16.33
16.43	Watford Jcn	16.55
17.54	Broad St	18.05
18.56	Richmond	19.15
20.06	Broad St	20.28
21.18	Richmond	21.30
22.17	Broad St	22.28
23.18	Richmond	23.43
23.57	Willesden HL	00.04
00.17	Mitre Bridge CS	

C/Working 38

Arr	Station	Dep
	Watford Jcn	06.44
07.47	Broad St	08.06
09.08	Watford Jcn	09.18
09.30	Croxley Gn CS	
	Berth	
	Croxley Gn CS	16.28
16.45	Bushey	16.46
17.26	Euston	17.40
18.22	Watford Jcn	18.38
19.23	Euston	

C/Working 39

Arr	Station	Dep
	Croxley Gn CS	05.57
06.07	Watford Jcn	06.18
07.03	Euston	07.16
08.04	Watford Jcn	08.23
09.13	Broad St	09.30
10.32	Watford Jcn	11.15
11.59	Euston	12.07
12.52	Watford Jcn	13.00
13.44	Euston	13.52
14.37	Watford Jcn	14.45
15.31	Euston	15.38
16.23	Watford Jcn	17.18
18.05	Euston	18.16
19.01	Watford Jcn	19.14
19.58	Euston	

C/Working 40

Arr	Station	Dep
	Croxley Gn CS	05.40
05.50	Watford Jcn	06.02
06.47	Euston	07.00
07.45	Watford Jcn	08.09
09.08	Broad St	09.14
09.58	Mitre Bridge CS	
	Berth	
	Mitre Bridge CS	16.05
16.18	Willesden HL	16.20
16.54	Broad St	17.09
18.07	Watford Jcn	18.15
18.25	Croxley Gn CS	

C/Working 41

Arr	Station	Dep
	Watford Jcn	07.46
08.38	Broad St	08.53
09.01	Dalston Jcn	
	Berth	
	Dalston Jcn	16.32
16.39	Broad St	16.53
17.54	Watford Jcn	18.06
18.17	Croxley Gn CS	

C/Working 42

Arr	Station	Dep
06.22	Watford Jcn	06.38
07.22	Euston	07.29
08.15	Watford Jcn	08.27
09.12	Euston	09.18
10.04	Watford Jcn	10.10
10.20	Croxley Gn CS	
	Berth	
	Croxley Gn CS	15.54
16.09	Bushey	16.10
16.52	Euston	17.02
17.48	Watford Jcn	17.58
18.08	Croxley Gn CS	

C/Working 43

Arr	Station	Dep
	Watford Jcn	07.03
07.11	Croxley Grn	07.15
07.28	Watford Jcn	07.48
07.55	Croxley Grn	08.01
08.48	Euston	08.56
09.41	Watford Jcn	09.48
09.58	Croxley Gn CS	
	Berth	
	Croxley Gn CS	14.25
14.35	Watford Jcn	15.00
15.45	Euston	15.52
16.38	Watford Jcn	16.46
17.33	Euston	17.52
18.36	Watford Jcn	

C/Working 44

Arr	Station	Dep
	Watford Jcn	06.57
07.42	Euston	07.52
08.36	Watford Jcn	08.52
09.00	Croxley Green	09.04
09.11	Watford Jcn	09.42
10.26	Euston	10.52
11.37	Watford Jcn	11.45
12.29	Euston	12.37
13.22	Watford Jcn	13.30
14.14	Euston	14.22
15.07	Watford Jcn	15.33
16.34	Broad St	16.44
17.36	Richmond	17.54
18.44	Broad St	19.05
20.07	Watford Jcn	

C/Working 45

Arr	Station	Dep
	Watford Jcn	08.15
09.00	Euston	09.08
09.54	Watford Jcn	10.15
10.59	Euston	11.07
11.52	Watford Jcn	12.00
12.44	Euston	12.52
13.37	Watford Jcn	13.45
14.29	Euston	14.37
15.22	Watford Jcn	16.11
16.57	Euston	17.16
18.01	Watford Jcn	18.18
19.03	Euston	19.12
19.56	Watford Jcn	20.12
20.57	Euston	21.07
21.52	Watford Jcn	22.00
22.45	Euston	23.05
23.49	Watford Jcn	00.10
00.20	Croxley Gn CS	

C/Working 46

Arr	Station	Dep
	Watford Jcn	07.05
08.08	Broad St	08.23
09.15	Richmond	09.28
10.16	Broad St	10.30
10.40	Dalston Jcn	
	Berth	
	Dalston Jcn	15.17
15.27	Broad St	15.37
16.27	Richmond	16.36
17.26	Broad St	17.40
18.32	Watford Jcn	

C/Working 47

Arr	Station	Dep
	Euston CS	06.35
06.40	Euston	06.53
07.40	Watford Jcn	07.57
08.56	Broad St	09.09
10.10	Watford Jcn	10.27
11.29	Euston	11.37
12.22	Watford Jcn	12.30
13.14	Euston	13.22
14.07	Watford Jcn	14.15
14.59	Euston	15.09
15.56	Watford Jcn	16.32
17.19	Euston	17.30
18.17	Watford Jcn	

C/Working 48

Arr	Station	Dep
	Croxley Gn CS	08.20
08.32	Watford Jcn	08.48
09.39	Broad St	09.55
10.43	Mitre Bridge CS	
	Berth	
	Mitre Bridge CS	16.40
16.55	Willesden HL	17.00
17.33	Broad St	17.43
18.46	Watford Jcn	

C/Working 49

Arr	Station	Dep
	Euston CS	05.55
06.00	Euston	06.15
07.02	Watford Jcn	07.19
08.20	Broad St	08.40
09.29	Richmond	09.45
10.33	Broad St	10.53
11.43	Richmond	11.56
12.44	Broad St	12.53
13.43	Richmond	13.56
14.44	Broad St	14.53
15.43	Richmond	16.16
17.05	Broad St	17.17
18.11	Watford Jcn	18.20
18.30	Croxley Gn CS	

C/Working 50

Arr	Station	Dep
	Broad St	05.09
05.24	Camden Road	05.33
05.48	Broad St	06.05
06.56	Richmond	07.10
08.00	Broad St	08.10
09.00	Richmond	09.15
10.03	Broad St	10.12
10.57	Mitre Bridge CS	
	Berth	
	Mitre Bridge CS	16.20
16.34	Willesden HL	16.37
17.12	Broad St	17.25
18.21	Croxley Green	18.25
18.40	Croxley Green CS	

C/Working 51

Arr	Station	Dep
	Watford Jcn	05.32
06.17	Euston	06.33
07.18	Watford Jcn	07.38
08.23	Euston	08.32
09.17	Watford Jcn	09.32
10.27	Broad St	10.45
11.35	Mitre Bridge CS	
	Berth	
	Mitre Bridge CS	16.30
17.20	Broad St	17.31
18.22	Richmond	18.38
19.29	Broad St	19.45
19.50	Dalston Jcn	

C/Working 52

Arr	Station	Dep
	Mitre Bridge CS	05.05
05.20	Kensal Green Sdg	05.30
05.32	Willesden HL	05.33
05.50	Richmond	06.03
06.53	Broad St	07.07
07.59	Richmond	08.15
09.04	Broad St	
	Berth	
	Broad St	16.22
17.21	Watford Jcn	17.38
18.24	Euston	18.44
19.30	Watford Jcn	19.44
20.00	Stonebridge Park CS	

C/Working 53

Arr	Station	Dep
	Mitre Bridge CS	04.15
04.29	Kensal Green Jn	04.33
04.36	Willesden New	04.48
05.02	Euston	05.10
05.57	Watford Jcn	06.14
07.16	Broad Street	07.28
08.30	Watford Jcn	08.40
09.24	Euston	09.34
10.19	Watford Jcn	10.26
10.36	Croxley Green CS	
	Berth	
	Croxley Green CS	15.22
15.32	Watford Jcn	15.55
16.41	Euston	16.50
17.35	Watford Jcn	17.45
17.55	Croxley Green CS	

C/Working 54

Arr	Station	Dep
	Broad Street	05.24
06.13	Richmond	06.23
07.12	Broad Street	07.22
08.14	Richmond	08.29
09.19	Broad Street	09.34
10.20	Mitre Bridge CS	

C/Working 55

Arr	Station	Dep
	Mitre Bridge CS	04.25
04.50	Willesden HL	04.52
05.07	Richmond	05.20
06.07	Broad St	06.35
07.26	Richmond	07.40
08.30	Broad St	08.47
09.48	Croxley Green	09.55
10.05	Croxley Green CS	
	Stable	
	Croxley Green CS	16.02
16.12	Watford Jcn	17.00
17.46	Euston	18.03
18.43	Bushey	18.44
18.54	Croxley Green CS	

C/Working 56

Arr	Station	Dep
	Croxley Green CS	14.45
14.55	Watford Jcn	15.10
15.56	Euston	16.10
16.56	Watford Jcn	17.06
18.09	Broad St	18.18
19.07	Richmond	19.53
19.43	Richmond	19.53
20.03	Acton Central	20.11
20.17	Willesden HL	20.23
20.50	Mitre Bridge CS	

C/Working 57

Arr	Station	Dep
	Watford Jcn	05.45
06.45	Broad St	07.03
07.50	Harrow	08.07
08.51	Broad St	09.06
	Mitre Bridge CS	
	Stable	
	Mitre Bridge CS	15.50
16.05	Kensal Grren Sdg	16.23
16.26	Willesden HL	16.27
16.43	Richmond	16.52
17.42	Broad St	17.56
18.55	Watford Jcn	19.59
20.16	Harrow	

C/Working 58

Arr	Station	Dep
	Harrow	06.58
07.13	Watford Jcn	07.25
08.10	Euston	08.18
09.03	Watford Jcn	09.15
09.58	Euston	10.10
	Watford Jcn	10.55
	Berth	
	Watford Jcn	15.04
16.04	Broad Street	16.33
17.24	Richmond	17.38
18.28	Broad Street	18.40
19.41	Watford Jcn	

C/Working 59

Arr	Station	Dep
	Mitre Bridge CS	05.55
06.08	Willesden HL	06.10
06.41	Broad St	06.54
07.55	Watford Jcn	08.58
09.53	Broad St	10.48
11.17	Willesden New	11.28
11.56	Broad St	12.18
12.47	Willesden New	12.58
13.26	Broad St	13.48
14.17	Willesden New	14.28
14.56	Broad St	16.00
16.51	Richmond	17.08
17.58	Broad St	18.09
19.10	Watford Jcn	19.23
20.24	Broad St	20.34
21.19	Mitre Bridge CS	

C/Working 60

Arr	Station	Dep
	Dalston Jcn	06.16
06.23	Broad Street	06.50
07.42	Richmond	07.56
08.45	Broad Street	08.58
09.49	Richmond	10.02
10.50	Broad Street	15.18
16.21	Watford Jcn	16.39
17.38	Broad Street	17.47
18.39	Richmond	18.55
19.45	Broad Street	20.40
20.45	Dalston Jcn	

C/Working 61

Arr	Station	Dep
	Croxley Green CS	07.35
07.53	Bushey	07.54
08.30	Euston	08.37
09.16	Bushey	09.17
09.24	Croxley Green CS	
	Berth	
	Croxley Green CS	16.02
16.12	Watford Jcn	17.28
18.13	Euston	18.33
19.19	Watford Jcn	

C/Working 62

Arr	Station	Dep
	Stonebridge Park CS	06.10
06.27	Willesden New	06.29
07.00	Broad Street	07.18
08.20	Watford Jcn	08.37
09.36	Broad Street	09.45
10.48	Watford Jcn	11.26
11.36	Croxley Green CS	
	Berth	
	Croxley Green CS	15.40
15.50	Watford Jcn	16.02
17.01	Broad Street	17.12
18.02	Richmond	18.23
19.14	Broad Street	19.42
20.43	Watford Jcn	22.57
23.07	Croxley Green CS	

C/Working 63

Arr	Station	Dep
	Watford Jcn	06.25
07.25	Broad Street	07.35
08.26	Richmond	08.44
09.33	Broad Street	09.47
10.35	Mitre Bridge CS	
	Stable	
	Mitre Bridge CS	14.50
15.04	Kensal Green Sdg	15.10
15.11	Willesden HL	15.12
15.28	Richmond	15.53
16.42	Broad Street	16.58
17.59	Watford Jcn	18.09
19.09	Broad Street	

C/Working 64

Arr	Station	Dep
	Croxley Green CS	15.27
15.44	Bushey	15.45
16.28	Euston	16.38
17.25	Watford Jcn	

C/Working 65

Arr	Station	Dep
	Mitre Bridge CS	05.20
05.41	Kensal Green Sdg	06.00
06.02	Willesden HL	06.05
06.19	Richmond	06.40
07.29	Broad Street	07.38
08.39	Watford Jcn	08.55
09.38	Euston	09.54
10.41	Watford Jcn	10.55
11.05	Croxley Green CS	
	Berth	
	Croxley Green CS	15.07
15.18	Watford Jcn	15.46
16.47	Broad Street	17.02
17.54	Richmond	18.06
18.58	Broad Street	19.21
20.22	Watford Jcn	00.10
00.20	Croxley Green CS	

C/Working 66

Arr	Station	Dep
06.03	Broad Street	06.20
07.12	Richmond	07.25
08.15	Broad Street	08.26
09.26	Watford Jcn	09.39
09.50	Croxley Green CS	
	Berth	
	Croxley Green CS	14.50
15.15	Watford Jcn	15.24
16.11	Euston	16.25
17.11	Watford Jcn	17.21
18.21	Broad Street	18.35
19.25	Richmond	19.50
20.40	Broad Street	20.58
21.49	Richmond	22.01
22.47	Broad Street	22.58
23.49	Richmond	00.04
00.35	Mitre Bridge CS	

C/Working 67

Arr	Station	Dep
	Croxley Green CS	06.35
06.47	Croxley Green	06.56
07.04	Watford Jcn	
07.24	Croxley Green	07.28
08.33	Broad Street	08.43
08.48	Dalston Jcn	
	Berth	
	Dalston Jcn	16.18
16.25	Broad Street	16.37
17.40	Watford Jcn	

C/Working 68

Arr	Station	Dep
	Croxley Green CS	08.10
08.25	Croxley Green	08.28
09.26	Broad Street	09.40
09.46	Dalston Jcn	
	Berth	
	Dalston Jcn	15.45
15.53	Broad Street	16.15
17.06	Richmond	17.23
18.12	Broad Street	18.23
19.20	Bushey	19.21
19.33	Croxley Green CS	

C/Working 69

Arr	Station	Dep
	Croxley Green CS	16.08
16.20	Bushey	16.21
17.16	Broad Street	17.28
18.45	Watford Jcn	18.45
18.52	Croxley Green	18.56
19.15	Croxley Green CS	